STUDY GUIDE
to accompany

MANAGERIAL ACCOUNTING
Tools for Business Decision Making
3RD Edition

Douglas W. Kieso PhD, CPA
Aurora University
Aurora, Illinois

Jerry J. Weygandt PhD, CPA
Arthur Andersen Alumni Professor of Accounting
University of Wisconsin
Madison, Wisconsin

Donald E. Kieso PhD, CPA
KPMG Peat Marwick Emeritus Professor of Accountancy
Northern Illinois University
DeKalb, Illinois

Paul D. Kimmel PhD, CPA
Associate Professor of Accounting
University of Wisconsin — Milwaukee
Milwaukee, Wisconsin

WILEY

JOHN WILEY & SONS, INC.

COVER PHOTO   © Gamma Ray Studio, Inc. / The Image Bank / Getty Images

To order books or for customer service call 1-800-CALL-WILEY (225-5945).

ISBN 0-471-68034-6

Printed in the United States of America

10 9 8 7 6 5 4 3 2 1

Printed and bound by Courier Kendallville, Inc.

CONTENTS

Chapter 1   Managerial Accounting

Chapter 2   Job Order Cost Accounting

Chapter 3   Process Cost Accounting

Chapter 4   Activity-Based Costing

Chapter 5   Cost-Volume-Profit

Chapter 6   Incremental Analysis

Chapter 7   Variable Costing: A Decision-Making Perspective

Chapter 8   Pricing

Chapter 9   Budgetary Planning

Chapter 10   Budgetary Control and Responsibility Accounting

Chapter 11   Standard Costs and Balanced Scorecard

Chapter 12   Planning for Capital Investments

Chapter 13   Statement of Cash Flows

Chapter 14   Financial Statement Analysis: The Big Picture

To The Student

This Study Guide will help in your study of *Managerial Accounting,* **3rd Edition** by Jerry J. Weygandt, Donald E. Kieso and Paul D. Kimmel. The material in the Study Guide is designed to reinforce your understanding of the principles and procedures presented in the textbook. **It is important to recognize that the Study Guide is a supplement to and not a substitute for the textbook.**

This Study Guide contains the following materials for each chapter in the textbook: (a) study objectives, (b) a preview of the chapter, (c) a chapter review consisting of 20-30 key points, (d) a demonstration problem, (e) 20 true—false statements, (f) 20 multiple choice questions, (g) a matching question pertaining to key terms, (h) 2-3 exercises, and (i) blank working papers for use in class. At the end of each chapter, answers to questions and exercises are provided in order to enable you to assess your comprehension of the material. Included are solutions explaining why the answer is what it is, so you get immediate feedback as to what, how, or why.

You will realize the maximum benefit from this Study Guide by following the approach suggested below.
1. Carefully read and study the chapter material in the textbook.
2. Read the chapter preview and review material in the Study Guide.
3. Answer the questions and exercises for the chapter in the Study Guide and compare your answers with those provided in the Study Guide. For any incorrect answers, refer back to the textbook for a discussion of the point you have missed.
4. Solve the end-of-chapter materials in the textbook assigned by your instructor.

The study guide should be helpful in preparing for examinations. The chapter review points and other materials may be used to determine your recollection of the information presented in specific chapters. When you have identified topics in need of further study, you can return to the textbook for a complete discussion of the subject matter.

I wish to acknowledge the valuable assistance of the proofer and checker of this Study Guide, James Emig of Villanova University, and our compositor, Mary Ann Benson.

Douglas W. Kieso

Chapter **1**

MANAGERIAL ACCOUNTING

The Navigator ✓
- ■ Scan Study Objectives ☐
- ■ Read Preview ☐
- ■ Read Chapter Review ☐
- ■ Work Demonstration Problem ☐
- ■ Answer True-False Statements ☐
- ■ Answer Multiple-Choice Questions ☐
- ■ Match Terms and Definitions ☐
- ■ Solve Exercises ☐

CHAPTER STUDY OBJECTIVES

After studying this chapter, you should be able to:
1. Explain the distinguishing features of managerial accounting.
2. Identify the three broad functions of management.
3. Define the three classes of manufacturing costs.
4. Distinguish between product and period costs.
5. Explain the difference between a merchandising and a manufacturing income statement.
6. Indicate how cost of goods manufactured is determined.
7. Explain the difference between a merchandising and a manufacturing balance sheet.
*8. Identify changes in managerial accounting.
*9. Prepare a work sheet and closing entries for a manufacturing company.

The Navigator

*Note: All **asterisked** (*) items relate to material contained in the Appendix to the chapter.

PREVIEW OF CHAPTER 1

Beginning with this chapter, we turn our attention to issues such as the costs of material, labor, and overhead and the relationship between costs and profits. In a previous financial accounting course, you should have studied the form and content of financial statements for external users such as stockholders and creditors. These statements represent the principal product of financial accounting. The chapters in this textbook focus primarily on the preparation of reports for internal users, such as the managers and officers of a company. These reports are the principal product of managerial accounting. The content and organization of this chapter are as follows:

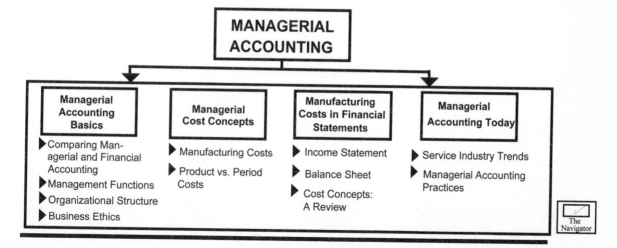

CHAPTER REVIEW

Managerial Accounting Basics

1. (S.O. 1) **Managerial accounting** is a field of accounting that provides economic and financial information for managers and other internal users. Managerial accounting applies to all types of businesses—service, merchandising, and manufacturing—and to all forms of business organizations—proprietorships, partnerships and corporations. Moreover, managerial accounting is needed in not-for-profit entities as well as in profit-oriented enterprises.

Comparing Managerial and Financial Accounting

2. There are both similarities and differences between managerial and financial accounting.
   a. Both fields of accounting deal with the economic events of a business and require that the results of that company's economic events be quantified and communicated to interested parties.
   b. The principal differences are the (1) primary users of reports, (2) types and frequency of reports, (3) purpose of reports, (4) content of reports, and (5) verification process.

3. The role of the managerial accountant has changed in recent years. Whereas in the past their primary concern used to be collecting and reporting costs to management, today they also evaluate how well the company is using its resources and providing information to cross-functional teams comprised of personnel from production, operations, marketing, engineering, and quality control.

Management Functions

4. (S.O. 2) Management performs three broad functions within an organization:
   a. Planning requires management to look ahead and to establish objectives.
   b. Directing involves coordinating a company's diverse activities and human resources to produce a smooth-running operation.
   c. Controlling is the process of keeping the firm's activities on track.

Organizational Structure

5. In order to assist in carrying out management functions, most companies prepare **organization charts** to show the interrelationships of activities and the delegation of authority and responsibility with the company.

   Stockholders own the corporation but manage the company through a **board of directors**. The **Chief Executive Officer (CEO)** has overall responsibility for managing the business. The **Chief Financial Officer (CFO)** is responsible for all of the accounting and finance issues the company faces. The CFO is supported by the **controller** and the **treasurer**.

Business Ethics

6. All employees are expected to act ethically in their business activities and an increasing number of organizations provide their employees with a code of business ethics.

7. Due to many fraudulent activities in recent years, U.S. Congress passed the Sarbanes-Oxley Act of 2002 which resulted in many implications for managers and accountants. CEOs and CFOs must certify the fairness of financial statements, top management must certify they maintain an adequate system of internal controls, and other matters.

Manufacturing Costs

8. (S.O. 3) Manufacturing consists of activities and processes that convert raw materials into finished goods.

9. Manufacturing costs are typically classified as either (a) direct materials, (b) direct labor or (c) manufacturing overhead.

10. **Direct materials** are raw materials that can be physically and conveniently associated with the finished product during the manufacturing process. **Indirect materials** are materials that (a) do not physically become a part of the finished product or (b) cannot be traced to their physical association with the finished product is too small in terms of cost to trace. Indirect materials are accounted for as part of manufacturing overhead.

11. The work of factory employees that can be physically and conveniently associated with converting raw materials into finished goods is considered **direct labor**. In contrast, the wages of maintenance people, timekeepers, and supervisors are usually identified as **indirect labor** because their efforts have no physical association with the finished product, or it is impractical to trace the costs to goods produced. Indirect labor is classified as manufacturing overhead.

12. **Manufacturing overhead** consists of costs that are indirectly associated with the manufacture of the finished product. Manufacturing overhead includes indirect materials, indirect labor, depreciation on factory buildings and machinery, insurance, taxes, and maintenance of factory facilities.

Product Versus Period Costs

13. (S.O. 4) **Product costs** are costs that are a necessary and integral part of producing the finished product. **Period costs** are costs that are matched with the revenue of a specific time period rather than included as part of the cost of a salable product. These are nonmanufacturing costs. Period costs include selling and administrative expenses.

Manufacturing Income Statement

14. (S.O. 5) The income statements of a merchandising company and a manufacturing com-pany differ in the cost of goods sold section.

15. The cost of goods sold section of the income statement for a manufacturing company shows:

Beginning Finished Goods Inventory	+	Cost of Goods Manufactured	-	Ending Finished Goods Inventory	=	Cost of Goods Sold

Determining Cost of Goods Manufactured

16. (S.O. 6) The determination of the cost of goods manufactured consists of the following:

    a. Beginning Work   Total Current   Total Cost of
        in Process   +   Manufacturing   =   Work in Process
        Inventory   Costs

    b. Total Cost of   Ending   Cost of Goods
        Work in   -   Work in Process =   Manufactured
        Process   Inventory

17. The costs assigned to the beginning work in process inventory are the manufacturing costs incurred in the prior period.

18. Total manufacturing costs is the sum of the direct materials costs, direct labor costs, and manufacturing overhead incurred in the current period.

19. Because a number of accounts are involved, the determination of costs of goods manufactured is presented in a Cost of Goods Manufactured Schedule. The cost of goods manufactured schedule shows each of the cost factors above. The format for the schedule is:

Beginning work in process		$XXXX
Direct materials used	$XXXX	
Direct labor	XXXX	
Manufacturing overhead	XXXX	
Total manufacturing costs		XXXX
Total cost of work in process		XXXX
Less: Ending work in process		XXXX
Cost of goods manufactured		$XXXX

Manufacturing Balance Sheet

20. (S.O. 7) The balance sheet for a manufacturing company may have three inventory accounts: finished goods inventory, work in process inventory, and raw materials inventory.

21. The manufacturing inventories are reported in the current asset section of the balance sheet.
    a. The inventories are generally listed in the order of their expected realization in cash.
    b. Thus, finished goods inventory is listed first.

22. Each step in the accounting cycle for a merchandising company is applicable to a manufacturing company.
    a. For example, prior to preparing financial statements, adjusting entries are required.
    b. Adjusting entries are essentially the same as those of a merchandising company.
    c. The closing entries for a manufacturing company are also similar to those of a merchandising company.

Contemporary Developments

23. (S.O. 8) Contemporary developments in managerial accounting involve: (a) a U.S. economy that has in general shifted toward an emphasis on providing services, rather than goods; and (b) efforts to manage the value chain and supply chain.

*Work Sheet

*24. (S.O. 9) When a work sheet is used in preparing financial statements, two additional columns are needed for the cost of goods manufactured schedule.
    a. The columns are labeled Cost of Goods Manufactured.
    b. The columns are inserted before the income statement columns.

*25. In the cost of goods manufactured columns,
    a. The beginning inventories of raw materials and work in process and all manufacturing costs are entered as debits.
    b. The ending inventories of raw materials and work in process are entered as credits.
    c. The balancing amount for these columns is the cost of goods manufactured and is entered as a credit. The same amount is also entered in the income statement debit columns.

*26. The income statement and balance sheet columns are basically the same as for a merchandising company.
    a. Beginning finished goods inventory is entered in the income statement debit column.
    b. Ending finished goods inventory is entered in the income statement credit column and the balance sheet debit column.

*27. In preparing closing entries, a Manufacturing Summary account is used to close all accounts that appear in the cost of goods manufactured schedule.
    a. Ending inventories of raw materials and work in process are debited and Manufacturing Summary is credited.
    b. Beginning inventories of raw materials and work in process and all manufacturing cost accounts are credited and Manufacturing Summary is debited.
    c. The balance in Manufacturing Summary is closed by debiting Income Summary and crediting Manufacturing Summary.

*28. As in the case of a merchandise company, all accounts shown in the income statement for a manufacturing company are closed to Income Summary.

The
Navigator

DEMONSTRATION PROBLEM (S.O. 6)

Indicate the missing amounts for the incomplete manufacturing costs, expenses, and selling data for the following four cases:

	Case			
	1	2	3	4
Direct Materials	$ 7,250	$ 5,500	$ 4,000	Q
Direct Labor	1,500	G	3,600	5,000
Manufacturing Overhead	3,700	11,000	L	5,700
Total Manufacturing Costs	A	23,400	13,000	17,000
Beginning Work in Process Inventory	3,200	H	2,600	R
Ending Work in Process Inventory	B	7,000	1,100	1,900
Sales	24,000	23,000	21,700	S
Sales Discounts	2,300	5,000	M	1,400
Cost of Goods Manufactured	14,400	18,400	N	19,800
Beginning Finished Goods Inventory	C	1,500	1,250	1,490
Goods Available for Sale	19,500	19,900	15,750	T
Cost of Goods Sold	D	14,500	O	U
Ending Finished Goods Inventory	1,300	I	1,300	2,000
Gross Profit	E	J	P	25,400
Operating Expenses	3,400	2,900	2,100	V
Net Income	F	K	2,400	2,700

The Navigator

SOLUTION TO DEMONSTRATION PROBLEM

A = $12,450 ($7,250 + $1,500 + $3,700).

B = $1,250 ($3,200 + $12,450 - $14,400).

C = $5,100 ($19,500 - $14,400).

D = $18,200 ($19,500 - $1,300).

E = $3,500 ($24,000 - $2,300 - $18,200).

F = $100 ($3,500 - $3,400).

G = $6,900 ($23,400 - $5,500 - $11,000).

H = $2,000 ($18,400 + $7,000 - $23,400).

I = $5,400 ($19,900 - $14,500).

J = $3,500 ($23,000 - $5,000 - $14,500).

K = $600 ($3,500 - $2,900).

L = $5,400 ($13,000 - $4,000 - $3,600).

M = $2,750 [$21,700 - ($14,450 + $4,500)].

N = $14,500 ($13,000 + $2,600 - $1,100).

O = $14,450 ($15,750 - $1,300).

P = $4,500 ($2,400 + $2,100).

Q = $6,300 ($17,000 - $5,000 - $5,700).

R = $4,700 ($19,800 - $17,000 + $1,900).

S = $46,090 ($25,400 + $19,290 + $1,400).

T = $21,290 ($19,800 + $1,490).

U = $19,290 ($21,290 - $2,000).

V = $22,700 ($25,400 - $2,700).

REVIEW QUESTIONS AND EXERCISES

TRUE—FALSE

Indicate whether each of the following is true (T) or false (F) in the space provided.

_____　1.　(S.O. 1)　Managerial accounting is primarily concerned with managers and external users.

_____　2.　(S.O. 1)　Managerial accountants assist management in evaluating how well the company is employing its resources.

_____　3.　(S.O. 2)　Managerial reports are required to follow generally accepted accounting principles.

_____　4.　(S.O. 2)　Planning involves coordinating the diverse activities and human resources of a company to produce a smooth running operation.

_____　5.　(S.O. 2)　Control involves performance evaluation by management.

_____　6.　(S.O. 2)　Directing involves coordinating the diverse activities and human resources of a company to produce a smooth running operation.

_____　7.　(S.O. 3)　When the physical association of raw materials with the finished product is too small to trace in terms of cost they are usually classified as indirect materials.

_____　8.　(S.O. 3)　The wages of maintenance employees, timekeepers, and supervisors are usually classified as direct labor.

_____　9.　(S.O. 3)　Manufacturing overhead consists of any costs that are directly associated with the manufacture of the finished goods.

_____　10.　(S.O. 4)　Product costs are also called inventoriable costs.

_____　11.　(S.O. 4)　Period costs are costs that are matched with the revenue of a specific time period.

_____　12.　(S.O. 4)　Product costs include selling and administrative expenses.

_____　13.　(S.O. 5)　The three components in determining cost of goods sold in a manufacturing company are beginning finished goods inventory, cost of goods manufactured, and ending finished goods inventory.

_____　14.　(S.O. 5)　Direct materials become a cost of the finished goods manufactured when they are acquired, not when they are used.

_____　15.　(S.O. 5)　In a manufacturing company, the calculation of cost of goods sold is the beginning finished goods inventory plus the cost of goods manufactured less the ending finished goods inventory.

_____ 16. (S.O. 6) The sum of the direct materials costs, direct labor costs, and beginning work in process is the total manufacturing costs for the year.

_____ 17. (S.O. 6) Beginning work in process inventory plus total current manufacturing costs incurred less ending work in process inventory equals the cost of goods manufactured.

_____ 18. (S.O. 6) The costs assigned to beginning work in process inventory are based on the manufacturing costs incurred in the prior period.

_____ 19. (S.O. 7) Raw Materials Inventory shows the cost of completed goods on hand.

_____ 20. (S.O. 7) In a manufacturing company balance sheet, manufacturing inventories are reported in the current asset section in the order of their expected use in production.

_____ *21. (S.O. 9) In a work sheet, the cost of goods manufactured is entered in the cost of goods manufactured credit column and the income statement debit column.

_____ *22. (S.O. 9) The Income Summary account is used to close all accounts that appear in the cost of goods manufactured schedule.

The Navigator

MULTIPLE CHOICE

Circle the letter that best answers each of the following statements.

1. (S.O. 1) Which of the following would **not** describe managerial accounting reports?
   a. They are internal reports.
   b. They provide general purpose information for all users.
   c. They are issued as frequently as the need arises.
   d. The reporting standard is relevance to the decision to be made.

2. (S.O. 1) Financial and managerial accounting are similar in that both:
   a. have the same primary users.
   b. produce general-purpose reports.
   c. have reports that are prepared quarterly and annually.
   d. deal with the economic events of an enterprise.

3. (S.O. 2) The function of coordinating the diverse activities and human resources of a company to produce a smooth running operation is:
   a. planning.
   b. directing.
   c. controlling.
   d. accounting.

4. (S.O. 2) The function that pertains to keeping the activities of the enterprise on track is:
    a. planning.
    b. directing.
    c. controlling.
    d. accounting.

5. (S.O. 2) The function that involves looking ahead and establishing objectives by management is:
    a. planning.
    b. directing.
    c. controlling.
    d. accounting.

6. (S.O. 4) Direct materials are a:

	Product Cost	Prime Cost
a.	No	Yes
b.	Yes	Yes
c.	No	No
d.	Yes	No

7. (S.O. 4) Direct labor is a(n):
    a. nonmanufacturing cost.
    b. indirect cost.
    c. product cost.
    d. period cost.

8. (S.O. 4) For a manufacturing company, which of the following is an example of a period cost rather than a product cost?
    a. Depreciation on factory equipment.
    b. Wages of salespersons.
    c. Wages of machine operators.
    d. Insurance on factory equipment.

9. (S.O. 4) Property taxes on a manufacturing plant are an element of:

	Product Cost	Period Cost
a.	Yes	No
b.	Yes	Yes
c.	No	Yes
d.	No	No

10. (S.O. 4) The salary of a plant manager would be considered a:

	Product Cost	Period Cost
a.	Yes	Yes
b.	Yes	No
c.	No	Yes
d.	No	No

11. (S.O. 5) For the year, Mahatma Company has cost of goods manufactured $325,000, beginning finished goods inventory $150,000, and ending finished goods inventory $175,000. The cost of goods sold is:
    a. $275,000.
    b. $300,000.
    c. $325,000.
    d. $350,000.

12. (S.O. 5) If the cost of goods manufactured is less than the cost of goods sold, which of the following is correct?
    a. Finished Goods Inventory has increased.
    b. Work in Process Inventory has increased.
    c. Finished Goods Inventory has decreased.
    d. Work in Process Inventory has decreased.

13. (S.O. 6) The account that shows the cost of production for those units that have been started in the manufacturing process, but that are not complete at the end of the accounting period is:
    a. Raw Materials Inventory.
    b. Work in Process Inventory.
    c. Finished Goods Inventory.
    d. Cost of Goods Sold.

14. (S.O. 6) Nehru Company has beginning and ending raw materials inventories of $32,000 and $40,000, respectively. If direct materials used were $130,000, what was the cost of raw materials purchased?
    a. $130,000.
    b. $140,000.
    c. $122,000.
    d. $138,000.

15. (S.O. 6) Ghindia Company has beginning and ending work in process inventories of $52,000 and $58,000 respectively. If total current manufacturing costs are $248,000, what is the total cost of work in process?
    a. $300,000.
    b. $306,000.
    c. $242,000.
    d. $254,000.

16. (S.O. 6) Mura Company has beginning work in process inventory of $72,000 and total current manufacturing costs of $318,000. If cost of goods manufactured is $320,000, what is the cost of the ending work in process inventory?
   a. $60,000.
   b. $74,000.
   c. $80,000.
   d. $70,000.

17. (S.O. 6) If the total manufacturing costs are greater than the cost of goods manufactured, which of the following is correct?
   a. Work in Process Inventory has increased.
   b. Finished Goods Inventory has increased.
   c. Work in Process Inventory has decreased.
   d. Finished Goods Inventory has decreased.

18. (S.O. 7) The inventory accounts that show the cost of completed goods on hand and the costs applicable to production that is only partially completed are, respectively
   a. Work in Process Inventory and Raw Materials Inventory.
   b. Finished Goods Inventory and Raw Materials Inventory.
   c. Finished Goods Inventory and Work in Process Inventory.
   d. Raw Materials Inventory and Work in Process Inventory.

19. (S.O. 7) In the current asset section of a balance sheet, manufacturing inventories are listed in the following sequence:

	Raw Materials Inventory	Work in Process Inventory	Finished Goods Inventory
a.	1	2	3
b.	2	3	1
c.	3	1	2
d.	3	2	1

*20. (S.O. 9) In a manufacturing work sheet, cost of goods manufactured for the period is entered in the following columns:

	Cost of Goods Manufactured		Income Statement	
	Dr.	Cr.	Dr.	Cr.
a.	Yes	No	No	Yes
b.	Yes	No	Yes	No
c.	No	Yes	Yes	No
d.	No	Yes	No	Yes

*21. (S.O. 9) The closing entries for a manufacturing company would **not** include:
   a. a credit to Finished Goods Inventory (Ending Balance).
   b. a debit to Manufacturing Summary.
   c. a credit to Manufacturing Summary.
   d. a credit to Raw Materials Inventory (Beginning Balance).

The Navigator

MATCHING

Match each term with its definition by writing the appropriate letter in the space provided.

Terms

_____ 1. Direct labor.

_____ 2. Period costs.

_____ 3. Indirect labor.

_____ 4. Managerial accounting.

_____ 5. Direct materials.

_____ 6. Product costs.

_____ 7. Indirect materials.

_____ 8. Manufacturing overhead.

Definitions

a. Costs that are matched with the revenue of a specific time period and charged to expense as incurred.

b. The work of factory employees that can be physically and conveniently associated with converting raw materials into finished goods.

c. A field of accounting that provides economic and financial information for managers and other internal users.

d. Raw materials that do not physically become part of the finished product or cannot be traced because their physical association with the finished product is too small.

e. Work of factory employees that has no physical association with the finished product, or it is impractical to trace the costs to the goods produced.

f. Costs that are a necessary and integral part of producing the finished product.

g. Manufacturing costs that are indirectly associated with the manufacture of the finished product.

h. Raw materials that can be physically and conveniently associated with manufacturing the finished product.

The Navigator

EXERCISES

EX. 1-1   (S.O. 6) At the end of 2006, the following information pertains to Norman Company:

Factory repairs	$10,000
Factory utilities	8,000
Factory insurance	7,500
Factory depreciation	6,000
Factory property taxes	5,500
Indirect labor	9,000
Raw Materials Inventory	
January 1	15,000
December 31	20,000
Direct labor	25,000
Work in Process Inventory	
January 1	32,000
December 31	30,000
Purchases of raw materials	48,000

Instructions
Prepare a Cost of Goods Manufactured Schedule for Norman Company.

NORMAN COMPANY
Cost of Goods Manufactured Schedule
For the Year Ended December 31, 2006

EX. 1-2   (S.O. 3 and 4)   The Svengooli Company specializes in manufacturing woodchuck traps. The company has a large number of orders to keep the factory production at 10,000 per month. Svengooli's monthly manufacturing costs and other expense data are as follows:

1.	Rent on factory equipment	$ 6,000
2.	Advertising for the traps	8,000
3.	Insurance on factory building	2,000
4.	Raw materials	24,000
5.	Supplies for the general office	500
6.	Wages for assembly line workers	39,700
7.	Depreciation on office equipment	800
8.	Miscellaneous factory materials	400
9.	Company president's salary	2,700
10.	Utility costs for the factory	900
11.	Maintenance costs for the factory	400
12.	Factory supervisor's salary	1,500
13.	Sales commissions	3,700
14.	Depreciation on factory building	900

Instructions
Enter each item and place an "X" mark under each of the following column headings.

Cost Item	Product Cost			Period Costs
	Direct Materials	Direct Labor	Manufacturing Overhead	
1.				
2.				
3.				
4.				
5.				
6.				
7.				
8.				
9.				
10.				
11.				
12.				
13.				
14.				

The Navigator

SOLUTIONS TO REVIEW QUESTIONS AND EXERCISES

TRUE-FALSE

1.	(F)	Managerial accounting relates primarily to managers and other internal users.
2.	(T)	
3.	(F)	The reporting standard for internal reports is relevance to the decision being made.
4.	(F)	Planning requires management to look ahead and to establish objectives. The statement given relates to the function of directing.
5.	(T)	
6.	(T)	
7.	(T)	
8.	(F)	The wages of these employees are usually identified as indirect labor because their efforts either have no physical association with the finished product or it is impractical to trace the costs to the goods produced.
9.	(F)	Manufacturing overhead consists of costs that are indirectly associated with the manufacture of the finished product.
10.	(T)	
11.	(T)	
12.	(F)	Period costs include selling and administrative expenses.
13.	(T)	
14.	(F)	Direct materials become a cost of the finished goods manufactured when they are used, not when they are acquired.
15.	(T)	
16.	(F)	The sum of the direct materials costs, direct labor costs, and manufacturing overhead incurred is the total manufacturing costs for the year.
17.	(T)	
18.	(T)	
19.	(F)	Raw Materials Inventory shows the cost of raw materials on hand. Finished Goods Inventory shows the cost of completed goods on hand.
20.	(F)	Manufacturing inventories are reported in the current asset section in order of their expected realization in cash.
*21.	(T)	
*22.	(F)	A Manufacturing Summary account is used to close all accounts that appear in the cost of goods manufactured schedule.

MULTIPLE CHOICE

1. (b) Managerial accounting reports are special-purpose reports for a particular user for a specific decision.

2. (d) Financial reports are for external users and managerial reports are for internal users (a). Financial reports are usually identified as general-purpose reports and managerial reports are for specific purposes (b). The financial reports are prepared quarterly and annually and managerial reports are issued as frequently as the need arises (c).

3. (b) Directing involves coordinating the diverse activities and human resources of a company in a manner that results in a smooth running operation.

4.   (c)   Controlling is the process of keeping the activities of the enterprise on track. Management determines whether planned goals are being met and what changes are necessary when there are deviations from targeted objectives.

5.   (a)   Planning requires management to look ahead and to establish future goals and objectives.

6.   (d)   Direct materials, direct labor, and manufacturing overhead are all referred to as manufacturing costs; and as such are also known as product costs.

7.   (c)   Direct labor is a product cost.

8.   (b)   Period costs are costs that are matched with the revenue of a specific time period rather than with production of a product. Therefore, the wages of salespersons are a period cost. The other answer choices are product costs.

9.   (a)   Property taxes on the manufacturing plant are considered a part of manufacturing overhead. Therefore, they are a product cost but not a period cost.

10. (b)   The salary of a plant manager would be a part of manufacturing overhead and a product cost.

11. (b)   The cost of goods sold is:

Beginning finished goods inventory......................	$150,000
Cost of goods manufactured	325,000
Cost of goods available for sale	475,000
Ending finished goods inventory...........................	175,000
Cost of goods sold...	$300,000

12. (c)   For cost of goods manufactured to be less than cost of goods sold, the beginning inventory of finished goods must be greater than the ending inventory of finished goods.

13. (b)   The Work in Process Inventory account represents the cost of production for those units that have been started in the manufacturing process, but which are not complete at the end of the accounting period.

14. (d)   Ending inventory $40,000 plus direct materials used $130,000 equals total cost of materials available for use, $170,000. $170,000 less the beginning inventory, $32,000 equals the cost of materials purchased, $138,000.

15. (a)   The total cost of work in process is the beginning work in process inventory $52,000 plus the total current manufacturing costs $248,000.

16. (d)   The cost of the ending work in process is the total cost of work in process $390,000 ($72,000 + $318,000) minus the cost of goods manufactured $320,000.

17. (a)   For total current manufacturing costs to be greater than the cost of goods manufactured, the beginning inventory of work in process must be less than the ending inventory of work in process.

18. (c) Finished goods Inventory shows the cost of completed goods on hand. Work in Process Inventory shows the costs applicable to production that is only partially completed.

19. (d) Manufacturing inventories are listed in the current asset section in the order of their expected realization in cash. Thus, the order is finished goods, work in process, and raw materials.

*20. (c) Cost of goods manufactured is entered in the cost of goods manufactured credit column and the income statement debit column.

*21. (a) Ending Finished Goods Inventory is closed by a debit, not a credit. Manufacturing Summary is both debited and credited when closing entries are prepared. Raw Materials Inventory (Beginning Balance) is credited when closing entries are prepared.

MATCHING

1. b
2. a
3. e
4. c

5. h
6. f
7. d
8. g

EXERCISES

EX. 1-1

NORMAN COMPANY
Cost of Goods Manufactured Schedule
For the Year Ended December 31, 2006

Work in process, January 1			$ 32,000
Direct materials			
Raw materials inventory, January 1	$15,000		
Raw materials purchases	48,000		
Total raw materials available for use	63,000		
Less: Raw materials inventory December 31	20,000		
Direct materials used		$43,000	
Direct labor		25,000	
Manufacturing overhead			
Factory repairs	10,000		
Indirect labor	9,000		
Factory utilities	8,000		
Factory insurance	7,500		
Factory depreciation	6,000		
Factory property taxes	5,500		
Total manufacturing overhead		46,000	
Total manufacturing costs			114,000
Total cost of work in process			146,000
Less: Work in process, December 31			30,000
Cost of goods manufactured			$116,000

EX. 1-2

| Cost Item | Product Cost | | | Period Costs |
	Direct Materials	Direct Labor	Manufacturing Overhead	
1.			X	
2.				X
3.			X	
4.	X			
5.				X
6.		X		
7.				X
8.			X	
9.				X
10.			X	
11.			X	
12.			X	
13.				X
14.			X	

Chapter 2

JOB ORDER COST ACCOUNTING

The Navigator	✓
■ Scan Study Objectives	☐
■ Read Preview	☐
■ Read Chapter Review	☐
■ Work Demonstration Problem	☐
■ Answer True-False Statements	☐
■ Answer Multiple-Choice Questions	☐
■ Match Terms and Definitions	☐
■ Solve Exercises	☐

CHAPTER STUDY OBJECTIVES

After studying this chapter, you should be able to:
1. Explain the characteristics and purposes of cost accounting.
2. Describe the flow of costs in a job order cost accounting system.
3. Explain the nature and importance of a job cost sheet.
4. Indicate how the predetermined overhead rate is determined and used.
5. Prepare entries for jobs completed and sold.
6. Distinguish between under- and overapplied manufacturing overhead.

The Navigator

PREVIEW OF CHAPTER 2

This chapter illustrates how manufacturing costs are assigned to specific jobs. We begin the discussion in this chapter with an overview of the flow of costs in a job order cost accounting system. We then use a case study to explain and illustrate the documents, entries, and accounts in this type of cost accounting system. The content and organization of this chapter are as follows:

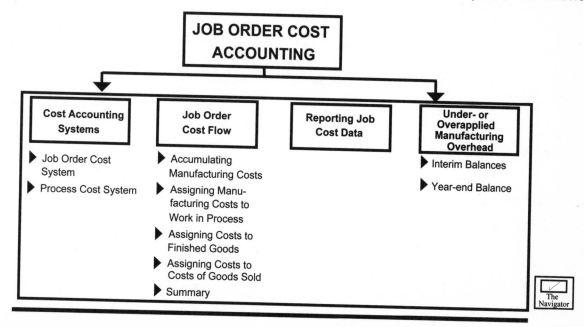

CHAPTER REVIEW

Cost Accounting Systems

1. (S.O. 1) **Cost accounting** involves the measuring, recording, and reporting of product costs. From the data accumulated, both the total cost and unit cost of each product is determined.

2. A **cost accounting system** consists of accounts for the various manufacturing costs. These accounts are fully integrated into the general ledger of a company. An important feature of a cost accounting system is the use of a perpetual inventory system. Such a system provides information immediately on the cost of a product. The two basic types of cost accounting systems are (a) a job order cost system and (b) a process cost system.

3. Under a **job order cost system,** costs are assigned to each job or to each batch of goods.

4. A **process cost system** is used when a large volume of similar products are manufactured. Process costing accumulates product-related costs for a period of time instead of assigning costs to specific products or job orders.

Job Order Cost Flow

5. (S.O. 2) The **flow of costs** in job order cost accounting parallels the physical flow of the materials as they are converted into finished goods. There are two major steps in the flow of costs: (a) accumulating the manufacturing costs incurred and (b) assigning the accumulated costs to the work done.

6. No effort is made when costs are incurred to associate the costs with specific jobs.

7. The **assignment of manufacturing costs** involves entries to Work in Process Inventory, Finished Goods inventory, and Cost of Goods Sold.

8. The costs of raw materials purchased are debited to **Raw Materials Inventory** when materials are received. This account is a **control account.** The subsidiary ledger consists of individual **materials inventory records** (stores ledger cards) for each item of raw materials.

9. **Factory labor costs** are debited to **Factory Labor** when they are incurred. The cost of factor labor consists of (1) gross earnings of factory workers, (2) employer payroll taxes on the earnings, and (3) fringe benefits incurred by the employer. Factory Labor is not a control account.

10. Manufacturing overhead costs are recognized daily as incurred and periodically through adjusting entries. The costs are debited to **Manufacturing Overhead** which is a control account. The subsidiary ledger consists of individual accounts for each type of cost.

Assigning Manufacturing Costs to Work in Process

11. (S.O. 3) The assignment of manufacturing overhead costs to work in process involves debits to Work in Process Inventory and credits to:
    a. Raw Materials Inventory based on **materials requisition slips.**
    b. Factory Labor based on **time tickets.**
    c. Manufacturing Overhead based on a predetermined overhead rate.

Job Cost Sheet

12. A **job cost sheet** is a form used to record the costs chargeable to a specific job and to determine the total and unit cost of the completed job. A separate job cost sheet is kept for each job. Each entry to Work in Process Inventory must be accompanied by a corresponding posting to one or more job cost sheets.

13. Raw materials costs are assigned when the materials are issued by the storeroom. Work in Process Inventory is debited for direct materials used, Manufacturing Overhead is debited for indirect materials used, and Raw Materials Inventory is credited.

14. Factory Labor costs are assigned to jobs on the basis of time tickets prepared when the work is performed. Work in Process Inventory is debited for direct labor costs, Manufacturing Overhead is debited for indirect labor costs, and Factory Labor is credited.

Manufacturing Overhead Costs

15. (S.O. 4) Manufacturing overhead relates to production operations as a whole and therefore cannot be assigned to specific jobs on the basis of actual costs incurred. Instead, manufacturing overhead is assigned to work in process and to specific jobs on an estimated basis through the use of a predetermined overhead rate.

16. The **predetermined overhead rate** is based on the relationship between estimated annual overhead costs and expected annual operating activity. This relationship is expressed in terms of a common activity base such as direct labor costs, direct labor hours, or machine hours.
    a. The formula for the predetermined overhead rate is:

$$\text{Estimated Annual Overhead Costs} \div \text{Expected Annual Operating Activity} = \text{Predetermined Overhead Rate}$$

    b. The use of a predetermined overhead rate enables the company to determine the approximate total cost of each job when the job is completed.
    c. In recent years, there has been a trend toward use of **machine hours** as the activity base due to increased reliance on automation in manufacturing operations.

17. At the end of each month, the balance in Work in Process Inventory should equal the sum of the costs shown on the job cost sheets for unfinished jobs.

Assigning Costs to Finished Goods

18. (S.O. 5) When a job is completed, the total cost is debited to Finished Goods Inventory and credited to Work in Process Inventory. Finished Goods Inventory is a control account that controls individual finished goods records in a finished goods subsidiary ledger.

19. **Cost of goods sold** is recognized when the sale occurs by a debit to Cost of Goods Sold and a credit to Finished Goods Inventory.

20. At the end of a period, financial statements are prepared that present aggregate data on all jobs manufactured and sold.

a. The cost of goods manufactured schedule has one new feature: in determining total manufacturing costs, **manufacturing overhead applied** is used instead of actual overhead costs.
b. The cost of goods manufactured schedule is prepared directly from the Work in Process Inventory account.

Under- or Overapplied Manufacturing Overhead

21. (S.O. 6) Manufacturing Overhead may be under- or overapplied. When Manufacturing Overhead has a **debit balance,** overhead is said to be underapplied. **Underapplied overhead** means that the overhead assigned to work in process is less than the overhead incurred. When manufacturing overhead has a credit balance, overhead is overapplied. **Overapplied overhead** means that the overhead assigned to work in process is greater than the overhead incurred.

22. At the **end of the year,** any balance in Manufacturing Overhead is eliminated through an adjusting entry, usually to Cost of Goods Sold.
a. Underapplied overhead is debited to Cost of Goods Sold.
b. Overapplied overhead is credited to Cost of Goods Sold.

The Navigator

DEMONSTRATION PROBLEM (S.O. 2, 3, 4, 5, and 6)

During April, Pam Lee Company works on two jobs: Numbers 101 and 102. Summary data concerning these jobs are as follows:

Manufacturing Costs Incurred
Purchased $68,000 of raw materials on account.
Factory labor of $100,000 plus $6,000 employer payroll taxes.
Manufacturing overhead exclusive of indirect materials and indirect labor of $72,500.

Assignment of Costs
Direct materials: Job 101-$36,000, Job 102-$30,000
Indirect materials: $4,000
Direct labor: Job 101-$68,000, Job 102-$34,500
Indirect labor: $3,500
Manufacturing overhead rate 70% of direct labor costs.

Job 101 was completed and sold on account for $184,000. Job 102 was only partially completed.

Instructions
(a)   Journalize the April transactions in the sequence followed in the chapter.
(b)   What was the amount of under- or overapplied manufacturing overhead?

SOLUTION TO DEMONSTRATION PROBLEM

(a) 1. Raw Materials Inventory 68,000
        Accounts Payable 68,000
        (Purchase of raw materials on account)

   2. Factory Labor.. 106,000
        Factory Wages Payable.. 100,000
        Payroll Taxes Payable 6,000
        (To record factory labor costs)

   3. Manufacturing Overhead 72,500
        Accounts Payable, Accumulated Depreciation,
          and Prepaid Insurance....................................... 72,500
        (To record overhead costs)

   4. Work in Process Inventory.. 66,000
      Manufacturing Overhead 4,000
        Raw Materials Inventory 70,000
        (To assign raw materials to production)

   5. Work in Process Inventory.. 102,500
      Manufacturing Overhead 3,500
        Factory Labor.. 106,000
        (To assign factory labor to production)

   6. Work in Process Inventory.. 71,750
        Manufacturing Overhead 71,750
        (To assign overhead to jobs: $102,500 X 70%)

   7. Finished Goods Inventory.. 151,600
        Work in Process Inventory 151,600
        [To record completion of Job 101: $36,000 +
          $68,000 + (68,000 X 70%)]

   8. Accounts Receivable 184,000
      Cost of Goods Sold... 151,600
        Sales.. 184,000
        Finished Goods Inventory..................................... 151,600
        (To record sale of Job 101)

(b) Manufacturing Overhead has a debit balance of $8,250 as shown below:

Manufacturing Overhead			
(3)	72,500	(6)	71,750
(4)	4,000		
(5)	3,500		
Bal.	8,250		

The manufacturing overhead is underapplied during the month.

REVIEW QUESTIONS AND EXERCISES

TRUE—FALSE

Indicate whether each of the following is true (T) or false (F) in the space provided.

_____ 1. (S.O. 1) Cost accounting involves the measuring, recording, and reporting of product costs and period costs.

_____ 2. (S.O. 1) A cost accounting system consists of manufacturing cost accounts that are fully integrated into the general ledger of a company.

_____ 3. (S.O. 1) An important feature of a cost accounting system is the use of a periodic inventory system.

_____ 4. (S.O. 1) A process cost system is best used when each job (or batch) has its own distinguishing characteristics.

_____ 5. (S.O. 1) A company cannot use both a job order system and a process cost system.

_____ 6. (S.O. 2) The flow of costs in job order cost accounting parallels the physical flow of the materials as they are converted into finished goods.

_____ 7. (S.O. 2) The cost of raw materials purchased is credited to Raw Materials Inventory when materials are received.

_____ 8. (S.O. 2) Raw materials Inventory is a control account.

_____ 9. (S.O. 2) Factory Labor is a control account.

_____ 10. (S.O. 3) A job cost sheet is a requisition form signed by an authorized employee for the issuance of materials.

_____ 11. (S.O. 3) Each entry to Work in Process must be accompanied by a corresponding posting to one or more job cost sheets.

_____ 12. (S.O. 3) Raw materials costs are assigned to Work in Process Inventory when the materials are purchased.

_____ 13. (S.O. 3) Requisitions for direct materials are posted daily to the individual job cost sheets.

_____ 14. (S.O. 3) Factory labor costs are assigned to jobs on the basis of time tickets prepared when work is performed.

_____ 15. (S.O. 4) The predetermined overhead rate is based on the relationship between estimated annual overhead costs and expected annual operating capacity expressed in terms of a common activity base.

_____ 16. (S.O. 4) The use of a predetermined overhead rate enables the company to determine the approximate total cost when the job still is in work in process.

_____ 17. (S.O. 5) Recognition of the cost of goods sold is made when each sale occurs.

_____ 18. (S.O. 6) Overapplied manufacturing overhead exists when the overhead assigned to work in process is less than the overhead incurred.

_____ 19. (S.O. 6) At the end of the year, underapplied overhead is usually credited to Cost of Goods Sold.

_____ 20. (S.O. 6) After the entry for underapplied or overapplied overhead is posted, Manufacturing Overhead will have a zero balance.

MULTIPLE CHOICE

Circle the letter that best answers each of the following statements.

1.   (S.O. 1) Cost accounting involves the following activities pertaining to product costs:
    a.   measuring.
    b.   recording.
    c.   reporting.
    d.   all of the above.

2.   (S.O. 1) Job order costing would **not** be used by a company that manufactures:
    a.   homes.
    b.   motion pictures.
    c.   cereal.
    d.   bridges.

3.   (S.O. 2) In a job order cost system, it would be correct in recording the purchase of raw materials to debit:
    a.   Work in Process Inventory.
    b.   Work in Process and Manufacturing Overhead.
    c.   Raw Materials Inventory.
    d.   Finished Goods Inventory.

4.   (S.O. 3) In a job order cost system, indirect labor costs are recognized in the ledger by a debit to:
    a.   Manufacturing Overhead.
    b.   Work in Process Inventory.
    c.   Finished Goods Inventory.
    d.   Accrued Payroll.

5. (S.O. 3) In job order costing, the basic form to accumulate the cost of each job is the:
   a. materials inventory record.
   b. finished goods inventory record.
   c. cost of goods sold record.
   d. job cost sheet.

6. (S.O. 3) In job order costing, when indirect materials are used in production:
   a. Work in Process Inventory is debited.
   b. Manufacturing Overhead is credited.
   c. Raw Materials Inventory is debited.
   d. Raw Materials Inventory is credited.

7. (S.O. 3) A cost that would not be included in the manufacturing overhead account is:
   a. factory utilities.
   b. direct labor.
   c. indirect labor.
   d. depreciation expense on factory machinery.

8. (S.O. 3) Which of the following is not a control account?
   a. Raw Materials Inventory.
   b. Factory Labor.
   c. Manufacturing Overhead.
   d. All of the above are control accounts.

9. (S.O. 4) In the Bono Company, the predetermined overhead rate is 70% of direct labor cost. During the month, $250,000 of factory labor costs are incurred of which $180,000 is direct labor and $70,000 is indirect labor. Actual overhead incurred was $130,000. The amount of overhead debited to Work in Process Inventory should be:
   a. $126,000.
   b. $130,000.
   c. $175,000.
   d. $180,000.

10. (S.O. 4) Jinnah Company applies overhead on the basis of 200% of direct labor cost. Job No. 501 is charged with $30,000 of direct materials costs and $40,000 of manufacturing overhead. The total manufacturing costs for Job No. 501 is:
    a. $70,000.
    b. $110,000.
    c. $90,000.
    d. $100,000.

11.   (S.O. 4) Patel Company manufactures customized chairs. The following pertains to Job 276:

Direct materials used	$4,200
Direct labor hours worked	300
Direct labor rate per hour	$ 8.00
Machine hours used	200
Applied factory overhead rate	
per machine hour	$15.00

What is the total manufacturing cost for Job 276?
a. $8,800.
b. $9,600.
c. $10,300.
d. $11,100.

12.   (S.O. 4) Ambedkar Inc. applies overhead to production at a predetermined rate of 90% based on direct labor cost. Job No. 343, the only job still in process at the end of August, has been charged with manufacturing overhead of $2,250. What was the amount of direct materials charged to Job 343 assuming the balance in Work in Process Inventory is $9,000?
a. $2,250.
b. $2,500.
c. $4,250.
d. $9,000.

13.   (S.O. 5) When a job is finished, the journal entry will include a:
a.   credit to Finished Goods Inventory.
b.   debit to Work in Process Inventory.
c.   debit to Manufacturing Overhead.
d.   debit to Finished Goods Inventory.

14.   (S.O. 5) When the units are sold, the journal entry will include a:
a.   credit to Finished Goods Inventory.
b.   debit to Work in Process Inventory.
c.   debit to Manufacturing Overhead.
d.   credit to Cost of Goods Sold.

15.   (S.O. 6) The Edge Company uses a predetermined overhead rate of $5 per direct labor hour. In December, actual overhead amounted to $650,000 and actual direct labor hours were 132,000. For the month, overhead was:
a. $50,000 overapplied.
b. $50,000 underapplied.
c. $10,000 overapplied.
d. $10,000 underapplied.

16.   (S.O. 6) Mountbatten Co. uses a predetermined overhead rate of $3 per direct labor hour. In July, actual overhead amounted to $325,000 and actual direct labor hours were 100,000. For the month, overhead was:
a. $30,000 overapplied.
b. $30,000 underapplied.
c. $25,000 overapplied.
d. $25,000 underapplied.

17.   (S.O. 6) Overapplied manufacturing overhead exists when overhead assigned to work in process is:
   a.   more than overhead incurred and there is a debit balance in Manufacturing Overhead at the end of a period.
   b.   less than overhead incurred and there is a debit balance in Manufacturing Overhead at the end of a period.
   c.   more than overhead incurred and there is a credit balance in Manufacturing Overhead at the end of a period.
   d.   less than overhead incurred and there is a credit balance in Manufacturing Overhead at the end of a period.

18.   (S.O. 6) At the end of the year, to transfer underapplied overhead to cost of goods sold, the journal entry will include a:
   a.   credit to Cost of Goods Sold.
   b.   debit to Cost of Goods Sold.
   c.   debit to Manufacturing Overhead.
   d.   debit to Factory Labor.

19.   (S.O. 6) At the end of the year, to transfer overapplied overhead to cost of goods sold, the journal entry will include a:
   a.   debit to Manufacturing Overhead.
   b.   credit to Manufacturing Overhead.
   c.   credit to Factory Labor.
   d.   debit to Work in Process Inventory.

20.   (S.O. 6) Which of the following statements about under- or overapplied manufacturing overhead is correct?
   a.   After the entry to transfer over- or under-applied overhead to Cost of Goods Sold is posted, Manufacturing Overhead will have a zero balance.
   b.   When Manufacturing Overhead has a credit balance, overhead is said to be underapplied.
   c.   At the end of the year, under- or overapplied overhead is eliminated by a closing entry.
   d.   When annual financial statements are prepared, overapplied overhead is reported in current liabilities.

The
Navigator

MATCHING

Match each term with its definition by writing the appropriate letter in the space provided.

<table>
<tr><td colspan="2">Terms</td><td colspan="2">Definitions</td></tr>
<tr><td>_____</td><td>1. Time ticket.</td><td>a.</td><td>An area of accounting that involves the measuring, recording, and reporting of product costs.</td></tr>
<tr><td>_____</td><td>2. Job order cost system.</td><td>b.</td><td>A rate based on the relationship between estimated annual overhead costs and ex-pected annual operating activity expressed in terms of a common activity base.</td></tr>
<tr><td>_____</td><td>3. Cost accounting.</td><td></td><td></td></tr>
<tr><td>_____</td><td>4. Cost accounting system.</td><td></td><td></td></tr>
<tr><td>_____</td><td>5. Job cost sheet.</td><td>c.</td><td>Manufacturing cost accounts that are fully integrated into the general ledger of a company.</td></tr>
<tr><td>_____</td><td>6. Materials requisition slip.</td><td>d.</td><td>Overhead assigned to work in process is less than the overhead incurred.</td></tr>
<tr><td>_____</td><td>7. Predetermined overhead rate.</td><td>e.</td><td>A form used to record the costs chargeable to a job and to determine the total and unit cost of the completed job.</td></tr>
<tr><td>_____</td><td>8. Underapplied overhead.</td><td>f.</td><td>A document authorizing the issuance of raw materials from the storeroom to production.</td></tr>
<tr><td>_____</td><td>9. Overapplied overhead.</td><td>g.</td><td>Overhead assigned to work in process is greater than the overhead incurred.</td></tr>
<tr><td></td><td></td><td>h.</td><td>A cost accounting system in which costs are assigned to each job or batch.</td></tr>
<tr><td></td><td></td><td>i.</td><td>A document indicating the time worked by an employee and the account and job to be charged.</td></tr>
</table>

The
Navigator

EXERCISES

EX. 2-1   (S.O. 2, 3, 4, 5, and 6) McEllen Company uses job order costing. Manufacturing overhead is applied to production at a predetermined rate of 150% of direct labor cost. Additional information is available as follows:

- Job 201 was the only job in process at January 31, 2006, with accumulated costs as follow:

Direct materials	$4,000
Direct labor	2,000
Manufacturing overhead	3,000
	$9,000

- Jobs 202, 203, and 204 were started during February.
- Direct materials requisitioned for February totaled $26,000.
- Direct labor cost of $20,000 was incurred for February.
- Actual manufacturing overhead was $32,000 for February.
- The only job still in process at February 28, 2006, was Job 204, with costs of $2,800 for direct materials and $1,800 for direct labor.

Instructions
(a)   Make the journal entry to record materials used.
(b)   Make the journal entry to assign factory labor to production.
(c)   Make the journal entry to assign overhead to jobs.
(d)   Make a combined journal entry to record the completion of Jobs No. 201, 202, and 203.
(e)   Prove the agreement of Work in Process Inventory with the costs of Job 204.

General Journal			J1
Date	Account Title	Debit	Credit

EX. 2-2   (S.O. 2, 4, 5, and 6)   Selected account balances as of January 1 for Remmers Company are: Raw Materials Inventory $220,000, Work in Process Inventory $160,000, and Finished Goods Inventory $350,000.

During 2006, the following transactions took place:

1. Purchased $820,000 of raw materials.
2. Incurred $680,000 of factory labor costs of which $630,000 relate to wages payable and $50,000 to employer payroll taxes payable.
3. Incurred overhead costs of $174,000 (Credit Accounts Payable $124,000 and Cash $50,000).
4. Used direct materials of $600,000 and indirect materials of $200,000.
5. Used direct labor of $650,000 and indirect labor of $30,000.
6. Applied overhead at 30% of direct labor cost.
7. Completed jobs totaling $1,100,000.
8. Sold jobs costing $1,000,000 for $1,400,000, on account.

Instructions
(a) Prepare the entries for Remmers Company for the above transactions assuming a job order cost accounting system is used. (Omit explanations.)
(b) At December 31, the ledger of Remmers Company shows underapplied manufacturing overhead of $5,000. Prepare the entry to transfer this balance to Cost of Goods Sold.

General Journal			J1
Date	Account Title	Debit	Credit

	General Journal		J
Date	Account Title	Debit	Credit

SOLUTIONS TO REVIEW QUESTIONS AND EXERCISES

TRUE-FALSE

1.   (F)   Cost accounting does not generally pertain to period costs.
2.   (T)
3.   (F)   An important feature of a cost accounting system is the use of a perpetual inventory system.
4.   (F)   A job order cost system is best used when each job (or batch) has its own distinguishing characteristics.
5.   (F)   A company can use both a job order system and a process cost system as General Motors does with different types of automobiles.
6.   (T)
7.   (F)   The cost of raw materials purchased is **debited** to Raw Materials Inventory when materials are received.
8.   (T)
9.   (F)   Factory Labor is not a control account.
10. (F)   A job cost sheet is a form used to record the costs chargeable to a specific job and to determine the total and unit cost of the job.
11. (T)
12. (F)   Raw materials costs are assigned to Work in Process Inventory when the materials are issued by the storeroom.
13. (T)
14. (T)
15. (T)
16. (F)   The use of a predetermined overhead rate enables the company to determine the approximate total cost of each job when the job is completed.
17. (T)
18. (F)   Overapplied manufacturing overhead exists when the overhead assigned to work in process is greater than the overhead incurred.
19. (F)   At the end of the year, underapplied overhead is usually debited to Cost of Goods Sold, and overapplied overhead is credited to Cost of Goods Sold.
20. (T)

MULTIPLE CHOICE

1.   (d)   Cost accounting involves the measuring, recording, and reporting of product costs.

2.   (c)   Job order costing would be used by a company that manufactures many jobs with distinguishing characteristics such as homes (a), motion pictures (b), and bridges (d). Process costing would be used for a homogeneous product such as cereal.

3.   (c)   Finished Goods Inventory is only debited for the cost of the completed job. The usual entry for the purchase of raw materials is Dr. Raw Materials Inventory, and Cr. Accounts Payable.

4.   (a)   Indirect labor costs are recorded by a debit to manufacturing overhead.

5.   (d)   A job cost sheet is a form used to record the cost charged to a specific job and to determine the total and unit cost of the completed job. Answers (a) and (b) pertain to subsidiary ledgers for raw materials and finished goods inventories. There is no cost of goods sold record (c).

6.   (d)   When indirect materials are used in production the following entry is made:

Manufacturing Overhead	XXX	
Raw Materials Inventory		XXX

7.   (b)   Factory utilities (a), indirect labor (c), and depreciation expense on factory machinery (d) are all included in the manufacturing overhead account. Direct labor is assigned directly to Work in Process Inventory.

8.   (b)   Raw Materials Inventory (a) and Manufacturing Overhead (c) are both control accounts. Factory Labor is not a control account.

9.   (a)   The debit to Work in Process Inventory is direct labor cost ($180,000) times the predetermined overhead rate of 70%.

10.   (c)   Manufacturing overhead is 200% of direct labor cost. Thus, direct labor cost is $20,000 ($40,000 ÷ 200%) and total costs are $90,000 ($30,000 + $20,000 + $40,000).

11.   (b)   The total manufacturing cost is calculated as follows:

Direct materials used	$4,200
Direct labor (300 X $8.00)	2,400
Manufacturing overhead (200 X $15.00)	3,000
Total manufacturing cost	$9,600

12.   (c)   If manufacturing overhead was $2,250, direct labor was $2,500 ($2,250 ÷ 90%). Therefore, direct materials must equal $4,250 [$9,000 - ($2,250 + $2,500)].

13.   (d)   When a job is finished, the following journal entry is made:

Finished Goods Inventory	XXX	
Work in Process Inventory		XXX

14.   (a)   When units are sold, the following journal entries are made:

Cost of Goods Sold	XXX	
Finished Goods Inventory		XXX
Accounts Receivable	XXX	
Sales		XXX

15.   (c)   The amount of overhead applied was $660,000 ($5 X 132,000). Therefore, there is $10,000 of overapplied overhead ($660,000 - $650,000).

16.   (d)   The amount of overhead applied was $300,000 ($3.00 X 100,000). Therefore, there is $25,000 of underapplied overhead ($325,000 - $300,000).

17.   (c)   Overapplied manufacturing overhead exists when overhead assigned to work in process is more than overhead incurred and results in a credit balance in Manufacturing Overhead at the end of the period.

18.   (b)   To transfer underapplied overhead to Cost of Goods Sold, the following entry is made:

Cost of Goods Sold   XXX
        Manufacturing Overhead   XXX

19.   (a)   To transfer overapplied overhead to Cost of Goods Sold, the following entry is made:

Manufacturing Overhead..   XXX
        Cost of Goods Sold   XXX

20.   (a)   Answer (b) is incorrect because when Manfacturing Overhead has a credit balance, overhead is said to be overapplied. At the end of the year, under- or overapplied overhead is eliminated by an adjusting entry (c), and it is not reported in the balance sheet (d).

MATCHING

1.	i	6.	f
2.	h	7.	b
3.	a	8.	d
4.	c	9.	g
5.	e		

EXERCISES

EX. 2-1

	General Journal		J1
Date	**Account Title**	**Debit**	**Credit**
(a)	Work in Process Inventory	26,000	
	Raw Materials Inventory		26,000
	(To record materials used)		
(b)	Work in Process Inventory	20,000	
	Factory Labor		20,000
	(To assign factory labor to production)		
(c)	Work in Process Inventory	30,000	
	Manufacturing Overhead		30,000
	(To assign overhead to jobs:		
	150% X $20,000)		
(d)	Finished Goods Inventory	77,700	
	Work in Process Inventory		77,700
	[$9,000 + $26,000 + $20,000 + $30,000 -		
	$2,800 - $1,800 - ($1,800 X 150%)]		

(e)

Work in Process Inventory			
Bal.	9,000	(d)	77,700
(a)	26,000		
(b)	20,000		
(c)	30,000		
Bal.	7,300		

Job 204

Direct materials	2,800
Direct labor	1,800
Manufacturing overhead	2,700*
Total	7,300

*$1800 X 150% = $2,700.

EX. 2-2

Date	Account Title	Debit	Credit
	General Journal		**J1**
(a)	1. Raw Materials Inventory	820,000	
	Accounts Payable		820,000
	2. Factory Labor	680,000	
	Factory Wages Payable		630,000
	Employer Payroll Taxes Payable		50,000
	3. Manufacturing Overhead	174,000	
	Accounts Payable		124,000
	Cash		50,000
	4. Work in Process Inventory	600,000	
	Manufacturing Overhead	200,000	
	Raw Materials Inventory		800,000
	5. Work in Process Inventory	650,000	
	Manufacturing Overhead	30,000	
	Factory Labor		680,000
	6. Work in Process Inventory	195,000	
	Manufacturing Overhead		195,000
	7. Finished Goods Inventory	1,100,000	
	Work in Process Inventory		1,100,000

| General Journal | | | J2 |
Date	Account Title	Debit	Credit
	8. Accounts Receivable	1,400,000	
	Sales		1,400,000
	Cost of Goods Sold	1,000,000	
	Finished Goods Inventory		1,000,000
(b)	Cost of Goods Sold	5,000	
	Manufacturing Overhead		5,000

Chapter 3

PROCESS COST ACCOUNTING

The Navigator ✓
- ■ Scan Study Objectives ☐
- ■ Read Preview ☐
- ■ Read Chapter Review ☐
- ■ Work Demonstration Problem ☐
- ■ Answer True-False Statements ☐
- ■ Answer Multiple-Choice Questions ☐
- ■ Match Terms and Definitions ☐
- ■ Solve Exercises ☐

CHAPTER STUDY OBJECTIVES

After studying this chapter, you should be able to:
1. Understand who uses process cost systems.
2. Explain the similarities and differences between job order cost and process cost systems.
3. Explain the flow of costs in a process cost system.
4. Make the journal entries to assign manufacturing costs in a process cost system.
5. Compute equivalent units.
6. Explain the four steps necessary to prepare a production cost report.
7. Prepare a production cost report.
*8. Compute equivalent units using the FIFO method.

*Note: All **asterisked** (*) items relate to material contained in the Appendix to the chapter.

The Navigator

PREVIEW OF CHAPTER 3

In contrast to job order cost accounting, which focuses on the individual job, process cost accounting focuses on the processes involved in mass-producing products that are identical or very similar in nature. The primary objective of the chapter is to explain and illustrate process cost accounting. The content and organization of this chapter are as follows:

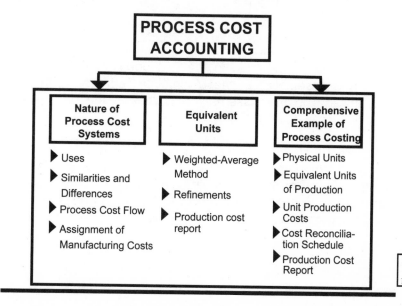

CHAPTER REVIEW

Process Manufacturing and Accounting

1. (S.O. 1) Process cost systems are used to apply costs to similar products that are mass produced in a continuous fashion, such as the production of ice cream, steel or soft drinks. In comparison, costs in a job order cost system are assigned to a specific job, such as the construction of a customized home, the making of a motion picture, or the manufacturing of a specialized machine.

2. (S.O. 2) Job order cost and process cost systems are similar in that (a) both use the same three manufacturing cost elements of direct materials, direct labor, and manufacturing overhead; (b) both accumulate costs of raw materials by debiting Raw Materials Inventory, factory labor by debiting Factory Labor, and manufacturing overhead costs by debiting Manufacturing Overhead; and (c) both flow costs to the same accounts of Work in Process, Finished Goods Inventory, and Cost of Goods Sold.

3. The major differences between a job order cost system and a process cost system are as follows:

Feature	Job Order Cost System	Process Cost System
Work in process accounts	One for each job	One for each process
Documents used	Job cost sheets	Production cost reports
Determination of total manufacturing costs	Each job	Each period
Unit-cost computations	Cost of each job ÷ Units produced for the job	Total manufacturing costs ÷ Equivalent Units produced during the period

Process Cost Flow

4. (S.O. 3) In the Tyler Company example in the text book, manufacturing consists of two processes: machining and assembly. In the Machining Department, the raw materials are shaped, honed, and drilled. In the Assembly Department, the parts are assembled and packaged.

5. Materials, labor, and manufacturing overhead can be added in both the Machining and Assembly Departments. When the Machining Department finishes its work, the partially completed units are transferred to the Assembly Department. In the Assembly Department, the goods are finished and are then transferred to the finished goods inventory. Upon sale, the goods are removed from the finished goods inventory.

Assignment of Manufacturing Costs

6. (S.O. 4) All raw materials issued for production are a materials cost to the producing department. Materials requisition slips may be used in a process cost system, but fewer requisitions are generally required than in a job order cost system, because the materials are used for processes rather than for specific jobs. The entry to record the materials used is:

Work in Process--Machining	XXXX	
Work in Process--Assembly	XXXX	
Raw Materials Inventory		XXXX

7. Time tickets may be used in determining the cost of labor assignable to the production departments. The labor cost chargeable to a process can be obtained from the payroll register or departmental payroll summaries. All labor costs incurred within a producing department are a cost of processing the raw materials. The entry to assign the labor costs is:

Work in Process--Machining	XXXX	
Work in Process--Assembly	XXXX	
Factory Labor		XXXX

8. The basis for allocating the overhead costs to the production departments in an objective and equitable manner is the activity that "drives" or causes the costs. A primary driver of overhead costs in continuous manufacturing operations is machine time used, not direct labor. Thus, machine hours are widely used in allocating manufacturing overhead costs. The entry to allocate overhead is:

Work in Process--Machining	XXXX	
Work in Process--Assembly	XXXX	
Manufacturing Overhead		XXXX

9. At the end of the period, the following transfer entries are needed:

Work in Process--Assembly	XXXX	
Work in Process--Machining		XXXX
Finished Goods Inventory	XXXX	
Work in Process--Assembly		XXXX
Cost of Goods Sold	XXXX	
Finished Goods Inventory		XXXX

Equivalent Units

10. (S.O. 5) A major step in process cost accounting is the calculation of equivalent units. **Equivalent units of production** measure the work done during the period, expressed in fully completed units. This concept is used to determine the cost per unit of completed product.

11. The formula to compute equivalent units of production is as follows:

Units Completed and Transferred Out	+	Equivalent Units of Ending Work in Process	=	Equivalent Units of Production

12. The method of computing equivalent units here is referred to as the weighted-average method. It considers the degree of completion (weighting) of the units completed and transferred out and the ending work in process. A lesser used method, called the FIFO method, is discussed in the appendix to this chapter.

13. To illustrate the computation of equivalent units using the weighted-average method, assume that materials are entered at the beginning of the process and the following information is provided for the Processing Department of the Silva Company:

	Physical Units	Percentage Complete Materials	Conversion Costs
Work in process, Beg.	2,500	100%	80%
Started into production	4,500		
Total units	7,000		
Units transferred out	6,000		
Work in process, End.	1,000	100%	60%
Total units	7,000		

14. The two equivalent unit computations are as follows:

	Equivalent Units Materials	Conversion Costs
Units transferred out	6,000	6,000
Work in process, End		
1,000 X 100%	1,000	
1,000 X 60%		600
Total equivalent units	7,000	6,600

Production Cost Report

15. (S.O. 6) A **production cost report** is the key document used by management to understand the activities in a department because it shows the production quantity and cost data related to that department. In order to be ready to complete a production cost report, the company must perform four steps:
     a. Compute the physical unit flow.
     b. Compute the equivalent units of production.
     c. Compute unit production costs.
     d. Prepare a cost reconciliation schedule.

16. The **computation of physical units** involves:
     a. adding the units started (or transferred) into production during the period to the units in process at the beginning of the period to determine the **total units to be accounted for**; and
     b. accounting for these units by determining the **output** for the period—which consists of units transferred out during the period and units in process at the end of the period.

In the example above, the **total units to be accounted for** and the **units accounted for** are both equal to 7,000 units for the Silva Company.

17. In computing unit costs, production costs are expressed in terms of equivalent units of production. When equivalent units are different for materials and conversion costs, the formulas for computing unit costs are as follows:

$$\text{Total Materials Cost} \div \text{Equivalent Units of Materials} = \text{Unit Materials Cost}$$

$$\text{Total Conversion Costs} \div \text{Equivalent Units of Conversion Costs} = \text{Unit Conversion Cost}$$

$$\text{Unit Materials Cost} + \text{Unit Conversion Cost} = \text{Total Manufacturing Cost per Unit}$$

18. The **cost reconciliation schedule** shows that the total costs accounted for equal the **total costs to be accounted for** as follows:

Costs to be accounted for		
Transferred out		$XXXX
Work in process, End		
Materials	$XXXX	
Conversion costs	XXXX	XXXX
Total costs		$XXXX

19. (S.O. 7) Assume the Processing Department of the Silva Company has the following additional cost information:

Work in process, Beg.	
Direct materials: 100% complete	$ 24,000
Conversion costs: 80% complete	19,620
Cost of work in process, Beg.	$ 43,620
Costs incurred during production	
Direct materials	$200,000
Conversion costs	150,000
Costs incurred	$350,000

20. The Silva Company's Processing Department Production Cost Report at the end of the period is as follows:

**Processing Department
Production Cost Report
For the Period Ended**

	Physical Units	Equivalent Units	
		Materials	Conversion Costs
QUANTITIES			
Units to be accounted for			
Work in process, Beg.	2,500		
Started into production	4,500		
Total units	7,000		
Units accounted for			
Transferred out	6,000	6,000	6,000
Work in process, End.	1,000	1,000	600 (1,000 x 60%)
Total units	7,000	7,000	6,600

		Materials	Conversion Costs	Total
COSTS				
Unit costs				
Costs during the period	(a)	$224,000	$169,620	$393,620
Equivalent units	(b)	7,000	6,600	
Unit costs [(a) ÷ (b)]		$32.00	$25.70	$57.70
Costs to be accounted for				
Work in process, Beg.				$ 43,620
Started into production				350,000
Total costs				$393,620

Cost Reconciliation Schedule

Costs accounted for			
Transferred out (6,000 X $57.70)			$346,200
Work in process, End.			
Materials (1,000 X $32.00)		$32,000	
Conversion costs (600 X $25.70)		15,420	47,420
Total costs			$393,620

Operations Costing

21. Companies often use a combination of a process cost and a job order cost system, called **operations costing.** Operations costing is similar to process costing in that standardized methods are used to manufacture the product. At the same time, the product may have some customized, individual features that require the use of a job order cost system.

Equivalent Units Using the FIFO Method

*22. (S.O. 8) To illustrate the computation of equivalent units using the FIFO method, assume that materials are entered at the beginning of the process and the following information is provided for the Processing Department of the Silva Company:

		Percentage Complete	
	Physical Units	Materials	Conversion Costs
Work in process, Beg.	2,500	100%	80%
Started into production	4,500		
Total units	7,000		
Units transferred out	6,000		
Work in process, End.	1,000	100%	60%
Total units	7,000		

*23. The equivalent units for material costs of the Processing Department under the FIFO method are computed as follows:

Processing Department

Production Data	Physical Units	Work Added This Period	Equivalent Units
Work in process, Beg.	2,500	0	
Started and finished	3,500	100%	3,500
Work in process, End.	1,000	100%	1,000
Total	7,000		4,500

*24. The equivalent units for conversion costs of the Processing Department under the FIFO method are computed as follows:

Processing Department

Production Data	Physical Units	Work Added This Period	Equivalent Units
Work in process, Beg.	2,500	20%	500
Started and completed	3,500	100%	3,500
Work in process, End.	1,000	60%	600
Total	7,000		4,600

Production Cost Report Using the FIFO Method

*25. Assume the Processing Department of the Silva Company has the following additional cost information:

Work in process, Beg.	
Direct materials: 100% complete	$ 24,000
Conversion costs: 80% complete	19,620
Cost of work in process, Beg.	$ 43,620
Costs incurred during the production	
Direct materials	$200,000
Conversion costs	150,000
Costs incurred	$350,000

*26. The Silva Company's Processing Department Production Cost Report at the end of the period using the FIFO method is as follows:

Processing Department
Production Cost Report
For the Period Ended

	Physical Units	Equivalent Units Materials	Equivalent Units Conversion Costs
QUANTITIES			
Units to be accounted for			
Work in process, Beg.	2,500		
Started into production	4,500		
Total units	7,000		
Units accounted for			
Completed and transferred out			
Work in process, Beg.	2,500	0	500
Started and completed	3,500	3,500	3,500
Work in process, End.	1,000	1,000	600
Total units	7,000	4,500	4,600

		Materials	Conversion Costs	Total
COSTS				
Unit costs				
Costs during the period	(a)	$200,000	$150,000	$350,000
Equivalent units	(b)	4,500	4,600	
Unit costs [(a)/(b)]		$44.444	$ 32.609	$77.053
Costs to be accounted for				
Work in process, Beg.				$ 43,620
Started into production				350,000
Total costs				$393,620

Cost Reconciliation Schedule

Costs accounted for			
Transferred out			
Work in process,			$ 43,620
Costs to complete beg. work in process			
Conversion costs (500 X $32.609)			16,305
Total costs			59,925
Units started and completed (3,500 X $77.053)			269,686
Total costs transferred out			329,611
Work in process, End			
Materials (1,000 X $44.444)		$44,444	
Conversion costs (600 X $32.609)		19,565	64,009
Total costs			$393,620

DEMONSTRATION PROBLEM (S.O. 5 and 6)

Assume data for the Stuart Cox Company for the Cutting Department for the month of November is as follows:

Units:	
Work in process, Nov. 1	21,000
Direct materials: 100% complete	
Conversion costs: 40% complete	
Units started into production during Nov.	500,000
Units completed and transferred out	450,000
Work in process, Nov. 30	71,000
Direct materials: 100% complete	
Conversion costs: 20% complete	
Costs:	
Work in process, Nov. 1	
Direct materials: 100% complete	$ 18,000
Conversion costs: 40% complete	16,600
Cost of work in process, Nov. 1	$ 34,600
Costs incurred during production in Nov.	
Direct materials	$262,000
Conversion costs	555,280
Costs incurred Nov.	$817,280

Instructions

Compute the physical unit flow, the equivalent units of production and unit production costs.

SOLUTION TO DEMONSTRATION PROBLEM

Cutting Department

	Physical Units
Units to be accounted for	
Work in process, Nov. 1	21,000
Started (transferred) into production	500,000
Total units	521,000
Units accounted for	
Completed and transferred out	450,000
Work in process, Nov. 30	71,000
Total units	521,000

	Equivalent Units	
	Materials	Conversion Costs
Units transferred out	450,000	450,000
Work in process, Nov. 30		
71,000 X 100%	71,000	
71,000 X 20%		14,200
Total equivalent units	521,000	464,200

Unit Materials Cost = ($18,000 + $262,000) ÷ 521,000 = $0.54
Unit Conversion Cost = ($16,600 + $555,280) ÷ 464,200 = $1.23

REVIEW QUESTIONS AND EXERCISES

TRUE—FALSE

Indicate whether each of the following is true (T) or false (F) in the space provided.

_____ 1. (S.O. 1)   Process cost accounting focuses on the individual job as opposed to job order costing which focuses on homogeneous products.

_____ 2. (S.O. 1)   In continuous process manufacturing, generally once the production begins, it continues until the finished product emerges.

_____ 3. (S.O. 1)   In process costing, there is usually only one work in process account.

_____ 4. (S.O. 2)   One similarity of process cost accounting with job order cost accounting is that both determine total manufacturing costs after each job.

_____ 5. (S.O. 2)   One difference of process costing with job order cost accounting is that they both track different manufacturing cost elements.

_____ 6. (S.O. 3)   The flow of costs in a process costing system require that materials be added in one department, labor added in another department and manufacturing overhead in a third department.

_____ 7. (S.O. 4)   Raw materials are usually added to production at the beginning of the first process.

_____ 8. (S.O. 4)   In process cost accounting, manufacturing costs are accumulated by debits to Raw Materials Inventory, Factory Labor, and Manufacturing Overhead.

_____ 9. (S.O. 4)   In process costing, there are usually more requisition slips because the materials are used for processes rather than jobs.

_____ 10. (S.O. 4)   The primary driver of overhead costs in continuous manufacturing operations is machine time used.

_____ 11. (S.O. 4)   When finished goods are sold, the entry to record the cost of goods sold is a debit to Finished Goods Inventory and a credit to Cost of Goods Sold.

_____ 12. (S.O. 5)   When computing physical units, the beginning inventory plus units started equals the units transferred out plus ending inventory.

_____ 13. (S.O. 5)   Equivalent units of production are a measure of the work done during the period.

_____ 14. (S.O. 5)   Equivalent Units of Production are equal to the Units Completed and Transferred Out and Equivalent Units of Ending Work in Process.

_____ 15. (S.O. 5)   When there is no beginning work in process and materials are entered at the beginning of the process, equivalent units of materials are the same as the units started into production.

_____ 16. (S.O. 5)   If 15,000 units are completed and transferred out and there are 5,000 units in ending inventory 60% complete, the equivalent units for conversion costs are 18,000.

_____ 17. (S.O. 5)   The unit conversion cost is equal to the total conversion costs divided by equivalent units of materials.

_____ 18. (S.O. 6)   A production cost report shows both production quantity and cost data for a production department.

_____ 19. (S.O. 6) In order to compute the physical unit flow, a company must first compute unit production costs.

_____ 20. (S.O. 7)   When calculating equivalent units of production, beginning work in process is generally included in the units "transferred out."

_____ *21. (S.O. 8)   Under the FIFO method, it is assumed that the beginning work in process is completed before new work is started.

The
Navigator

MULTIPLE CHOICE

Circle the letter that best answers each of the following statements.

1. (S.O. 1) Which of the following is an **incorrect** statement concerning process cost accounting?
   a. Individual work in process accounts are maintained for each production department or manufacturing process.
   b. The summarization of manufacturing costs is performed on production cost reports.
   c. The focus is on the individual job.
   d. The system is used by companies that manufacture products through a series of continuous processes or operations.

2. (S.O. 2) Which of the following is considered a difference between a job order cost and a process cost system?
   a. The manufacturing cost elements.
   b. Documents used to track costs.
   c. The accumulation of the costs of materials, labor, and overhead.
   d. The flow of costs.

3. (S.O. 2) Which of the following is considered a similarity between a job order cost and a process cost system?
   a. The flow of costs.
   b. The number of work in process accounts used.
   c. The point at which costs are totaled.
   d. Unit cost computations.

4. (S.O. 5) Total physical units to be accounted for are equal to the units:
   a. started (or transferred) into production.
   b. started (or transferred) into production plus the units in beginning work in process.
   c. started (or transferred) into production less the units in beginning work in process.
   d. completed and transferred out.

5. (S.O. 5) Equivalent units of production are a measure of:
   a. completed and transferred out.
   b. units transferred out.
   c. units in ending work in process.
   d. the work done during the period expressed in fully completed units.

6. (S.O. 6) In Saint-Simon, Inc., the Assembly Department started 6,000 units and completed 7,000 units. If beginning work in process was 3,000 units, how many units are in ending work in process?
   a. 0.
   b. 1,000.
   c. 2,000.
   d. 4,000.

7. (S.O. 6) In the Blanc Company, the Cutting Department had beginning work in process of 4,000 units, transferred out 9,000 units, and an ending work in process of 2,000 units. How many units were started by Blanc during the month?
    a. 6,000.
    b. 7,000.
    c. 9,000.
    d. 11,000.

8. (S.O. 6) In the Camria Company, materials are entered at the beginning of the process. If there is no beginning work in process, but there is an ending work in process inventory, the number of equivalent units as to material costs will be:
    a. the same as the units started.
    b. the same as the units completed.
    c. less than the units started.
    d. less than the units completed.

9. (S.O. 6) In its first month of operation, the Molding Department started 20,000 units into production. During the month, 18,000 units were transferred out and the 2,000 units in work in process were 100% complete as to materials and 40% complete as to conversion costs. Equivalent units for conversion costs are:
    a. 20,000.
    b. 18,000.
    c. 18,800.
    d. 19,200.

10. (S.O. 6) Equivalent units of production for conversion costs:
    a. includes all of the beginning work in process units transferred out.
    b. includes only conversion costs performed on beginning work in process during the period.
    c. includes all of the ending work in process units started during the period.
    d. excludes all of the ending work in process units.

11. (S.O. 6) The Cutting Department for Babeuf Company began the period with 4,000 units that were 75% complete, transferred out 14,000 units, and ended with 6,000 units that were 40% complete. The number of equivalent units of conversion costs is:
    a. 13,400.
    b. 14,600.
    c. 15,400.
    d. 16,400.

12. (S.O. 6) The Molding Department of the Smith Company has the following production data: beginning work in process 20,000 units (60% complete), started into production 340,000 units, completed and transferred out 320,000 units, and ending work in process 40,000 units (40% complete). Assuming materials are entered at the beginning of the process, equivalent units for materials are:
    a. 360,000.
    b. 300,000.
    c. 320,000.
    d. 380,000.

13. (S.O. 6) Using the data in question 12 and assuming conversion costs are incurred uniformly during the process, the equivalent units for conversion costs are:
    a. 320,000.
    b. 324,000.
    c. 336,000.
    d. 360,000.

14. (S.O. 6) Malthus Company has the following equivalent units for July: materials 10,000 and conversion costs 9,000. Production cost data are:

	Materials	Conversion
Work in process, July 1	$ 9,600	$ 4,500
Costs added in July	75,600	63,000

    The unit production costs for July are:

	Materials	Conversion Costs
a.	$7.56	$7.50
b.	8.52	7.00
c.	7.56	7.00
d.	8.52	7.50

15. (S.O. 6) For the Assembly Department, unit materials cost is $8 and unit conversion cost is $12. If there are 4,000 units in ending work in process 75% complete as to conversion costs, the costs to be assigned to the inventory are:
    a. $80,000.
    b. $68,000.
    c. $60,000.
    d. $72,000.

16. (S.O. 6) In the Shaping Department of the Hendrix Company, the unit materials cost is $5.00 and the unit conversion cost is $3.00. The department transferred out 8,000 units and had 1,000 units in ending work in process 20% complete. If all materials are added at the beginning of the process, what is the total cost to be assigned to the ending work in process?
    a. $1,600.
    b. $5,000.
    c. $5,600.
    d. $8,000.

17. (S.O. 7) In a production cost report, which one of the following sections is **not** shown under Costs?
    a. Unit costs.
    b. Costs to be accounted for.
    c. Costs during the period.
    d. Units accounted for.

18. (S.O. 7) Which of the following statements about the production cost report is **incorrect**?
    a. Units accounted for must equal units to be accounted for.
    b. The report only provides a basis for determining whether unit costs and total costs are correct.
    c. Total costs should reconcile.
    d. There are four steps in preparing the report.

19. (S.O. 6)   When materials are added at the beginning of the process and costs are transferred in from another department, unit materials cost is based on the:
    a.   sum of the materials costs in the beginning work in process plus the cost of materials added during the period.
    b.   materials costs added during the period.
    c.   sum of the materials costs in the work in process plus materials costs added during the period plus the costs transferred in.
    d.   costs transferred in.

20. (S.O. 6) The Finishing Department of the Monica Company has 27,500 equivalent units of materials in June. An analysis of the work in process account shows: materials cost in beginning work in process $25,000, materials cost added during the period $50,000, and costs transferred in from assembly $200,000. The unit materials cost for June is:
    a. $10.
    b. $8.
    c. $2.
    d. $3.

*21. (S.O. 8) The Molding Department of the Smith Company has the following production data: beginning work in process 20,000 units (60% complete), started into production 340,000 units, completed and transferred out 320,000 units, and ending work in process 40,000 units (40% complete). Assuming materials are entered at the beginning of the process, the equivalent units under the FIFO method are:
    a.   340,000.
    b.   300,000.
    c.   320,000.
    d.   380,000.

*22. (S.O. 8) Using the data in question 21, the equivalent units under the FIFO method for conversion costs are:
    a.   320,000.
    b.   324,000.
    c.   350,000.
    d.   360,000.

The
Navigator

MATCHING

Match each term with its definition by writing the appropriate letter in the space provided.

Terms	**Definitions**

Terms

_____ 1. Production cost report.

_____ 2. Physical units.

_____ 3. Process cost accounting.

_____ 4. Operations costing.

_____ 5. Unit production costs.

_____ 6. Weighted average method.

_____ 7. Equivalent units of production.

_____ 8. Total units (costs) to be accounted for.

_____ 9. Total units (costs) accounted for.

Definitions

a. An accounting system used to apply costs to similar products that are mass-produced in a continuous fashion.

b. The sum of the units (costs) started (or transferred) into production during the period plus the units (costs) in process at the beginning of the period.

c. A measure of the work done during the period, expressed in fully completed units.

d. Method used to compute equivalent units of production which considers the degree of completion (weighting) of the units completed and transferred out and the ending work in process.

e. Actual units to be accounted for during a period irrespective of any work performed.

f. Costs expressed in terms of equivalent units of production.

g. An internal report that shows both production quantity and production costs.

h. A combination of a process cost and a job order cost system, in which products are manufactured primarily by standardized methods, with some customization.

i. The sum of the units (costs) transferred out during the period plus the units (costs) in process at the end of the period.

The
Navigator

EXERCISES

EX. 3-1   Avanti Manufacturing Company has two production departments: Molding and Assembly.   March 1 inventories are Raw Materials $3,600, Work in Process—Molding $2,200, Work in Process—Assembly $8,800 and Finished Goods $26,000.   During March, the following transactions occurred:

1.   Purchased $28,400 of raw materials on account.
2.   Incurred $48,000 of factory labor. (Credit Wages Payable.)
3.   Incurred $62,000 of manufacturing overhead; $39,000 was paid and the remainder is unpaid.
4.   Requisitioned materials for Molding $12,300 and Assembly $7,200.
5.   Used Factory labor for Molding $26,000 and Assembly $22,000.
6.   Applied overhead at the rate of $18 per machine hour. Machine hours were Molding 1,540 and Assembly 1,430.
7.   Transferred goods costing $62,000 from the Molding Department to the Assembly Department.
8.   Transferred goods costing $122,600 from Assembly to Finished Goods.
9.   Sold goods costing $110,000 for $185,000 on account.

Instructions
Journalize the transactions. (Omit explanations.)

EX. 3-2   (S.O. 5 and 6) Sismondi Company has a process cost accounting system. During May, the Assembly and Finishing Departments had the following data concerning physical units:

Assembly:

Work in process, May 1	3,000
Started into process during the month	65,000
Work in process, May 31	7,000

Finishing:

Work in process, May 1	6,000
Transferred in from Assembly Department during the month	?
Work in process, May 31	4,000

Instructions
Compute the physical units transferred out and in process for each department.

SISMONDI COMPANY

	Assembly	Finishing
Units to be accounted for		

Units accounted for		

EX. 3-3   (S.O. 5, 6, and 7) The Muller Company reports the following physical units for its Polishing Department for the month ended July 31, 2006.

Units to be accounted for	Physical Units
Work in process, July 1	1,000
Transferred in	11,000
Total units	12,000

Units accounted for	
Completed and transferred out	10,500
Work in process, July 31 (30% complete)	1,500
Total units	12,000

Work in process July 1 was $3,000 for direct materials and $1,920 for conversion costs. Costs incurred in July were: materials $59,400, labor $23,520, and overhead $9,600.   The percentage complete refers to conversion costs.   Materials and transferred in units are added at the beginning of the process.

Instructions
Prepare the production cost report.

MULLER COMPANY
Polishing Department
Production Cost Report
For the Month Ended July 31, 2006

		Equivalent Units	
QUANTITIES	**Physical Units**	**Materials**	**Conversion Costs**
Units to be accounted for			
Units accounted for			

COSTS

Unit costs	**Materials**	**Conversion Costs**	**Total**

Costs to be accounted for

Cost Reconciliation Schedule

SOLUTIONS TO REVIEW QUESTIONS AND EXERCISES

TRUE-FALSE

1. (F) Job order costing focuses on the individual job, while process cost accounting focuses on the processes involved in producing homogeneous products.

2. (T)

3. (F) A distinctive feature of process cost accounting is that individual work in process accounts are maintained for each production department or manufacturing process.

4. (F) Under process cost accounting, the determination of total manufacturing costs is made for each accounting period.

5. (F) Both job order costing and process costing track the same three manufacturing cost elements—direct materials, direct labor, and manufacturing overhead.

6. (F) The flow of costs indicates that materials, labor, and manufacturing overhead can be added in any or all departments.

7. (T)

8. (T)

9. (F) Fewer requisitions are generally required because the materials are used for processes rather than jobs.

10. (T)

11. (F) When finished goods are sold, the entry to record the cost of goods sold is a debit to Cost of Goods Sold and a credit to Finished Goods Inventory.

12. (T)

13. (T)

14. (T)

15. (T)

16. (T)

17. (F) The unit conversion cost is equal to the total conversion costs divided by equivalent units of conversion costs.

18. (T)

19. (F) The order of calculation in a production cost report requires that the computation of the physical unit flow come before the computation of the unit production costs.

20. (T)

*21. (T)

MULTIPLE CHOICE

1. (c) Process cost accounting focuses on the process involved in producing homogeneous products not on individual jobs. Answers (a), (b), and (d) are all correct statements concerning process cost accounting.

2. (b) One of the differences between a job order cost and a process cost system is the documents used to track costs. Answers a., c., and d., are all considered to be examples of similarities between the two systems.

3. (a) One of the similarities between a job order cost and a process cost system is the flow of costs. Answers b., c., and d. are all considered to be examples of differences between the two systems.

4.   (b)   Total physical units are equal to the sum of the units started (or transferred) into production plus the units in beginning work in process.

5.   (d)   Equivalent units of production are a measure of the work done during the period expressed in fully completed units.

6.   (c)   The number of units in ending work in process is:

Beginning work in process...	3,000
Started..	6,000
Total units to be accounted for	9,000
Less: Units completed	7,000
Ending work in process	2,000

7.   (b)   The number of units started is:

Transferred out..	9,000
Ending work in process	2,000
Total units accounted for	11,000
Less: Beginning work in process..................................	4,000
Number of units started	7,000

8.   (a)   Because the inventory is 100% complete as to materials costs, the number of equivalent units would be equal to the number of units started into production. All of the units started (even units not completed) have 100% of the materials used.

9.   (c)   Equivalent units are equal to the 18,000 units transferred out plus 800 units of ending work in process (2,000 X 40%).

10.   (a)   Equivalent units of production for conversion costs includes all the units transferred out which usually includes all of the beginning work in process units.

11.   (d)   The number of equivalent units is:

Units transferred out..	14,000
Ending work in process (6,000 X .40).............................	2,400
Total equivalent units...	16,400

12.   (a)   Equivalent units for materials are:

Units transferred out..	320,000
Ending work in process (40,000 X 100%)	40,000
Total equivalent units...	360,000

13.   (c)   Equivalent units for conversion costs are:

Units transferred out..	320,000
Ending work in process (40,000 X 40%)	16,000
Total equivalent units...	336,000

14.   (d)   Total materials cost ($9,600 + $75,600) divided by 10,000 units is $8.52 and total conversion costs ($4,500 + $63,000) divided by 9,000 units is $7.50.

15.   (b)   The materials cost is $32,000 (4,000 X $8) and the conversion cost is $36,000 (3,000 equivalent units X $12).

16. (c) The total cost to be assigned to the ending work in process is:

Materials	1,000 X 100% X $5.00 =		$5,000
Conversion costs	1,000 X 20% X $3.00 =		600
Total			$5,600

17. (d) Units accounted for are reported under Quantities in the production cost report.

18. (b) The report is generally used for evaluating the productivity of a department.

19. (c) When materials are added at the beginning of the process, transferred in costs are considered to be a materials cost. The base for computing unit materials cost is the sum of the materials cost added during the period plus the costs transferred in.

20. (a) Transferred in costs are considered to be a materials cost. Thus, the total materials cost is $275,000 and the unit materials cost is $10 ($275,000 ÷ 27,500).

*21. (a) Equivalent units for materials are:

Units started and completed	300,000
Ending work in process (40,000 X 100%)	40,000
Total equivalent units	340,000

*22. (b) Equivalent units for conversion costs are:

Beg. work in process (20,000 X 40%)	8,000
Units started and completed	300,000
Ending work in process (40,000 X 40%)	16,000
Total equivalent units	324,000

MATCHING

1.	g		6.	d
2.	e		7.	c
3.	a		8.	b
4.	h		9.	i
5.	f			

EXERCISES

EX. 3-1

1.	Raw Materials	28,400	
	Accounts Payable		28,400
2.	Factory Labor	48,000	
	Wages Payable		48,000

3.	Manufacturing Overhead	62,000	
	Cash		39,000
	Accounts Payable		23,000
4.	Work in Process—Molding	12,300	
	Work in Process—Assembly	7,200	
	Raw Materials Inventory		19,500
5.	Work in Process—Molding	26,000	
	Work in Process—Assembly	22,000	
	Factory Labor..		48,000
6.	Work in Process—Molding	27,720	
	Work in Process—Assembly	25,740	
	Manufacturing Overhead		53,460
7.	Work in Process—Assembly	62,000	
	Work in Process—Molding		62,000
8.	Finished Goods Inventory...	122,600	
	Work in Process—Assembly		122,600
9.	Cost of Goods Sold..	110,000	
	Finished Goods Inventory......................................		110,000
	Accounts Receivable	185,000	
	Sales..		185,000

EX. 3-2

SISMONDI COMPANY

	Assembly	Finishing
Units to be accounted for		
Beginning work in process	3,000	6,000
Started into production	65,000	61,000
Total units	68,000	67,000
Units accounted for		
Transferred out	61,000	63,000
Ending work in process	7,000	4,000
Total units	68,000	67,000

EX. 3-3

MULLER COMPANY
Polishing Department
Production Cost Report
For the Month Ended July 31, 2006

	Physical Units	Equivalent Units	
		Materials	Conversion Costs
QUANTITIES			
Units to be accounted for			
Work in process, July 1	1,000		
Transferred in	11,000		
Total units	12,000		
Units accounted for			
Transferred out	10,500	10,500	10,500
Work in process, July 31	1,500	1,500	450 (1,500 X 30%)
Total units	12,000	12,000	10,950

COSTS

		Materials	Conversion Costs	Total
Unit costs				
Costs in July	(a)	$62,400*	$35,040**	$97,440
Equivalent units	(b)	12,000	10,950	
Unit costs (a) ÷ (b)		$5.20	$3.20	$8.40

Costs to be accounted for		
In process, July 1		$ 4,920
Costs in July		92,520
Total costs charged		$97,440

Cost Reconciliation Schedule

Costs accounted for		
Transferred out (10,500 X $8.40)		$88,200
Work in process, July 30		
Materials (1,500 X $5.20)	7,800	
Conversion costs (450 X $3.20)	1,440	9,240
Total costs accounted for		$97,440

*Work in process $3,000 + materials added $59,400.

** Work in process $1,920 + labor $23,520 + overhead $9,600.

Chapter 4

The Navigator ✓
- ■ Scan Study Objectives ☐
- ■ Read Preview ☐
- ■ Read Chapter Review ☐
- ■ Work Demonstration Problem ☐
- ■ Answer True-False Statements ☐
- ■ Answer Multiple-Choice Questions ☐
- ■ Match Terms and Definitions ☐
- ■ Solve Exercises ☐

ACTIVITY-BASED COSTING

CHAPTER STUDY OBJECTIVES

After studying this chapter, you should be able to:
1. Recognize the difference between traditional costing and activity-based costing.
2. Identify the steps in the development of an activity-based costing system.
3. Know how companies identify the activity cost pools used in activity-based costing.
4. Know how companies identify and use the activity cost drivers in activity-based costing.
5. Understand the benefits and limitations of activity-based costing.
6. Differentiate between value-added and nonvalue-added activities.
7. Understand the value of using activity levels in activity-based costing.
8. Apply activity-based costing to service industries.
*9. Explain just-in-time (JIT) processing.

*Note: All **asterisked** (*) items relate to material contained in the Appendix to the chapter.

The Navigator

PREVIEW OF CHAPTER 4

Traditional costing systems are not the best answer for every company. Sometimes a traditional system can mask significant differences in its real cost structure. New management tools have been developed that allow businesses to gather more accurate data for decision-making purposes, including **activity-based costing (ABC).** The content and organization of this chapter are as follows:

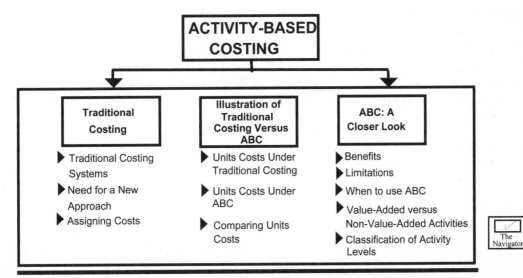

CHAPTER REVIEW

Traditional Costing And Activity-Based Costing

1. (S.O. 1) Often the most difficult part of computing accurate unit costs is determining the proper amount of overhead cost to assign each product, service, or job. For job order costing we assumed the direct labor cost was the relevant activity base for assigning overhead costs to a job and for process costing we assumed that machine hours was the relevant activity base.

2. **Activity-based costing (ABC)** allocates overhead to multiple activity cost pools and assigns the activity cost pools to products and services by means of cost drivers. In ABC, an **activity** is any event, action, transaction, or work sequence that causes the incurrence of cost in producing a product or providing a service. A **cost driver** is any factor or activity that has a direct cause-effect relationship with the resources consumed.

3. ABC allocates overhead in a two-stage process: In the first stage, overhead costs are allocated to activity cost pools, rather than to departments. Each is a distinct type of activity. In the second stage, the overhead allocated to the activity cost pools is assigned to products using cost drivers which represent and measure the number of individual activities undertaken or performed to produce products or provide services.

4. (S.O. 2) Activity-based costing involves the following four steps:
    a. Identify and classify the major activities involved in the manufacture of specific products and allocate manufacturing overhead costs to the appropriate cost pools.
    b. Identify the cost driver that has a strong correlation to the costs accumulated in the cost pool.
    c. For each cost pool, compute the activity-based overhead rate per cost driver.
    d. Assign manufacturing overhead costs for each cost pool to products, using the overhead rates (cost per driver).

Unit Costs Under ABC

5. (S.O. 3) A well designed activity-based costing system starts with an analysis of the activities performed to manufacture a product or provide a service. This analysis should identify all resource-consuming activities. It requires a detailed, step-by-step walk through of each operation, documenting every activity undertaken to accomplish a task.

6. (S.O. 4) After costs are allocated to the activity cost pools, the cost drivers for each cost pool must be identified. The cost driver must accurately measure the actual consumption of the activity by the various products. To achieve accurate costing, a **high degree of correlation** must exist between the cost driver and the actual consumption of the overhead costs in the cost pool.

7. An **activity-based overhead rate** per cost driver is computed by dividing the total estimated overhead per activity by the number of cost drivers expected to be used per activity. The formula for this computation is as follows:

$$\frac{\text{Estimated Overhead Per Activity}}{\text{Expected Use of Cost Driver Per Activity}} = \frac{\text{Activity Based}}{\text{Overhead Rate}}$$

8. In assigning overhead costs, it is necessary to know the expected use of cost drivers **for each product.** To assign overhead costs to each product, the activity-based overhead rates are multiplied by the number of cost drivers expected to be used per product.

Benefits of ABC

9. (S.O. 5) The primary benefit of ABC is more accurate product costing because:
    a. ABC leads to more cost pools.
    b. ABC leads to enhanced control over overhead costs.
    c. ABC leads to better management decisions.

Limits of ABC

10. Although ABC systems often provide better product cost data than traditional volume-based systems, there are the following limitations:
    a. ABC can be expensive.
    b. Some arbitrary allocations continue.

When to Use ABC

11. The presence of one or more of the following factors would point to possibly using ABC:
    a. Product lines differ greatly in volume and manufacturing complexity.
    b. Product lines are numerous, diverse, and require differing degrees of support services.
    c. Overhead costs constitute a significant portion of total costs.
    d. The manufacturing process or the number of products has changed significantly.
    e. Production or marketing managers are ignoring data provided by the existing system and are instead using "bootleg" costing data or other alternative data when pricing or making other product decisions.

Value-Added Versus Non-Value-Added Activities

12. (S.O. 6) **Activity-based management (ABM)** is an extension of ABC from a product costing system to a management function that focuses on reducing costs and improving processes and decision making.
    a. **Value-added activities** increase the worth of a product or service to customers. Examples include engineering design, machining, assembly, painting, and packaging.
    b. **Non-value-added activities** are product- or service-related activities that simply add cost to, or increase the time spent on, a product or service without increasing its market value. Examples include repair of machines, the storage of inventory, the moving of raw materials, assemblies, and finished product; building maintenance; inspections; and inventory control. Examples for service enterprises might include taking appointments, reception, bookkeeping, billing, traveling, ordering supplies, advertising, cleaning, and computer repair.

13. The purpose of ABM is to reduce or eliminate the time and cost devoted to non-value-added activities.

Classification of Activity Levels

14. (S.O. 7) The recognition that some activity costs are not driven by output units has led to the development of a classification of ABC activities, consisting of four levels. The four levels are classified and defined as follows:
    a. **Unit-level activities.** Activities performed for each unit of production.
    b. **Batch-level activities.** Activities performed for each batch of products rather than each unit.
    c. **Product-level activities.** Activities performed in support of an entire product line, but are not always performed every time a new unit or batch of products is produced.
    d. **Facility-level activities.** Activities required to support or sustain an entire production process.

Activity-Based Costing in Service Industries

15. (S.O. 8) The general approach to identifying activities, activity cost pools, and cost drivers is the same for service companies and for manufacturers. Also, the labeling of activities as value-added and non-value-added, and the attempt to reduce or eliminate non-value-added activities as much as possible is just as valid in service industries as in manufacturing operations.

16. Implementation of activity-based costing in service industries is sometimes more difficult because there is a larger proportion of overhead costs which are company-wide costs that cannot be directly traced to specific services provided by the company.

Just-In-Time Processing

*17. (S.O. 9) Just-in-time (JIT) manufacturing is dedicated to having the right amount of materials, products, or parts at the time they are needed. Under JIT processing, raw materials are received just in time for use in production, subassembly parts are completed just in time for use in finished goods, and finished goods are completed just in time to be sold.

*18. A primary objective of JIT is to eliminate all manufacturing inventories. Inventories are considered to have an adverse effect on net income because they tie up funds and storage space that could be made available for more productive purposes.

*19. There are three important elements in JIT processing:
    a. A company must have dependable suppliers who are willing to deliver on short notice exact quantities of raw materials according to precise quality specifications. This may even include multiple deliveries within the same day.
    b. A multiskilled work force must be developed.
    c. A total quality control system must be established throughout the manufacturing operations.

*20. The major benefits of implementing JIT processing are:
   a. Manufacturing inventories are significantly reduced or eliminated.
   b. Product quality is enhanced.
   c. Rework costs and inventory storage costs are reduced or eliminated.
   d. Production cost savings are realized from the improved flow of goods through the processes.

DEMONSTRATION PROBLEM (S.O. 4)

Trujillo Stereos manufactures two high fidelity speaker models: the Sonic which sells for $500 per speaker, and the Boom which sells for $450 per speaker. The production cost computed per unit under traditional costing for each model in 2006 was as follows:

	Sonic	Boom
Direct materials	$150	$140
Direct labor ($20 per hour)	80	60
Manufacturing overhead ($30 per DLH)	120	90
Total	$350	$290

In 2006, Trujillo manufactured 80,000 units of the Sonic and 60,000 units of the Boom. The overhead rate of $30 per direct labor hour was determined by dividing total expected manufacturing overhead of $15,000,000 by the total direct labor hours (500,000) for the two models.

Under traditional costing, the gross profit on the models was: Sonic $150 ($500 - $350) and Boom $160 ($450 - $290). Because of this difference, management is considering phasing out the Sonic model and increasing the production of the Boom model.

Before finalizing its decision, management asks the controller of Trujillo to prepare an analysis using activity-based costing (ABC). The controller accumulates the following information about overhead for the year ended December 31, 2006.

Activity	Cost Driver	Estimated Overhead	Expected Use of Cost Drivers Per Activity	Activity Based Overhead Rate
Purchasing	Number of orders	$3,000,000	120,000	$25
Machine setups	Number of setups	2,000,000	40,000	50
Machining	Machine hours	9,000,000	200,000	45
Quality control	Number of inspections	1,000,000	25,000	40

The cost drivers used for each product were:

Cost Driver	Sonic	Boom	Total
Purchase orders	80,000	40,000	120,000
Machine setups	30,000	10,000	40,000
Machining	90,000	110,000	200,000
Quality control	15,000	10,000	25,000

Instructions

(a)   Assign the total 2006 manufacturing overhead costs to the two products using activity-based costing (ABC).

(b)   What was the cost per unit and gross profit of each model using ABC costing?

(c)   Are management's future plans for the two models sound?

The Navigator

SOLUTION TO DEMONSTRATION PROBLEM

(a)   The allocation of total manufacturing overhead using activity-based costing is as follows:

	Sonic		Boom		
Overhead Rate	**Drivers Used**	**Cost Assigned**	**Drivers Used**	**Cost Assigned**	**Total Overhead**
Purchase orders @ $25	80,000	$2,000,000	40,000	$1,000,000	$3,000,000
Machine setups @ $50	30,000	1,500,000	10,000	500,000	2,000,000
Machine hours @ $45	90,000	4,050,000	110,000	4,950,000	9,000,000
Inspections @ $40	15,000	600,000	10,000	400,000	1,000,000
Total assigned costs (a)		$8,150,000		$6,850,000	$15,000,000
Units produced (b)		80,000		60,000	
Cost per unit (a) ÷ (b)		$101.875		$114.167	

(b)   The cost per unit and gross profit of each model under ABC costing were:

	Sonic	Boom
Direct materials	$150.00	$140.00
Direct labor	80.00	60.00
Manufacturing overhead	101.88	114.17
Total cost per unit	$331.88	$314.17
Sales price per unit	$500.00	$450.00
Cost per unit	331.88	314.17
Gross profit	$168.12	$135.83

(c)   Management's plans for the two speaker models are not sound. Under ABC costing, the Sonic model is $32.29 per unit more profitable than the Boom model.

REVIEW QUESTIONS AND EXERCISES

TRUE—FALSE

Indicate whether each of the following is true (T) or false (F) in the space provided.

_____ 1. (S.O. 1)   The amount of direct labor used in many industries is now greatly increased, and total overhead costs (for depreciation on expensive equipment and machinery, utilities, repair, and maintenance) have significantly decreased.

_____ 2. (S.O. 1)   Activity-based costing (ABC) allocates overhead to multiple cost pools and assigns the cost pools to products by means of cost drivers.

_____ 3. (S.O. 1)   A cost driver is used by retailers to offer low discounts to drive down sales prices.

_____ 4. (S.O. 2)   Under activity-based costing, one of the steps is to identify the cost drivers that accurately measure each activity's contribution to the finished product and compute the activity-based overhead rate.

_____ 5. (S.O. 4)   One of the advantages of activity-based costing is that accurate costing can be achieved without a high degree of correlation between the cost driver and the actual consumption of the cost pool.

_____ 6. (S.O. 4)   An activity-based overhead rate per cost driver is computed by dividing the total number of cost drivers expected to be used per cost pool by the total estimated overhead per activity.

_____ 7. (S.O. 4)   In assigning overhead costs under activity-based costing, it is necessary to know the expected use of cost drivers for each product.

_____ 8. (S.O. 5)   Activity-based costing relies on volume-of-output, unit level allocation bases.

_____ 9. (S.O. 5)   Under activity-based costing, many overhead costs can be traced directly to activities, thus some indirect costs become direct costs.

_____ 10. (S.O. 5)   Activity-based costing changes the amount of total overhead costs.

_____ 11. (S.O. 5)   One of the advantages of activity-based costing is that it is inexpensive to use.

_____ 12. (S.O. 5)   Even though more overhead costs can be assigned directly to products through multiple activity cost pools, certain overhead costs remain to be allocated by means of some arbitrary volume-based cost driver such as labor or machine hours.

_____ 13. (S.O. 5)   When product lines are few, similar, and require the same support services, activity-based costing is generally the better costing system.

_____ 14. (S.O. 5)   When overhead costs constitute a significant portion of total costs, activity-based costing is generally the better costing system.

_____ 15. (S.O. 6)   Value-added activities are production- or service-related activities that simply add cost to, or increase the time spent on, a product or service without increasing its market value.

_____ 16. (S.O. 6)   Not all activities labeled non-value-added are totally wasteful.

_____ 17. (S.O. 7)   Product design and engineering changes are considered product-level activities.

_____ 18. (S.O. 7)   The classification of activity levels provides managers a structured way of thinking about the relationship between activities and the resources they consume.

_____ 19. (S.O. 8)   One of the difficulties of implementing activity-based costing in service industries is that a larger proportion of overhead costs are company-wide costs that cannot be directly traced to specific services provided by the company.

_____ *20. (S.O. 9)   Just-in-time processing strives to eliminate inventories by using a push approach in manufacturing.

The Navigator

MULTIPLE CHOICE

Circle the letter that best answers each of the following statements.

1. (S.O. 1) Which of the following is **not** considered a step in activity-based costing?
    a.   Allocate overhead costs to activity cost pools.
    b.   The overhead allocated to the activity cost pools is assigned to products using cost drivers.
    c.   Identify a single overhead rate as the predetermined overhead rate.
    d.   Identify and classify the major activities involved in the manufacture of specific products.

2. (S.O. 1) Which of the following statements is **incorrect** concerning activity-based costing?
    a.   ABC may be used with either a job order or process cost accounting system.
    b.   ABC assumes all costs related to the activity should respond proportionally to changes in the activity level of the cost driver.
    c.   The primary benefit of ABC is more accurate and meaningful product costing.
    d.   ABC focuses on units of production.

3.   (S.O. 4) Duncan Company uses activity-based costing and one of its activity cost pools is inspecting the product. The total estimated overhead for inspecting is estimated to be $400,000. If the total expected inspections is 80,000, then what is the activity-based overhead rate?
     a. $400,000.
     b. $500.
     c. $50.
     d. $5.

4.   (S.O. 4) To assign overhead costs to each product, the activity-based overhead rates are multiplied by
     a.   the predetermined overhead rate.
     b.   the average number of cost drivers expected to be used.
     c.   the units produced.
     d.   the number of cost drivers expected to be used per product.

The following information pertains to questions 5 through 8.

Bodhi Company has three cost pools and two doggie products (leashes and collars). The activity cost pool of **ordering** has the cost driver of purchase orders. The activity cost pool of **assembly** has a cost driver of parts. The activity cost pool of **supervising** has the cost driver of labor hours. The accumulated data relative to those cost drivers is as follows:

| | | | Expected Use of | |
| | Total Expected | Estimated | Cost Drivers by Product | |
Cost Drivers	Cost Drivers	Overhead	Leashes	Collars
Purchase orders	130,000 orders	$260,000	70,000	60,000
Parts	800,000 parts	400,000	300,000	500,000
Labor hours	25,000 hours	300,000	15,000	10,000
		$960,000		

5.   (S.O. 4) The activity-based overhead rates are:

	per order	per part	per hour
a.	$2.40	$0.50	$ 6.00
b.	$2.00	$0.50	$12.00
c.	$1.00	$2.00	$12.00
d.	$1.00	$0.50	$ 6.00

6.   (S.O. 4) The costs assigned to leashes for supervising are:
     a. $ 90,000.
     b. $180,000.
     c. $120,000.
     d. $ 60,000.

7.   (S.O. 4) The costs assigned to collars for ordering are:
     a. $ 30,000.
     b. $ 35,000.
     c. $120,000.
     d. $130,000.

8. (S.O. 4) The total costs assigned are:

	Leashes	Collars
a.	$270,000	$360,000
b.	$270,000	$470,000
c.	$490,000	$470,000
d.	$470,000	$490,000

9. (S.O. 5) Which of the following is **not** considered a benefit of activity-based costing?
    a. ABC leads to better management decisions.
    b. ABC leads to enhanced control over overhead costs.
    c. Some arbitrary allocations continue.
    d. ABC leads to more cost pools.

10. (S.O. 5) Which of the following is **not** a factor that would indicate ABC as the possible costing system:
    a. Overhead costs constitute an insignificant portion of total costs.
    b. Product lines differ greatly in volume and manufacturing complexity.
    c. Product lines are numerous, diverse, and require differing degrees of support services.
    d. The manufacturing process or the number of products has changed significantly.

11. (S.O. 6) Which of the following would be considered a value-added activity?
    a. Repair of machines.
    b. Storage of inventory.
    c. Engineering design.
    d. Bookkeeping.

12. (S.O. 6) Which of the following would be considered a non-value-added activity?
    a. Machining.
    b. Painting.
    c. Packaging.
    d. Advertising.

13. (S.O. 7) An example of a batch-level activity is:
    a. Drilling.
    b. Engineering changes.
    c. Inspection.
    d. Property taxes.

14. (S.O. 7) An example of a cost associated with a product-level activity is:
    a. Building depreciation.
    b. Equipment setup costs.
    c. Material handling costs.
    d. Product design.

15. (S.O. 7) Which of the following statements about the classification of activity levels is **incorrect**?
   a. Setting up a classification of activity levels provides managers a structured way of thinking about the relationship between activities and the resources they consume.
   b. The number of activities performed at the batch level goes up as the number of units within the batches changes.
   c. Facility-sustaining activity costs are not dependent upon the number of products, batches, or units produced.
   d. The number of activities performed at the batch level goes up as the number of batches rises.

16. (S.O. 8) Which of the following statements about activity-based costing (ABC) in service industries is **incorrect**?
   a. The overall objective of ABC in service firms is no different than it is in a manufacturing company.
   b. The classification of activities into unit-level, batch-level, product-level, and facility-level activities also applies to service industries.
   c. The general approach to identifying activities, activity cost pools, and cost drivers is the same for service companies and for manufacturers.
   d. ABC is usually easier to implement in a service industry because there is a smaller proportion of overhead costs that are company-wide costs.

17. (S.O. 8) A cost driver more likely to be associated with a service industry than a manufacturing industry is:
   a. Number of inspections.
   b. Number of parts painted.
   c. Number of working paper pages.
   d. Number of machine hours.

*18. (S.O. 9) Which of the following statements about just-in-time (JIT) processing is **incorrect?**
   a. Primarily in response to foreign competition, many U.S. firms have switched to JIT processing.
   b. Under JIT processing, sub-assembly parts are completed just in time for use in finished goods.
   c. Inventories of raw materials are maintained just in case some items are of poor quality.
   d. Finished goods are completed just in time to be sold.

*19. (S.O. 9) Which of the following statements about just-in-time (JIT) processing is **incorrect**?
   a. JIT strives to eliminate all manufacturing inventories by using a push approach.
   b. A primary objective of JIT is to eliminate all manufacturing inventories.
   c. JIT strives to eliminate inventories by using a pull approach.
   d. An important element in JIT processing is that a multiskilled work force must be developed.

*20.   (S.O. 9) Which of the following is **not** a major benefit of implementing JIT processing?
    a.   Manufacturing inventories are significantly reduced or eliminated.
    b.   Inventories of raw materials are maintained if a key supplier is shut down by a strike.
    c.   Product quality is enhanced.
    d.   Rework costs and inventory storage costs are reduced or eliminated.

MATCHING

Match each term with its definition by writing the appropriate letter in the space provided.

Terms		Definitions	
_____	1. Activity-based costing.	a.	An activity that adds cost to, or increases the time spent on, a product or service without increasing its market value.
_____	2. Activity-based management.	b.	Activities performed for each batch of products.
_____	3. Activity cost pool.	c.	Activities required to support or sustain an entire production process and not dependent on number of products, batches, or units produced.
_____	4. Cost driver.		
_____	5. Non-value-added activity.	d.	An overhead cost allocation system that allocates overhead to multiple activity cost pools and assigns the activity cost pools to products or services by means of cost drivers.
_____	6. Value-added activity.		
_____	7. Batch-level activities.	e.	Activities performed for and identifiable with an entire product line.
_____	8. Facility-level activities.	f.	The overhead cost allocated to a distinct type of activity or related activities.
_____	9. Product-level activities.	g.	An activity that increases the worth of a product or service.
_____	10. Unit-level activities.	h.	An extension of ABC from a product costing system to a management function that focuses on reducing costs and improving processes and decision making.
		i.	Any factor or activity that has a direct cause-effect relationship with the resources consumed.
		j.	Activities performed for each unit of production.

EXERCISES

EX. 4-1   (S.O. 1, 4, 6, and 8) Doggi Chew company uses a traditional product costing system to assign overhead costs uniformly to all products. To meet government regulations and to assure dogs of safe, sanitary, and nutritious food, Doggi Chew engages in quality control. Doggi Chew assigns its quality-control overhead costs to all products at a rate of 15% of direct-labor costs. Its direct-labor cost for the month of February for its puppy food product line is $30,000. Doggi Chew is going to change its costing method to activity-based costing. Data relating to the puppy food line for the month of February is as follows:

Activity Cost Pool	Cost Driver	Overhead Rate	Number of Cost Drivers Used
In-house inspection	Number of pounds	$0.24 per pound	12,500 pounds
Government inspection	Number of servings	$0.05 per serving	1,000 servings
Certification	Customer orders	$0.32 per order	550 orders

Instructions
(a)   Compute the quality-control overhead cost to be assigned to the puppy food product line for the month of February; (1) using the traditional product costing system (direct labor cost is the cost driver), and (2) using activity-based costing.
(b)   By what amount does the traditional product costing system undercost or overcost the puppy food product line?
(c)   Classify each of the activities as value-added or non-value-added.
(d)   For each activity, identify the activity level as unit, batch, product or facility level.

EX. 4-2   (S.O. 4) Fastchip, Inc. manufactures two computers: the FC-PC which sells for $2,000, and the FC-laptop, which sells for $4,200. The production cost per unit for each computer in 2006 was as follows:

	FC-PC	FC-laptop
Direct Materials	$1,260	$3,040
Direct labor ($25 per hour)	200	300
Manufacturing overhead ($10 per DLH)	80	120
Total per unit cost	$1,540	$3,460

In 2006, Fastchip manufactured 20,000 units of the FC-PC and 15,000 units of the FC-laptop. The overhead rate of $10 per direct labor hour was determined by dividing the total expected manufacturing overhead of $3,400,000 by the total direct labor hours (340,000) for the two computers.

The gross profit and gross profit rate on the computers were: FC-PC $460 ($2,000 - $1,540) and 23% ($460/$2,000); and FC-laptop $740 ($4,200 - $3,460) and 17.62% ($740/$4,200). Because of the lower profit margin on the FC-laptop, management is considering phasing out the FC-laptop and increasing the production of the FC-PC.

Before finalizing its decision, management asks the controller of Fastchip to prepare an analysis using activity-based costing. The controller accumulates the following information about overhead for the year ended December 31, 2006:

Activity	Cost Driver	Total Cost	Cost Driver Volume	Overhead Rate
Ordering raw materials	# of orders	$ 100,000	80	$1,250
Receiving raw materials	# of shipments	$ 120,000	75	$1,600
Materials handling	weight of materials	$ 600,000	60,000 lbs.	$ 10
Production scheduling	# of orders	$ 100,000	35,000	$ 2.86
Machining	machine hours	$ 800,000	2,000	$ 400
Quality control inspections	# of inspections	$1,200,000	10,000	$ 120
Factory supervision	# of employees	$ 480,000	250	$1,920

The cost driver volume for each product was:

Cost Driver	FC-PC	FC-laptop	Total
# of orders	60	20	80
# of shipments.	50	25	75
weight of materials	40,000 lbs.	20,000 lbs.	60,000 lbs.
# of orders	20,000	15,000	35,000
machine hours	1,100	900	2,000
# of inspections	8,000	2,000	10,000
# of employees	150	100	250

Instructions
(a)   Assign the total 2006 manufacturing overhead costs to the two products using activity-based costing (ABC).
(b)   What was the cost per unit, gross profit, and gross profit rate of each model using ABC costing?

The Navigator

SOLUTIONS TO REVIEW QUESTIONS AND EXERCISES

TRUE-FALSE

1. (F)   Because of advances in technology, the amount of direct labor used in many industries is now greatly reduced, and total overhead costs (for depreciation on expensive equipment and machinery, utilities, repair, and maintenance) have significantly increased.
2. (T)
3. (F)   A cost driver is any factor or activity that has a direct cause-effect relationship with the resources consumed.
4. (T)
5. (F)   To achieve accurate costing, a high degree of correlation must exist between the cost driver and the actual consumption of the cost pool.
6. (F)   An activity-based overhead rate per cost driver is computed by dividing the estimated overhead per activity by the number of cost drivers expected to be used per activity.
7. (T)
8. (F)   Unlike traditional costing which relies on volume-of-output, unit level allocation bases, activity-based costing introduces a variety of bases—whatever drives the activity and consumes resources.
9. (T)
10. (F)   Activity-based costing does not, in and of itself, change the amount of overhead costs, but it does in certain circumstances allocate those costs in a more accurate manner.
11. (F)   One of the limitations of activity-based costing is that it may be expensive to use.
12. (T)
13. (F)   When product lines are numerous, diverse, and require differing degrees of support services, activity-based costing is generally the better costing system.
14. (T)
15. (F)   Value-added activities increase the worth of a product or service to customers; they involve resource usage and related costs that customers are willing to pay for. Non-value-added activities are production- or service-related activities that simply add cost to, or increase the time spent on, a product or service without increasing its market value.
16. (T)
17. (T)
18. (T)
19. (T)
*20. (F) Just-in-time processing strives to eliminate inventories by using a pull approach in manufacturing.

MULTIPLE CHOICE

1. (c) Identifying a single overhead rate as the predetermined overhead rate is typically the method of allocating overhead costs under job order costing and process costing. Answers a., b., and d., are all considered steps in activity-based costing.

2. (d) Conventional cost systems focus on units of production. ABC focuses on the activities performed to produce specific products. Answers a., b., and c. are all correct statements about ABC.

3. (d) The activity-based overhead rate is calculated by dividing estimated overhead per activity by expected use of cost driver per activity ($400,000 ÷ 80,000).

4. (d) To assign overhead costs to each product, the activity-based overhead rates are multiplied by the number of cost drivers expected to be used per product.

5. (b) The computations of the activity-based overhead rates are as follows:

Estimated Overhead		Total Expected Cost Drivers		Activity-Based Overhead Rates
$260,000	÷	130,000	=	$2.00 per order
$400,000	÷	800,000	=	$0.50 per part
$300,000	÷	25,000	=	$12.00 per hour

6. (b) The cost assigned to leases for supervising is calculated by multiplying the estimated use of cost drivers per product by the activity-based overhead rate (15,000 X $12.00 = $180,000).

7. (c) The cost assigned to collars for ordering and receiving is calculated by multiplying the estimated use of cost drivers per product by the activity-based overhead rate (60,000 X $2.00 = $120,000).

8. (d) The assignment of activity cost pools to products and the total costs assigned are as follows:

Activity Cost Pools	Leashes Expected Use of Cost Drivers	Overhead Rate	Cost Assigned	Collars Expected Use of Cost Drivers	Overhead Rate	Cost Assigned
Ordering	70,000 X	$ 2.00 =	$140,000	60,000 X	$ 2.00 =	$120,000
Assembly	300,000 X	.50 =	150,000	500,000 X	.50 =	250,000
Supervising	15,000 X	$12.00 =	180,000	10,000 X	12.00 =	120,000
Total Costs			$470,000			$490,000

9. (c) The primary benefit of ABC is more accurate product costing because (1) ABC leads to more cost pools, (2) ABC leads to enhanced control over overhead costs, and (3) ABC leads to better management decisions. Limitations of ABC include: (1) ABC can be expensive to use, and (2) some arbitrary allocations continue.

10. (a) A fact that would indicate the use of ABC as the possible costing system is when overhead costs constitute a significant portion of total costs.

11.   (c)   Engineering design would be considered a value-added activity. Repair of machines, storage of inventory, and bookkeeping would all be considered non-value-added activities.

12.   (d)   Advertising would be considered a non-value-added activity. Machining, painting and packaging would all be considered value-added activities.

13.   (c)   Inspection is an example of a batch-level activity. Drilling is considered a unit-level activity, engineering changes are considered product-level activities, and property taxes are a facility-level activity.

14.   (d)   Product design costs are an example of a cost associated with product-level activities. Building depreciation is a cost associated with facility-level activities, and equipment set-up costs and material handling costs are associated with batch-level activities.

15.   (b)   The number of activities performed at the batch level goes up as the number of batches rises (d)—not as the number of units within the batches changes. Answers a. and c. are correct statements.

16.   (d)   ABC is usually more difficult to implement in a service industry because there is a larger proportion of overhead costs that are company-wide costs.

17.   (c)   The number of working paper pages would be a cost driver more likely to be associated with the service industry than with the manufacturing industry. Inspections, parts painted, and machine hours (answers a., b., and d.) are all cost drivers more likely to be associated with a manufacturing company.

*18.   (c)   Maintaining inventories of raw materials just in case some items are of poor quality is not considered to be a part of the just-in-case philosophy. Answers a., b., and d. are all correct statements.

*19.   (a)   JIT strives to eliminate inventories by using a pull approach (c). Answers b. and d. are correct statements.

*20.   (b)   JIT processing usually does not maintain inventories if a key supplier is shut down by a strike. Answers a., c., and d. are all major benefits of implementing JIT processing.

MATCHING

1.	d		6.	g
2.	h		7.	b
3.	f		8.	c
4.	i		9.	e
5.	a		10.	j

EXERCISES

EX. 4-1

(a) (1) Traditional product costing system:
$30,000 X .15 = $4,500 Quality-control overhead costs assigned in February to the puppy food product line.

(2) Activity-based costing system:

Activity Cost Pool	Cost Drivers Used	Overhead Rate	Overhead Cost Assigned
In-house inspection	12,500	$0.24	$3,000
Government inspection	1,000	$0.05	50
Certification	550	$0.32	176
Total assigned cost			$3,226

(b) As compared to ABC, the traditional product costing system overcosts the quality-control overhead cost assigned to the puppy food product line by $1,274 ($4,500 - $3,226) in the month of February. That is a 39% overstatement.

(c) All three activities, as quality-control related activities, are non-value-added activities.

(d) In-house inspections and government inspections are unit-level activities (number of pounds and number of servings) while certification appears to be a batch-level activity (customer orders).

EX. 4-2

(a)

Cost Driver	Rate	FC-PC Number	FC-PC Cost	FC-laptop Number	FC-laptop Cost	Cost
# of orders	$1,250	60	$ 75,000	20	$ 25,000	$ 100,000
# of shipments	1,600	50	80,000	25	40,000	120,000
weight of materials	10	40,000	400,000	20,000	200,000	600,000
# of orders	2.86	20,000	57,200	15,000	42,900	100,100*
machine hours	400	1,100	440,000	900	360,000	800,000
# of inspections	120	8,000	960,000	2,000	240,000	1,200,000
# of employees	1,920	150	288,000	100	192,000	480,000
Total assigned costs			$2,300,200		$1,099,900	$3,400,100*
Units produced			20,000		15,000	
Overhead cost per unit			$ 115.01		$ 73.33	

*rounding error of $100.

(b)

	FC-PC	FC-laptop
Direct Materials	$1,260.00	$3,040.00
Direct labor ($25 per hour)	200.00	300.00
Manufacturing overhead	115.01	73.33
Total per unit cost	$1,575.01	$3,413.33

FC-PC
Gross profit: $2,000 - $1,575.01 = $424.99
Gross profit rate: $424.99/$2,000 = 21.25%

FC-laptop
Gross profit: $4,200 - $3,413.33 = $786.67
Gross profit rate: $786.67/$4,200 = 18.73%

The Navigator ✓
- Scan Study Objectives ☐
- Read Preview ☐
- Read Chapter Review ☐
- Work Demonstration Problem ☐
- Answer True-False Statements ☐
- Answer Multiple-Choice Questions ☐
- Match Terms and Definitions ☐
- Solve Exercises ☐

COST-VOLUME-PROFIT

CHAPTER STUDY OBJECTIVES

After studying this chapter, you should be able to:
1. Distinguish between variable and fixed costs.
2. Explain the significance of the relevant range.
3. Explain the concept of mixed costs.
4. List the five components of cost-volume-profit analysis.
5. Indicate what contribution margin is and how it can be expressed.
6. Identify the three ways to determine the break-even point.
7. Give the formulas for determining sales required to earn target net income.
8. Define margin of safety, and give the formulas for computing it.

PREVIEW OF CHAPTER 5

Management must understand how costs respond to changes in sales volume and the effect of the interaction of costs and revenues on profits. A prerequisite to understanding cost-volume-profit (CVP) relationships is knowledge of how costs behave. In this chapter, we first explain the considerations involved in cost behavior analysis. The content and organization of the chapter are as follows:

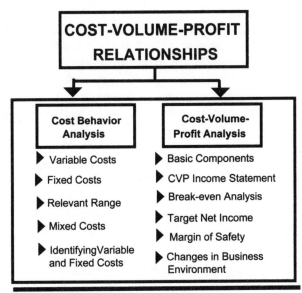

CHAPTER REVIEW

Cost Behavior Analysis

1. **Cost behavior analysis** is the study of how specific costs respond to changes in the level of business activity. A knowledge of cost behavior helps management plan operations and decide between alternative courses of action.

2. The **activity index** identifies the activity that causes changes in the behavior of costs; examples include direct labor hours, sales dollars, and units of output. Once an appropriate activity index is chosen, costs can be classified as variable, fixed or mixed.

Variable and Fixed Costs

3. (S.O. 1) **Variable costs** are costs that **vary in total** directly and proportionately with changes in the activity level. Examples of variable costs include direct materials and direct labor, cost of goods sold, sales commissions, and freight out. A variable cost may also be defined as a cost that **remains the same per unit** at every level of activity.

4. **Fixed costs** are costs that remain the same in total regardless of changes in the activity level. Examples include property taxes, insurance, rent, supervisory salaries, and depreciation. Fixed costs per unit vary inversely with activity; as volume increases, unit cost declines and vice versa.

Relevant Range

5. (S.O. 2) The range over which a company expects to operate during the year is called the **relevant range.** Within the relevant range a **straight-line relationship** exists for both variable and fixed costs.

Mixed Costs

6. (S.O. 3) **Mixed costs** are costs that contain both a variable element and a fixed element; they increase in total as the activity level increases, but not proportionately. For purposes of CVP analysis, mixed costs must be classified into their fixed and variable elements.

7. The **high-low method** uses the total costs incurred at the high and low levels of activity. The difference in costs represents variable costs, since only the variable cost element can change as activity levels change.

8. The steps in computing fixed and variable costs under the high-low method are:
    a. Determine variable cost per unit from the following formula:

    $$\frac{\text{Change in}}{\text{Total Costs}} \div \frac{\text{High minus Low}}{\text{Activity Level}} = \frac{\text{Variable Cost}}{\text{per Unit}}$$

    b. Determine the fixed cost by subtracting the total variable cost at either the high or the low activity level from the total cost at that activity level.

Cost-Volume-Profit Analysis

9. (S.O. 4) **Cost-volume-profit (CVP) analysis** is the study of the effects of changes in costs and volume on a company's profits. It is a critical factor in such management decisions as profit planning, setting selling prices, determining product mix, and maximizing use of production facilities.

10. CVP analysis considers the interrelationships among the following **components**: (a) volume or level of activity, (b) unit selling prices, (c) variable cost per unit, (d) total fixed costs, and (e) sales mix.

Basic CVP Components

11. The following **assumptions** underlie each CVP analysis:
    a. The behavior of both costs and revenues is linear throughout the relevant range of the activity index.
    b. All costs can be classified as either variable or fixed with reasonable accuracy.
    c. Changes in activity are the only factors that affect costs.
    d. All units produced are sold.
    e. When more than one type of product is sold, the sales mix will remain constant. That is, the percentage that each product represents of total sales will stay the same.

Contribution Margin

12. (S.O. 5) **Contribution margin** is the amount of revenue remaining after deducting variable costs. The formula for contribution margin per unit is:

$$\text{Unit Selling Price} - \text{Unit Variable Costs} = \text{Contribution Margin Per Unit}$$

13. Contribution margin per unit indicates the amount available to cover fixed costs and contribute to income. The formula for the **contribution margin ratio** is:

$$\text{Contribution Margin Per Unit} \div \text{Unit Selling Price} = \text{Contribution Margin Ratio}$$

    The ratio indicates the portion of each sales dollar that is available to apply to fixed costs and to contribute to income.

Break-Even Analysis

14. (S.O. 6) The **break-even point** is the level of activity at which total revenue equals total costs (both fixed and variable). Knowledge of the break-even point is useful to management when it decides whether to introduce new product lines, change sales prices on established products, or enter new market areas.

15. A common equation used for CVP analysis is as follows:

$$\text{Sales} = \text{Variable Costs} + \text{Fixed Costs} + \text{Net Income}$$

16. Under the **contribution margin technique,** the break-even point can be computed by using either the contribution margin per unit or the contribution margin ratio.

17. The formula, using unit contribution margin, is:

$$\begin{array}{ccc} \text{Fixed} & \text{Contribution} & \text{Break - even} \\ \text{Costs} \div & \text{Margin per Unit} = & \text{Point in Units} \end{array}$$

18. The formula using the contribution margin is:

$$\begin{array}{ccc} \text{Fixed} & \text{Contribution} & \text{Break - even} \\ \text{Costs} \div & \text{Margin Ratio} = & \text{Point in Dollars} \end{array}$$

19. A chart (or graph) can also be used as an effective means to determine and illustrate the break-even point. A cost-volume-profit (CVP) graph is as follows:

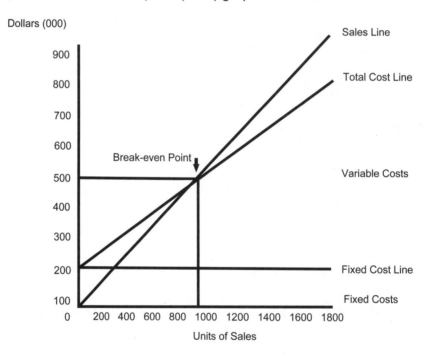

Target Net Income

20. (S.O. 7) **Target net income** is the income objective for individual product lines. The following equation is used to determine target net income sales:

Required Sales = Variable Costs + Fixed Costs + Target Net Income

Margin of Safety

21.   (S.O. 8) **Margin of safety** is the difference between actual or expected sales and sales at the break-even point.

a.   The formula for stating the margin of safety in dollars is:

$$\text{Actual (Expected) Sales} - \text{Break-Even Sales} = \text{Margin of Safety in Dollars}$$

b.   The formula for determining the margin of safety ratio is:

$$\text{Margin of Safety in Dollars} \div \text{Actual (Expected) Sales} = \text{Margin of Safety Ratio}$$

The higher the dollars or the percentage, the greater the margin of safety.

The
Navigator

DEMONSTRATION PROBLEM (S.O. 1, 6, 7, and 8)

The Valley Video Shop has two employees. The manager, J.J., is paid $2,200 per month. The other employee, Bob, is paid $1,200 per month. In addition, Bob is paid a commission of 20 cents per video that is rented. Other monthly costs are: store rent $1,000 plus 10 cents per rented video, depreciation on videos $1,000, utilities $400, and advertising $400. The rental fee for a movie is $2.00.

Instructions
(a)   Determine the variable cost per rented video and the total monthly fixed costs.
(b)   Compute the break-even point in units and dollars.
(c)   Determine the rentals required to earn net income of $2,000.
(d)   Determine the margin of safety and margin of safety ratio, assuming 5,000 videos are rented in a month.

SOLUTION TO DEMONSTRATION PROBLEM

(a)   Variable Cost = .30 (.20 cents + .10 cents)
       Fixed Cost = $6,200 ($2,200 + $1,200 + $1,000 + $1,000 + $400 + $400)

(b)   Break-even Point: $6,200/($2.00 - $.30) = 3,648 rented videos
                            (3,648 X $2.00) = $7,296 in sales dollars

(c)   Required sales: ($6,200 + $2,000) ÷ $2.00 - $.30 = 4,824 rentals or $9,648.

(d)   (1) $10,000 - $7,296 = $2,704.
       (2) $2,704 ÷ $10,000 = 27.04%

REVIEW QUESTIONS AND EXERCISES

TRUE—FALSE

Indicate whether each of the following is true (T) or false (F) in the space provided.

_____   1. (S.O. 1)   The activity level is represented by an activity index such as direct labor hours, units of output, or sales dollars.

_____   2. (S.O. 1)   Variable cost per unit changes as the level of activity changes.

_____   3. (S.O. 1)   Fixed costs remain the same in total regardless of changes in the activity index.

_____   4. (S.O. 1)   The trend in most companies is to have more variable costs and fewer fixed costs.

_____   5. (S.O. 2)   Within the relevant range, it is assumed costs are curvilinear.

_____   6. (S.O. 2)   Most companies operate at 100 percent capacity.

_____   7. (S.O. 3)   For purposes of CVP analysis, mixed costs must be classified into their fixed and variable elements.

_____   8. (S.O. 3)   The high-low method is a mathematical method that uses total costs incurred at the high and low levels of activity.

_____   9. (S.O. 3)   Under the high-low method, the variable cost per unit is computed by dividing the change in total costs by the high minus low activity level.

_____   10. (S.O. 4)   One assumption of CVP analysis is that changes in activity are not the only factors that affect costs.

_____   11. (S.O. 4)   One assumption of CVP analysis is that all costs can be classified as either variable or fixed with reasonable accuracy.

_____   12. (S.O. 5)   The contribution margin per unit is the unit selling price less the fixed costs per unit.

_____   13. (S.O. 5)   The contribution margin ratio of 30% means that 70 cents of each sales dollar is available to cover fixed costs and to produce a profit.

_____   14. (S.O. 6)   Break-even occurs where total sales equal variable costs plus fixed costs.

_____   15. (S.O. 6)   If the contribution margin ratio is 60% and the amount of fixed costs are $400,000, then the sales dollars at the break-even point are $666,667.

_____   16. (S.O. 6)   At the break-even point, contribution margin must equal total fixed costs.

_____ 17. (S.O. 6)   A cost-volume-profit graph shows the amount of net income or loss at each level of sales.

_____ 18. (S.O. 7)   If variable costs per unit are 70% of sales, fixed costs are $290,000, and target net income is $70,000, required sales are $1,200,000.

_____ 19. (S.O. 8)   The margin of safety is the difference between fixed costs and variable costs.

_____ 20. (S.O. 8)   The margin of safety ratio is equal to the margin of safety in dollars divided by the actual or (expected) sales.

MULTIPLE CHOICE

Circle the letter that best answers each of the following statements.

1. (S.O. 1) Costs that vary in total directly and proportionately with changes in the activity level are:
   a. variable costs.
   b. fixed costs.
   c. mixed costs.
   d. semivariable costs.

2. (S.O. 1) Fixed costs are costs that:
   a. remain the same in total regardless of changes in the activity level.
   b. vary inversely with activity on a per unit basis.
   c. both (a) and (b).
   d. neither (a) nor (b).

3. (S.O. 2) Within the relevant range, the variable cost per unit:
   a. differs at each activity level.
   b. remains constant at each activity level.
   c. increases as production increases.
   d. decreases as production increases.

4. (S.O. 3) In the Gabbana Company, maintenance costs are a mixed cost. At the low level of activity (40 direct labor hours), maintenance costs are $600. At the high level of activity (100 direct labor hours), maintenance costs are $1,100. Using the high-low method, what is the variable maintenance cost per unit and the total fixed maintenance cost?

	Variable Cost Per Unit	Total Fixed Cost
a.	$8.33	$267
b.	$8.33	$500
c.	$11.00	$220
d.	$15.00	$400

5. (S.O. 4) Which of the following is **not** an underlying assumption of cost-volume-profit analysis?
    a. All costs can be classified as either variable or fixed with reasonable accuracy.
    b. When more than one type of product is sold, total sales will be in a constant sales mix.
    c. Changes in activity and other factors affect costs.
    d. The behavior of both costs and revenues is linear throughout the entire range of the activity index.

6. (S.O. 5) The contribution margin ratio increases when:
    a. fixed costs increase.
    b. fixed costs decrease.
    c. variable costs as a percentage of sales decrease.
    d. variable costs as a percentage of sales increase.

7. (S.O. 5) The contribution margin per unit decreases when unit selling price remains the same and:
    a. fixed costs increase.
    b. fixed costs decrease.
    c. variable costs per unit increases.
    d. variable cost per unit decreases.

8. (S.O. 6) A formula for break-even point in sales dollars is:
    a. Contribution margin per unit divided by fixed costs.
    b. Fixed costs divided by contribution margin per unit.
    c. Contribution margin ratio divided by fixed costs.
    d. Fixed costs divided by contribution margin ratio.

9. (S.O. 6) Which of the following is **correct?**
    a. Contribution Margin Ratio ÷ Fixed Costs = Break-even in Dollars
    b. Fixed Costs ÷ Contribution Margin Ratio = Break-even in Dollars
    c. Contribution Margin Ratio ÷ Fixed Costs = Break-even in Units
    d. Fixed Costs ÷ Contribution Margin Ratio = Break-even in Units

10. (S.O. 6) Livingston Co. has fixed costs of $60,000 and a contribution margin ratio of 30%. How much in dollar sales does Livingston Co. need to have to break-even?
    8. 0.
    9. $60,000.
    10. $180,000.
    11. $500,000.

11. (S.O. 6) Dolce Company is planning to sell 400,000 hammers for $1.50 per unit. The contribution margin ratio is 20%. If Dolce will break even at this level of sales, what are the fixed costs?
    a. $120,000.
    b. $280,000.
    c. $400,000.
    d. $480,000.

12. (S.O. 6) At the break-even point, fixed costs are:
     a.   less than the contribution margin.
     b.   equal to the contribution margin.
     c.   more than the contribution margin.
     d.   indeterminate of the contribution margin.

Items 13 and 14 are based on the following data for the Mizrahi Company.

Sales (50,000 units) $1,000,000, direct materials and direct labor $300,000, other variable costs $50,000, and fixed costs $130,000.

13. (S.O. 6) What is Mizrahi's break-even point in units?
     a.   9,848.
     b.   10,000.
     c.   18,571.
     d.   26,000.

14. (S.O. 6) What is Mizrahi's contribution margin ratio?
     a.   66%.
     b.   65%.
     c.   59%.
     d.   35%.

15. (S.O. 6) Versace Company is contemplating an expansion program based on expected sales $600,000, variable costs $420,000, and fixed costs $120,000. What is the amount of break-even sales?
     a. $400,000.
     b. $420,000.
     c. $540,000.
     d. $660,000.

16. (S.O. 6) Mugler Company sells radios for $50 per unit. The fixed costs are $210,000 and the variable costs are 60% of the selling price. As a result of new automated equipment, it is anticipated that fixed costs will increase by $50,000 and variable costs will be 50% of the selling price. The new break-even point in units is:
     a.   10,500.
     b.   10,400.
     c.   10,300.
     d.   8,400.

Items 17 and 18 are based on the following data:

Moschino Company sells cassette players for $60 each. Variable costs are $40 per unit, and fixed costs total $30,000.

17. (S.O. 7) How many cassette players must Moschino sell to earn net income of $70,000?
     a.   5,000.
     b.   3,500.
     c.   2,500.
     d.   1,500.

18. (S.O. 6) What sales are needed by Moschino to break even?
     a. $40,000.
     b. $75,000.
     c. $90,000.
     d. $120,000.

19. (S.O. 7) Lagerfeld Company reported the following results from the sale of 5,000 hammers in May: sales $200,000, variable costs $120,000, fixed costs $60,000, and net income $20,000. Assume that Lagerfeld increases the selling price of hammers by 10% on June 1. How many hammers will have to be sold in June to maintain the same level of net income?
     a.   4,000.
     b.   4,300.
     c.   4,500.
     d.   5,000.

20. (S.O. 8) Gaultier Company had actual sales of $800,000 when break-even sales were $600,000. What is the margin of safety ratio?
     a.   25%.
     b.   33%.
     c.   67%.
     d.   75%.

The
Navigator

MATCHING

Match each term with its definition by writing the appropriate letter in the space provided.

<table>
<tr><td colspan="2">Terms</td><td colspan="2">Definitions</td></tr>
<tr><td>_____</td><td>1. Contribution margin.</td><td>a.</td><td>The study of how specific costs respond to changes in the level of activity.</td></tr>
<tr><td>_____</td><td>2. Relevant range.</td><td>b.</td><td>The level of activity at which total revenues equal total costs.</td></tr>
<tr><td>_____</td><td>3. Variable costs.</td><td>c.</td><td>Costs that contain both variable and a fixed cost element.</td></tr>
<tr><td>_____</td><td>4. CVP income statement.</td><td>d.</td><td>The income objective for individual product lines.</td></tr>
<tr><td>_____</td><td>5. Mixed costs.</td><td>e.</td><td>A statement for internal use that classifies costs and expenses as fixed or variable and reports contribution margin.</td></tr>
<tr><td>_____</td><td>6. Margin of safety.</td><td>f.</td><td>The difference between actual or expected sales and sales at the break-even point.</td></tr>
<tr><td>_____</td><td>7. Cost behavior analysis.</td><td>g.</td><td>Costs that remain the same in total regardless of changes in the activity level.</td></tr>
<tr><td>_____</td><td>8. Target net income.</td><td>h.</td><td>The amount of revenue remaining after deducting variable costs.</td></tr>
<tr><td>_____</td><td>9. Cost-volume-profit (CVP) analysis.</td><td>i.</td><td>The study of the effects of changes in costs and volume on a company's profits.</td></tr>
<tr><td>_____</td><td>10. High-low method.</td><td>j.</td><td>The range of the activity index over which the company expects to operate during the year.</td></tr>
<tr><td>_____</td><td>11. Fixed costs.</td><td>k.</td><td>Costs that vary in total directly and proportionately with changes in the activity level.</td></tr>
<tr><td>_____</td><td>12. Break-even point.</td><td>l.</td><td>A mathematical method that uses the total costs incurred at the high and low levels of activity.</td></tr>
</table>

The Navigator

EXERCISES

EX. 5-1   (S.O. 3) Galliano Company has accumulated the following information pertaining to maintenance costs for the last eight months.

Month	Direct Labor Hours	Maintenance Cost
January	2,800	$15,000
February	1,000	7,000
March	2,500	13,000
April	4,000	22,000
May	3,000	18,000
June	3,500	19,000
July	1,500	8,000
August	2,000	10,000

Instructions
Using the high-low method, compute (1) variable cost per direct labor hour and (2) the fixed cost per month.

EX. 5-2   (S.O. 5, 6, 7, and 8) Rykiel Company sells radios. For the year its revenues and costs were: sales $550,000 (11,000 units), variable costs $330,000, and fixed costs $150,000.

Instructions
(a)   Compute the contribution margin per unit.
(b)   Compute the contribution margin ratio.
(c)   Compute the break-even point in dollars using the contribution margin ratio.
(d)   Compute the break-even point in units using the unit contribution margin.
(e)   Compute the number of units that must be sold to earn net income of $100,000.
(f)   Compute the margin of safety ratio.

(a)   _____

_____

_____

_____

_____

_____

(b)   _____

_____

_____

_____

_____

_____

(c)   _____

_____

_____

_____

_____

_____

(d)

(e)

(f)

SOLUTIONS TO REVIEW QUESTIONS AND EXERCISES

TRUE-FALSE

1. (T)
2. (F)   A variable cost remains the same per unit at every level of activity.
3. (T)
4. (F)   Because of increased use of automation and less use of the work force, the trend in most companies is to have more fixed costs and fewer variable costs.
5. (F)   Within the relevant range, costs are assumed to be linear.
6. (F)   For most companies, operating at almost zero or 100 percent capacity is the exception rather than the rule.
7. (T)
8. (T)
9. (T)
10. (F)   One assumption of CVP analysis is that changes in activity are the only factors that affect costs.
11. (T)
12. (F)   The contribution margin per unit is the unit selling price less the variable costs per unit.
13. (F)   The contribution margin ratio of 30% means that 30 cents of each sales dollar is available to cover fixed costs and to produce a profit.
14. (T)
15. (T)
16. (T)
17. (T)
18. (F)   The margin of safety is the difference between actual or expected sales and sales at the break-even point.
19. (T)
20. (T)

MULTIPLE CHOICE

1. (a)   Fixed costs remain the same in total as activity levels change (a). Mixed costs and semivariable costs are the same; they increase in total but not proportionately.

2. (c)   In total, a fixed cost remains the same regardless of changes in the activity level. However, as volume increases, unit cost declines and vice versa.

3. (b)   The variable cost per unit remains constant at different levels of activity. The total variable cost changes in proportion and direction with the change in the activity level.

4. (a)   To determine the variable cost per unit, the following formula is used:

Change in Total Costs	÷	High minus Low Activity Level	=	Variable Cost per Unit
($1,100 - $600)	÷	(100 - 40)	=	$8.33

The fixed cost ($267) is determined by subtracting the total variable cost at either activity level from the total cost at that activity level: High = $1,100 - (100 X $8.33); Low = $600 - (40 X $8.33).

5. (c)   Answers a., b., and d., are all underlying assumptions of cost-volume-profit analysis. Answer (c) is not an underlying assumption because the assumption is that changes in activity are the only factor that affects costs.

6. (c)   The following format can be used to visualize the effect on the contribution margin ratio:

	Dollars	Percentage
Sales	$100	100%
Variable costs	60	60%
Contribution margin	$ 40	40%

Thus, if variable costs as a percentage of sales decreases, the contribution margin ratio will increase. The changes in fixed costs are not relevant.

7. (c)   The following format represents the contribution margin per unit of a hypothetical product:

	Per Unit
Sales	$10.00
Variable costs	6.00
Contribution margin	$ 4.00

If the variable cost per unit increases, then the contribution margin decreases. Fixed costs are not a factor in computing contribution margin.

8. (d)   Fixed costs divided by the contribution margin ratio equals the break-even point in dollars. Fixed costs divided by the contribution margin per unit equals the break-even point in units.

9. (b)   Fixed Costs ÷ Contribution Margin Ratio = Break-even in Dollars. All the other answers are incorrect.

10. (d)   Livingston Co. needs $500,000 in dollar sales to break-even ($60,000 ÷ 30%).

11. (a)   At the break-even point, fixed costs equal the contribution margin. The contribution margin is $120,000 [20% X (400,000 x $1.50)], which is also the amount of fixed costs.

12. (b)   If fixed costs and the contribution margin are not equal, then the net income is not equal to zero and therefore the company is not at break-even point.

13. (b)   The contribution per unit is unit selling price $20 ($1,000,000 ÷ 50,000) less unit variable costs $7 [($300,000 + $50,000) ÷ 50,000] or $13. Break-even sales in units equals fixed costs $130,000 ÷ contribution margin per unit $13 or 10,000 units.

14. (b)   The contribution margin ratio is equal to the contribution margin per unit $13 divided by unit selling price $20 or 65%.

15. (a)   Break-even sales in dollars is equal to fixed costs divided by the contribution margin ratio. The contribution margin ratio is 30% [($600,000 - $420,000) ÷ $600,000]. Therefore, break-even sales are $400,000 ($120,000 ÷ .30).

16. (b)   Using the mathematical equation, the computation is: $50X = $25X + $260,000 ($210,000 + $50,000). Therefore,

$$X = 10,400 \text{ units}$$

17. (a)   The required unit sales are determined by dividing fixed costs plus target net income by the contribution margin per unit. The contribution margin per unit is $20 ($60 - $40). Therefore, required unit sales are 5,000 ($100,000 ÷ $20).

18. (c)   The break-even point in sales dollars is equal to fixed costs divided by the contribution margin ratio. The contribution margin ratio is equal to 33.3% [($60 - $40) ÷ $60]. Therefore, the break-even point is $90,000 ($30,000 ÷ .333).

19. (a)   The selling price per unit during the month of May was $40 ($200,000 ÷ 5,000). During June the selling price increases to $44 ($40 X 110%). The variable cost per unit remains the same in June as it was in May, $24 ($120,000 ÷ 5,000). Therefore, during June the contribution margin per unit is equal to $20. Required sales in units is the sum of the fixed costs plus target net income divided by the contribution margin per unit. Thus, the required units are 4,000 [($60,000 + $20,000) ÷ $20].

20. (a)   The margin of safety in dollars is equal to actual (expected) sales less break-even sales, $200,000 ($800,000 - $600,000). The margin of safety ratio is equal to the margin of safety in dollars $200,000 divided by actual (expected) sales $800,000, or 25%.

MATCHING

1.	h	5.	c	9.	i
2.	j	6.	f	10.	l
3.	k	7.	a	11.	g
4.	e	8.	d	12.	b

EXERCISES

EX. 5-1

(1) Variable cost per unit is computed by dividing the change in total costs by the high minus low activity index. ($22,000 - $7,000) ÷ (4,000 - 1,000) = $5.00

(2) The fixed cost per month can be computed by subtracting the total variable cost at either activity level from the total cost at that activity level.

    Low $ 7,000 - ($5.00 X 1,000) = $2,000.
    High $22,000 - ($5.00 X 4,000) = $2,000.

EX. 5-2

(a) Contribution margin per unit is: $220,000 ÷ 11,000 = $20.

(b) Contribution margin ratio is: $220,000 ÷ $550,000 = 40%.

(c) The break-even point in dollars is: $150,000 ÷ .40 = $375,000.

(d) The break-even point in units is: $150,000 ÷ $20 = 7,500.

(e) The number of units to earn net income of $100,000 is: ($150,000 + $100,000) ÷ $20 = 12,500.

(f) The margin of safety is: $550,000 - $375,000 = $175,000.
    The margin of safety ratio is: $175,000 ÷ $550,000 = 32% (rounded).

Chapter 6

The Navigator ✓
- Scan Study Objectives ☐
- Read Preview ☐
- Read Chapter Review ☐
- Work Demonstration Problem ☐
- Answer True-False Statements ☐
- Answer Multiple-Choice Questions ☐
- Match Terms and Definitions ☐
- Solve Exercises ☐

*I*NCREMENTAL ANALYSIS

CHAPTER STUDY OBJECTIVES

After studying this chapter, you should be able to:
1. Identify the steps in management's decision-making process.
2. Describe the concept of incremental analysis.
3. Identify the relevant costs in accepting an order at a special price.
4. Indicate the relevant costs in a make-or-buy decision.
5. Identify the relevant costs in determining whether to sell or process materials further.
6. Identify the relevant costs to be considered in retaining or replacing equipment.
7. Identify the relevant costs in deciding whether to eliminate an unprofitable segment.
8. Determine sales mix when a company has limited resources.

The Navigator

PREVIEW OF CHAPTER 6

An important purpose of management accounting is to provide management with relevant information for decision making. This chapter explains management's decision-making process, and a decision-making approach called incremental analysis. The content and organization of this chapter are as follows:

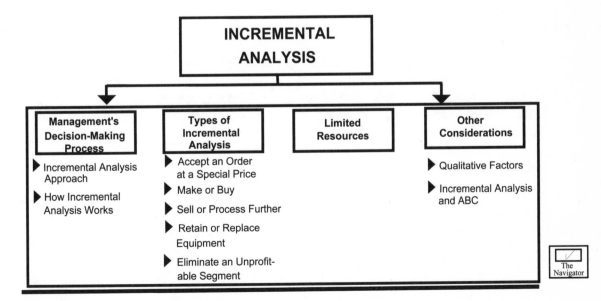

CHAPTER REVIEW

<u>Incremental Analysis</u>

1. (S.O. 1) **Management's decision-making process** frequently involves the following steps:
    a. Identify the problem and assign responsibility.
    b. Determine and evaluate possible courses of action.
    c. Make a decision.
    d. Review the results of the decision.

    Accounting's contribution to the decision-making process occurs primarily in steps (b) and (d).

2. (S.O. 2) Business decisions involve a choice among alternative courses of action. In making such decisions, management ordinarily considers both financial and nonfinancial information. The process used to identify the financial data that change under alternative courses of action is called **incremental analysis.**
    a. Incremental analysis involves not only identifying relevant revenues and costs, but also determining the probable effects of the decision on **future earnings.**
    b. Data for incremental analysis involves estimates and uncertainty.
    c. Gathering data may involve market analysts, engineers, and accountants.

3. In incremental analysis, **both costs and revenues** may change. However, in some cases (1) variable costs may not change under the alternative courses of action, and (2) fixed costs may change.

<u>Accept an Order at a Special Price</u>

4. (S.O. 3) An **order at a special price** should be accepted when the incremental revenue from the order exceeds the incremental costs.
    a. It is assumed that sales in other markets will not be affected by the special order.
    b. If the units can be produced within existing plant capacity, generally only variable costs will be affected.

<u>Make or Buy</u>

5. (S.O. 4) In a **make or buy** decision, management must determine the costs which are different under the two alternatives. If there is an opportunity to use the productive capacity for another purpose, opportunity cost should be considered. **Opportunity cost** is the potential benefit that may be obtained by following an alternative course of action. This cost is an additional cost of making the component.

<u>Sell or Process Further</u>

6. (S.O. 5) The basic decision rule in a **sell or process further** decision is: Process further as long as the incremental revenue from such processing exceeds the incremental processing costs. Incremental revenue is the increase in sales which results from processing the product further.

Retain or Replace Equipment

7. (S.O. 6) In a decision to **retain or replace equipment,** management compares the costs which are affected by the two alternatives. Generally, these are variable manufacturing costs and the cost of the new equipment.
    a. The **book value** of the old machine is a sunk cost which does not affect the decision. A **sunk cost** is a cost that cannot be changed by any present or future decision.
    b. However, any **trade-in allowance** or **cash disposal value** of the existing asset must be considered.

Eliminate an Unprofitable Segment

8. (S.O. 7) In deciding whether to **eliminate an unprofitable segment,** management should choose the alternative which results in the highest net income. Often fixed costs allocated to the unprofitable segment must be absorbed by the other segments. It is possible, therefore, for net income to **decrease** when an unprofitable segment is eliminated.

Limited Resources

9. (S.O. 8) When a company has limited resources (floor space, raw materials, or machine hours), management must decide which products to make and sell in order to maximize net income. In an allocation of limited resources decision, a company does this by finding the **contribution margin per unit of limited resource.**
    a. This is obtained by dividing the contribution margin per unit of each product by the number of units of the limited resource required for each product. For example, if the unit contribution margin for a product is $6 and three machine hours are required, the contribution margin per unit of limited resource is $2 ($6 ÷3).
    b. Production should be geared to the product with the highest contribution margin per unit of limited resource.

10. Many of the decisions involving incremental analysis also have important qualitative features.

The
Navigator

DEMONSTRATION PROBLEM (S.O. 7)

Lynn Devers, a recent graduate of Smith's accounting program, evaluated the operating performance of Knutson Company's six divisions. Lynn made the following presentation to Knutson's Board of Directors and suggested the Adams Division be eliminated. "If the Adams Division is eliminated," she said, "Our net income would increase by $23,200."

	The Other Five Divisions	Adams Division	Total
Sales	$2,422,600	$249,400	$2,672,000
Cost of goods sold	1,712,500	199,300	1,911,800
Gross profit	710,100	50,100	760,200
Operating expenses	456,000	73,300	529,300
Net income	$ 254,100	$(23,200)	$ 230,900

The cost of goods sold for Adams Division is 30% fixed, and its operating expenses are 60% fixed. None of Adams Division's fixed costs will be eliminated if the division is discontinued.

Instructions
Is Lynn right about eliminating the Adams Division? Prepare a schedule to support your answer.

The Navigator

SOLUTION TO DEMONSTRATION PROBLEM

No, net income would decrease $80,570 ($230,900 - $150,330).

	The Other Five Divisions	Adams Division	Total
Sales	$2,422,600	$ -0-	$2,422,600
Cost of goods sold	1,712,500	59,790*	1,772,290
Gross profit	710,100	(59,790)	650,310
Operating expenses	456,000	43,980**	499,980
Net income	$ 254,100	$(103,770)	$ 150,330

*$199,300 X 30% = $59,790 fixed.
**$73,300 X 60% = $43,980 fixed.

REVIEW QUESTIONS AND EXERCISES

TRUE—FALSE

Indicate whether each of the following is true (T) or false (F) in the space provided.

_____ 1. (S.O. 1) Accounting contributes to management's decision making process through internal reports that review the actual impact of the decision.

_____ 2. (S.O. 1) In making business decisions, management ordinarily considers both financial and nonfinancial information.

_____ 3. (S.O. 2) The process used to identify the financial data that change under alternative courses of action is called allocation of limited resources.

_____ 4. (S.O. 2) Incremental analysis involves only identifying relevant revenues and costs.

_____ 5. (S.O. 2) Costs and revenues that differ across alternatives are called relevant costs.

_____ 6. (S.O. 2) Variable costs may not change under alternative courses of action, while fixed costs may change.

_____ 7. (S.O. 3) When deciding whether to accept an order at a special price, management should make its decision on the basis of the total cost per unit and the expected revenue.

_____ 8. (S.O. 3) If a company is operating at full capacity, the incremental costs of a special order will likely include fixed manufacturing costs.

_____ 9. (S.O. 4) An example of an incremental analysis decision is make or buy.

_____ 10. (S.O. 4) Opportunity cost is the potential benefit that may be obtained by following an alternative course of action.

_____ 11. (S.O. 5) The basic decision rule in a sell or process further decision is: sell without further processing as long as the incremental revenue from processing exceeds the incremental processing costs.

_____ 12. (S.O. 5) Sell-or-process-further decisions are particularly applicable to production processes that produce multiple products simultaneously.

_____ 13. (S.O. 6) An important factor to be considered in a retain or replace equipment decision is the book value of the old equipment.

_____ 14. (S.O. 6) A trade-in allowance or cash disposal value of an existing asset in a retain or replace equipment decision is irrelevant.

_____ 15. (S.O. 7) In deciding on the future status of an unprofitable segment, management should recognize that net income could decrease by eliminating the unprofitable segment.

_____ 16. (S.O. 8) The contribution margin per unit of limited resource is obtained by dividing the number of units of the limited resource per unit of product by the contribution margin per unit of each product.

_____ 17. (S.O. 8) During incremental analysis, qualitative features that are not easily measured should be ignored.

_____ 18. (S.O. 8) An example of a qualitative factor is the effect on employees and the community when deciding whether to use outsourcing.

_____ 19. (S.O. 8) Because activity-based costing will result in better identification of relevant costs, management can conduct better incremental analysis.

_____ 20. (S.O. 8) The concepts in this chapter are inconsistent with activity-based costing.

The
Navigator

MULTIPLE CHOICE

Circle the letter that best answers each of the following statements.

1. (S.O. 2) A number of different types of decisions may be made by management that involve incremental analysis. Which of the following types of decisions do **not** involve incremental analysis?
   a. Retain or replace equipment.
   b. Make or buy.
   c. Sell products or process them further.
   d. All of the above are considered to involve incremental analysis.

2. (S.O. 3) It costs Crabbe Company $26 per unit ($18 variable and $8 fixed) to produce their product, which normally sells for $38 per unit. A foreign wholesaler offers to purchase 2,000 units at $21 each. Crabbe would incur special shipping costs of $2 per unit if the order were accepted. Crabbe has sufficient unused capacity to produce the 2,000 units. If the special order is accepted, what will be the effect on net income?
   a. $2,000 decrease.
   b. $2,000 increase.
   c. $6,000 increase.
   d. $36,000 increase.

3. (S.O. 3) Its costs Pineda Company $38 per unit ($25 variable and $13 fixed) to produce its product, which normally sells for $52 per unit. A foreign wholesaler offers to purchase 4,000 units at $30 each. Pineda would incur special shipping costs of $4 per unit if the order were accepted. Pineda has sufficient unused capacity to produce the 4,000 units. If the special order is accepted, what will be the effect on net income?
   a. $4,000 increase.
   b. $2,000 decrease.
   c. $4,000 decrease.
   d. $8,000 decrease.

4. (S.O. 3) Geis Company produces 40,000 printers per month, which is 80% of plant capacity. Variable manufacturing costs are $80 per unit, and fixed manufacturing costs are $1,200,000, or $30 per unit. The printers are normally sold directly to retailers at $150 each. Geis has an offer from a foreign wholesaler to purchase an additional 4,000 printers at $100 per unit. Acceptance of the offer would not affect normal sales of the product, and the additional units can be manufactured without increasing plant capacity. What is the amount of increase (decrease) to net income if Geis accepts the order?
   a. ($200,000)
   b. ($ 40,000)
   c. $ 40,000
   d. $ 80,000

5. (S.O. 4) Which of the following would generally **not** affect a make or buy decision?
   a. Selling expenses.
   b. Direct labor.
   c. Variable manufacturing costs.
   d. Opportunity cost.

6. (S.O. 4) Opportunity cost is:
   a. the total difference in costs for two alternatives.
   b. the potential benefit that may be obtained by following an alternative course of action.
   c. a cost that cannot be changed by any present or future decision.
   d. the annual cash inflow from a capital investment.

7. (S.O. 4) McAlister Corporation incurs the following annual costs in producing 30,000 floppy drives for computers:

Direct materials	$ 60,000
Direct labor	100,000
Variable manufacturing overhead	80,000
Fixed manufacturing overhead	90,000
Total manufacturing costs	$330,000

   However, if McAlister purchases the floppy drives from another company at a price of $10, what is the increase (decrease) in net income for McAlister?
   a. ($90,000)
   b. ($60,000)
   c. $30,000
   d. $60,000

8. (S.O. 5) Which of the following would generally **not** affect a sell or process further decision?
   a. Sales.
   b. Direct materials.
   c. Direct labor.
   d. Fixed manufacturing overhead.

9. (S.O. 6) A cost that cannot be changed by any present or future decision is a (an)
    a. incremental cost.
    b. opportunity cost.
    c. sunk cost.
    d. variable cost.

10. (S.O. 7) If an unprofitable segment is eliminated:
    a. it is impossible for net income to decrease.
    b. fixed expenses allocated to the eliminated segment will be eliminated.
    c. variable expenses of the eliminated segment will be eliminated.
    d. it is impossible for net income to increase.

11. (S.O. 8) The contribution margin per unit of limited resource is calculated by:
    a. dividing the limited resource per unit by the contribution margin per unit.
    b. multiplying the limited resource per unit with the contribution margin per unit.
    c. multiplying the contribution margin per unit with the sales revenue per unit.
    d. dividing the contribution margin per unit by the limited resource per unit.

12. (S.O. 8) In the Rossetto Company, contribution margin per unit is $6 for Product X and $10 for Product Y. Product X requires 4 machine hours and Product Y requires 8 machine hours. What is the contribution margin per unit of limited resource for each product?

	X	Y
a.	$1.50	$1.25
b.	$2.50	$1.50
c.	$1.25	$ .75
d.	$2.50	$ .75

13. (S.O. 8) The Irvine Company has limited resources and therefore management must decide between two products—plates and cups—to make and sell in order to maximize net income. Relevant data consist of the following:

	Plates	Cups
Contribution margin per unit	$2.00	$1.50
Machine hours required per unit	.04	.05

    What is the contribution margin per unit of the limited resource?

	Plates	Cups
a.	$0.08	$0.075
b.	$1.20	$1.25
c.	$25	$15
d.	$50	$30

14.   (S.O. 8)   The Anteater Company has limited resources and therefore management must decide between two products—shirts and pants—to make and sell in order to maximize net income.   Relevant data consist of the following:

	Shirts	Pants
Contribution margin per unit	$8.00	$7.50
Machine hours required per unit	.2	.15

What is the contribution margin per unit of the limited resource?

	Shirts	Pants
a.	$10.00	$12.00
b.	$11.50	$12.50
c.	$40.00	$50.00
d.	$43.25	$30.15

15.   (S.O. 8)   Many decisions involving incremental analysis have important qualitative features that, while not easily measured, should not be ignored.   Which of the following is a qualitative factor that is not easily measured?
a.   Rent expense.
b.   Lost morale amongst employees when a line of business is eliminated.
c.   Increased direct labor costs.
d.   The opportunity to use productive capacity in some other manner.

The
Navigator

MATCHING

Match each term with its definition by writing the appropriate letter in the space provided.

Terms	Definitions
_____ 1. Incremental analysis.	a. The process of identifying the financial data that change under alternative courses of action.
_____ 2. Relevant cost.	b. The potential benefit that may be obtained by following an alternative course of action.
_____ 3. Opportunity cost.	c. A cost that cannot be changed by any present or future decision.
_____ 4. Sunk cost.	d. The costs that differ across alternatives.

EXERCISES

EX. 6-1   (S.O. 4) Calvin Company manufactures its own subassembly units known by the code name "ekrob." Calvin incurs the following annual costs in producing 40,000 ekrobs:

Direct materials	$ 60,000
Direct labor	90,000
Variable overhead	50,000
Fixed overhead	80,000
Total	$280,000

Calvin can purchase the ekrobs from Hobbes Corporation for $6.00 per unit. If they purchase the ekrobs, only $30,000 of the fixed overhead will be eliminated. However, the vacant factory space can be used to increase production of another product, which would generate annual income of $22,000.

Instructions
Prepare an incremental analysis to determine whether Calvin should make or buy ekrobs.

	Make	Buy	Net Income Incr. (Decr.)

EX. 6-2   (S.O. 6) King Enterprises is a research analysis firm for television advertisements. On January 1, 2006, management is considering updating its computer system with new software that is estimated to cut labor costs by 10 percent. King's labor costs for the current year are estimated to be $400,000 and would be expected to remain the same the following two years. In addition, the new software has a filing system that will allow for a decrease in the storage of the hardcopy of documents within the facilities by 30 percent. The space opened up from the storage of documents will be used to decrease rent expense by $1,000 per month. If the new software costs $70,000 and is expected to be useful for three years, should King Enterprises purchase it?

_____

_____

_____

_____

_____

_____

_____

The
Navigator

SOLUTIONS TO REVIEW QUESTIONS AND EXERCISES

TRUE-FALSE

1. (T)
2. (T)
3. (F)   The process used to identify the financial data that change under alternative courses of action is called incremental analysis.
4. (F)   Incremental analysis involves not only identifying relevant revenues and costs, but also determining the probable effects of decisions on future earnings.
5. (T)
6. (T)
7. (F)   When deciding whether to accept an order at a special price, management should make its decision on the basis of the incremental cost per unit and the expected revenue.
8. (T)
9. (T)
10. (T)
11. (F)   The basic decision rule is: process further as long as the incremental revenue from such processing exceeds the incremental processing costs.
12. (T)
13. (F)   In a retain or replace equipment decision, the book value of the old machine is a sunk cost which does not affect the decision.
14. (F)   Any trade-in allowance or cash disposal value of an existing asset in a retain or replace equipment decision is relevant.
15. (T)
16. (F)   The contribution margin per unit of limited resource is obtained by dividing the contribution margin per unit of each product by the number of units of limited resource per unit of product.
17. (F)   Many of the decisions involving incremental analysis have important qualitative features that, while not easily measured, should not be ignored.
18. (T)
19. (T)
20. (F)   The concepts in this chapter are consistent with Activity-Based Costing.

MULTIPLE CHOICE

1. (d) Common types of management decisions that involve incremental analysis are (1) acceptance of an order at a special price, (2) make or buy, (3) sell or process further, (4) retain or replace equipment, and (5) elimination of an unprofitable segment.

2. (b) The incremental analysis is:

	Reject Order	Accept Order	Net Income Increase (Decrease)
Revenues	$ -0-	$42,000	$ 42,000
Costs: Manufacturing	-0-	(36,000)	(36,000)
Shipping	-0-	(4,000)	(4,000)
Net income	$ -0-	$ 2,000	$ 2,000

3. (a) The incremental analysis is:

	Reject Order	Accept Order	Net Income Increase (Decrease)
Revenues	$ -0-	$120,000	$120,000
Costs: Manufacturing	-0-	(100,000)	(100,000)
Shipping	-0-	(16,000)	(16,000)
Net income	$ -0-	$ 4,000	$ 4,000

4. (d) The amount of increase would be $80,000 [4,000 X ($100 - $80)]. The fixed manufacturing costs would not be included in the decision because there is no increase in plant activity by taking the order.

5. (a) Selling expenses should not change under the two alternatives (make or buy). Choices (b), (c) and (d) all represent incremental costs which could change depending upon which alternative is chosen.

6. (b) Opportunity cost is the potential benefit that may be obtained by following an alternative course of action. Choice (a) is the incremental cost, (c) is a sunk cost, and (d) is simply called annual cash inflow.

7. (b) If McAlister purchases the floppy drives from another company, McAlister will still have to incur its fixed manufacturing overhead costs with the following result:

	Make	Buy	Net Income Increase (Decrease)
Direct materials	$ 60,000	$-0-	$ 60,000
Direct labor	100,000	-0-	100,000
Variable manufacturing overhead	80,000	-0-	80,000
Fixed manufacturing overhead	90,000	90,000	-0-
Purchase price (30,000 X $10)	-0-	300,000	(300,000)
Total manufacturing costs	$330,000	$390,000	$(60,000)

8. (d) Generally, total fixed manufacturing overhead will be the same whether the product is sold or processed further. Choices (a), (b) and (c) would usually change under the two alternatives.

9. (c) A sunk cost is a cost that cannot be changed by any present or future decision.

10. (c) If an unprofitable segment is eliminated, the segment's variable costs will be completely eliminated. Net income may increase or decrease, depending on the situation (a). The fixed expenses which are allocated to the eliminated segment will have to be absorbed by the other segments (b).

11. (d) The contribution margin per unit of limited resource is calculated by dividing the contribution margin per unit by the limited resource per unit.

12. (a) The contribution margin per unit of limited resource for each product is:

	X	Y
Contribution margin per unit (a)	$6.00	$10.00
Machine hours required (b)	4.00	8.00
Contribution margin per unit of limited resource (a) ÷ (b)	$1.50	$1.25

13. (d) The contribution margin per unit of limited resource is $50 for plates ($2.00 ÷ .04) and $30 for cups ($1.50 ÷ .05).

14. (c) The contribution margin per unit of limited resource is $40 for shirts ($8.00 ÷ .2) and $50 for pants ($7.50 ÷ .15).

15. (b) It is often difficult to measure the cost associated with the lost morale amongst employees when a line of business is eliminated. Answers a., c., and d. are all examples of factors which are quantified during incremental analysis.

MATCHING

1. a
2. d
3. b
4. c

EXERCISES

EX. 6-1

	Make	Buy	Net Income Incr. (Decr.)
Direct materials	$ 60,000	$ -0-	$ 60,000
Direct labor	90,000	-0-	90,000
Variable overhead	50,000	-0-	50,000
Fixed overhead	80,000	50,000	30,000
Purchase price (40,000 X $6)		240,000	(240,000)
Opportunity cost	22,000		22,000
Total annual cost	$302,000	$290,000	$ 12,000

The analysis indicates that if the ekrobs are purchased from Hobbes, Calvin will increase net income by $12,000.

EX. 6-2

Yes, the incremental savings of the new software is $86,000 and is calculated as follows:

	Retain	Replace	Net Income Incr. (Decr.)
Purchase new software	-0-	($70,000)	($70,000)
Decrease in labor costs ($400,000 X 10% X 3)	-0-	120,000	120,000
Decrease in rent expense ($1,000 X 12 X 3)	-0-	36,000	36,000
Total	-0-	$86,000	$ 86,000

Chapter 7

VARIABLE COSTING: A DECISION-MAKING PERSPECTIVE

The Navigator ✓
- ■ Scan Study Objectives ☐
- ■ Read Preview ☐
- ■ Read Chapter Review ☐
- ■ Work Demonstration Problem ☐
- ■ Answer True-False Statements ☐
- ■ Answer Multiple-Choice Questions ☐
- ■ Match Terms and Definitions ☐
- ■ Solve Exercises ☐

CHAPTER STUDY OBJECTIVES

After studying this chapter, you should be able to:
1. Explain the difference between absorption costing and variable costing.
2. Discuss the effect that changes in production level and sales level have on net income measured under absorption costing versus variable costing.
3. Discuss the relative merits of absorption costing versus variable costing for management decision making.
4. Explain the term sales mix and its effect on break-even sales.
5. Understand how operating leverage affects profitability.

PREVIEW OF CHAPTER 7

In order to better track and understand the impact of cost structure on corporate profitability, some companies use an approach called variable costing. The purpose of this chapter is to show how variable costing can be helpful in making sound business decisions. The content and organization of this chapter are as follows:

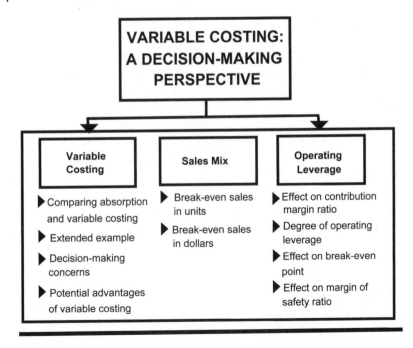

VARIABLE COSTING: A DECISION-MAKING PERSPECTIVE

Variable Costing
- ▶ Comparing absorption and variable costing
- ▶ Extended example
- ▶ Decision-making concerns
- ▶ Potential advantages of variable costing

Sales Mix
- ▶ Break-even sales in units
- ▶ Break-even sales in dollars

Operating Leverage
- ▶ Effect on contribution margin ratio
- ▶ Degree of operating leverage
- ▶ Effect on break-even point
- ▶ Effect on margin of safety ratio

CHAPTER REVIEW

Variable Costing vs. Absorption Costing

1. (S.O. 1) There are two approaches to **product costing.**
   a. Under **full or absorption costing** all manufacturing costs are charged to the product. This is also the approach required under generally accepted accounting principles.
   b. Under **variable costing** only direct materials, direct labor, and variable manufacturing overhead costs are treated as product costs; fixed manufacturing overhead costs are recognized as period costs (expenses) when incurred.

2. The primary difference between variable and absorption costing is that under variable costing the fixed manufacturing overhead is charged as an expense in the current period. The result is that absorption costing will show a higher net income number than variable costing whenever units produced exceed units sold. The reason: the cost of the ending inventory is higher under absorption costing than under variable costing.

3. (S.O. 2) The effects of the alternative costing methods on income from operations are:

Circumstance	Effects on Income From Operations
Units produced exceed units sold	Income under absorption costing is higher than under variable costing
Units produced are less than units sold	Income under absorption costing Is lower than under variable costing
Units produced equal units sold	Income will be equal under both approaches

4. (S.O. 3) One of the problems with absorption costing is that management may be tempted to overproduce in a given period in order to increase net income. Therefore, to avoid this overproduction, variable costing is often used internally to evaluate management decision-making.

5. The following are potential advantages of variable costing:
   a. The use of variable costing is consistent with cost-volume-profit and incremental analysis.
   b. Net income computed under variable costing is unaffected by changes in production levels.
   c. Net income computed under variable costing is closely tied to changes in sales levels giving a more realistic assessment of a company's success or failure.
   d. The presentation of fixed and variable cost components on the face of the variable costing income statement makes it easier to identify these costs and understand their effect on the business.

Sales Mix

6. (S.O. 4) Sales mix is the relative percentage in which each product is sold when a company sells more than one product. For example, if 3 units of Product A are sold for every 2 units of Product B, the sales mix of the product is 3:2.

7.   Break-even sales can be computed for a mix of two or more products by determining the **weighted average unit contribution margin of all the products**. At any level of units sold, net income will be greater if more high contribution margin units are sold than low contribution margin units. An analysis of these relationships generally shows that a shift from low-margin sales to high-margin sales may increase net income, even though there is a decline in total units sold.

8.   The formula for computing the break-even point in dollars is fixed costs divided by the weighted-average contribution margin ratio. To compute a company's weighted-average contribution ratio, multiply each division's contribution margin ratio by its percentage of total sales and then sum these amounts.

Cost Structure and Operating Leverage

9.   (S.O. 5) **Cost structure** refers to the relative proportion of fixed versus variable costs that a company incurs. In most cases, increased reliance on fixed costs increases a company's risk. When sales are increasing, profits can increase at a high rate, but when sales decline, losses can also increase at a high rate. Companies can change their cost structure by using more sophisticated robotic equipment and reducing it later, or vice versa. The equipment would increase the fixed costs whereas labor increases variable costs.

DEMONSTRATION PROBLEM (S.O. 1 and 2)

Thibodeau Company manufactures candy bars and has the following information:

Volume Information	**2005**
Candy bars in beginning inventory	20,000
Candy bars produced	40,000
Candy bars sold	30,000

Financial Information	
Selling price per candy bar	$1.00
Variable manufacturing cost per candy bar	$ .40
Fixed manufacturing cost per year	$12,000
Fixed manufacturing cost per candy bar	$ .30
Variable selling and administrative expense per candy bar	$ .05
Fixed selling and administrative expense	$ 4,000

Instructions
(a) Prepare an absorption costing income statement.
(b) Prepare a variable costing income statement.

SOLUTION TO DEMONSTRATION PROBLEM

(a)

Thibodeau Company
Income Statement
For the Year Ended 2005
Absorption Costing

Sales (30,000 X $1.00)		$30,000
Cost of goods sold [30,000 X ($.40 + $.30)]		21,000
Gross profit		9,000
Variable selling and administrative expenses (30,000 X $.05)	$1,500	
Fixed selling and administrative expenses	4,000	5,500
Net income		$ 3,500

(b)

Thibodeau Company
Income Statement
For the Year Ended 2005
Variable Costing

Sales (30,000 X $1.00)		$30,000
Variable costs of good sold (30,000 X $.40)	$12,000	
Variable selling and administrative expenses (30,000 X $.05)	1,500	13,500
Contribution margin		16,500
Fixed manufacturing overhead	12,000	
Fixed selling and administrative expense	4,000	16,000
Net income		$ 500

REVIEW QUESTIONS AND EXERCISES

TRUE—FALSE

Indicate whether each of the following is true (T) or false (F) in the space provided.

_____ 1. (S.O. 1) Absorption costing and variable costing differ in the treatment of all manufacturing costs.

_____ 2. (S.O. 1) Under variable costing, fixed manufacturing overhead is charged as an expense in the current period.

_____ 3. (S.O. 1) When units produced exceed units sold, income is lower under absorption costing than under variable costing.

_____ 4. (S.O. 2) When units produced equal units sold, income is the same under both absorption costing and variable costing.

_____ 5. (S.O. 2) The use of variable costing is only acceptable for internal use by management.

_____ 6. (S.O. 2) One of the problems with absorption costing is that managers may have greater incentive to underproduce inventories.

_____ 7. (S.O. 3) A potential advantage of variable costing is net income being computed with no effect by changes in production levels.

_____ 8. (S.O. 4) Sales mix is the relative percentage in which each product is sold when a company sells more than one product.

_____ 9. (S.O. 4) Break-even sales can be computed for a mix of two or more products by determining the weighted average unit contribution margin of all the products.

_____ 10. (S.O. 4) At any level of units sold, net income will be greater if more low contribution margin units are sold than high contribution margin units.

_____ 11. (S.O. 4) The formula for computing the break-even point in dollars is the weighted-average contribution margin ratio divided by fixed costs.

_____ 12. (S.O. 4) To compute a company's weighted average contribution margin, multiply each division's contribution margin ratio by its percentage of total sales and then sum these amounts.

_____ 13. (S.O. 5) Cost structure refers to the proportion of assets purchased by cash versus those purchased by increasing liabilities.

_____ 14. (S.O. 5) When a company's sales revenue is increasing, high operating leverage is a good thing because its means that profits will increase rapidly.

_____ 15. (S.O. 5) A cost structure that relies on higher fixed costs is always bad.

The
Navigator

MULTIPLE CHOICE

Circle the letter that best answers each of the following statements.

1. (S.O. 1) Klotz Co. manufactures a dog shampoo called Cleanfur. Relevant data for Cleanfur in January 2005, the first month of production, are as follows:

Selling price	$26 per unit
Units	Produced 20,000; sold 15,000; beginning inventory zero
Variable manufacturing unit costs	$10
Fixed costs	Manufacturing overhead $140,000 Selling and administrative expenses $30,000

The per unit costs under both absorption and variable costing are:

	Absorption	**Variable**
a.	$10	$7
b.	$ 7	$10
c.	$17	$7
d.	$17	$10

2. (S.O. 1) Ebbinghaus Company produces basketballs. In 2005, 100,000 units are produced and 80,000 units sold. Variable costs per unit are $10 and fixed manufacturing costs are $200,000. The per unit cost for both absorption and variable costing are as follows:

	Absorption Costing	**Variable Costing**
a.	$8	$10
b.	$10	$18
c.	$12	$18
d.	$12	$10

3. (S.O. 1) In the Klein Company, 50,000 units are produced and 40,000 units are sold. Variable manufacturing costs per unit are $8 and fixed manufacturing costs are $160,000. The cost of the ending finished goods inventory under each costing approach is:

	Absorption Costing	**Variable Costing**
a.	$112,000	$ 80,000
b.	$112,000	$100,000
c.	$120,000	$80,000
d.	$120,000	$100,000

4. (S.O. 2) When units produced are less than units sold, income under absorption costing will be:
   a. higher than under variable costing.
   b. the same as under variable costing.
   c. lower than under variable costing.
   d. indeterminate compared to variable costing.

5. (S.O. 2) When units produced and sold are the same, income under variable costing will be:
    a.   higher than under absorption costing.
    b.   the same as under absorption costing.
    c.   lower than under absorption costing.
    d.   indeterminate compared to absorption costing.

6. (S.O. 2) In the Hermes Company, sales are $800,000, cost of goods under absorption costing is $600,000 and total operating expenses are $120,000. If cost of goods sold is 70% variable and total operating expenses are 60% fixed, what is the contribution margin under variable costing?
    a. $380,000.
    b. $332,000.
    c. $308,000.
    d. $260,000.

7. (S.O. 3) Variable costing is:
    a.   not compatible with responsibility accounting.
    b.   acceptable under generally accepted accounting principles.
    c.   acceptable for income tax purposes.
    d.   only acceptable for internal use by management.

8. (S.O. 3) One of the problems with absorption costing is that management may be tempted to increase income by:
    a   overproducing.
    b.   decreasing inventories.
    c.   underproducing.
    d.   falsifying the records.

9. (S.O. 3) Which of the following is **not** considered an advantage of variable costing?
    a.   Net income computed under variable costing is unaffected by changes in production levels.
    b.   It is allowed under generally accepted accounting principles.
    c.   The use of variable costing is consistent with cost-volume-profit and incremental analysis.
    d.   The presentation of fixed and variable cost components on the face of the variable costing income statement makes it easier to identify these costs and understand their effect on the business.

10. (S.O. 4) Break-even sales can be computed for a mix of two or more products by determining the:
    a.   sales revenue of the two products divided by the number of products sold.
    b.   weighted average unit contribution margin of all the products.
    c.   cost of goods sold less the variable costs.
    d.   weighted average unit gross profit margin of all the products.

The following information pertains to questions 11 and 12.

Jennifer Company sells both chairs and tables at the following per unit data:

Unit Data	Tables	Chairs
Selling price	$200	$50
Variable costs	120	35
Contribution margin	$ 80	$15
Sales mix	1	4

11. (S.O. 4) Assuming $210,000 fixed costs, how many tables and chairs should Jennifer Company sell to break even?

	Tables	Chairs
a.	500	2,000
b.	1,000	4,000
c.	1,500	6,000
d.	2,000	8,000

12. (S.O. 4) Assuming $118,580 fixed costs, what is the total revenues in chairs Jennifer Company needs to break even?
   a. $154,800
   b. $169,400
   c. $175,200
   d. $188,600

The following information pertains to questions 13 and 14.

Sheltie Company sells both lamps and clocks at the following per unit data:

Unit Data	Lamps	Clocks
Selling price	$75	$45
Variable costs	48	30
Contribution margin	$27	$15
Sales mix	3	1

13. (S.O. 4) Assuming $312,000 fixed costs, how many lamps and clocks should Sheltie Company sell to break even?

	Lamps	Clocks
a.	9,600	3,200
b.	9,750	3,250
c.	12,000	4,000
d.	12,900	4,300

14. (S.O. 4) Assuming $149,952 fixed costs, what is the total revenues in lamps Sheltie Company needs to break even?
   a. $289,800
   b. $333,720
   c. $351,450
   d. $377,600

15. (S.O. 4) At any level of units sold, net income will be greater if:
    a.   more low contribution margin units are sold than high contribution margin units.
    b.   more high contribution margin units are sold than low contribution margin units.
    c.   fixed costs equal the dollar amount of sales.
    d.   variable costs equal fixed costs.

16. (S.O. 5) Operating leverage refers to:
    a.   the operating expense in comparison to advertising expenses.
    b.   the change that a company experiences in net income when there is a change in its production levels.
    c.   the change that a company experiences in net income when there is a change in its variable costs.
    d.   the change that a company experiences in net income when there is a change in its sales revenue.

17. (S.O. 5) Because of operating leverage, the more a company relies on fixed costs,
    a.   the greater a company's risk.
    b.   the less a company's risk.
    c.   the less net profit it will experience when sales increase.
    d.   the less net loss it will experience when sales decrease.

The
Navigator

MATCHING

Match each term with its definition by writing the appropriate letter in the space provided.

Terms

_____ 1. Absorption costing.

_____ 2. Variable costing.

_____ 3. Sales mix.

_____ 4. Weighted-average unit contribution margin.

_____ 5. Cost structure.

_____ 6. Operating leverage.

Definitions

a. The change that a company experiences in net income when there is a change in its sales revenue.

b. A method of calculating net income where all manufacturing costs are charged to the product.

c. The relative percentage in which each product is sold when a company sells more than one product.

d. A method of calculating net income that only includes variable costs and excludes fixed manufacturing overhead.

e. The relative proportion of fixed versus variable costs that a company incurs.

f. Total contribution margin divided by the number of units in the sales mix.

The Navigator

EXERCISES

EX. 7-1   (S.O. 1 and 2) During March of 2006 Fendi Company produced 3,000 units but only sold 2,500 units. The company had no beginning inventory. The unit selling price was $4,000. Manufacturing costs were: variable $2,000 per unit produced and fixed $1,800,000. Selling and administrative expenses were: variable $80 per unit of sales and fixed $300,000.

Instructions
(a)   Compute the manufacturing cost of one unit of product using (1) absorption costing and (2) variable costing.
(b)   Prepare an income statement for March using the variable costing approach.

(a) _____

_____

_____

_____

_____

(b) _____

_____

_____

_____

_____

_____

_____

_____

_____

_____

_____

_____

EX. 7-2 (S.O. 4) Smuthers Company manufactures and sells three products. Selling price and variable cost data for the models are as follows:

		Product	
	Yellow	**Blue**	**Red**
Unit selling price	$36	$40	$44
Unit variable costs	26	30	36
Contribution margin	$10	$10	$ 8
Sales mix	1	2	3

Instructions
(a)   Compute the break-even point in units, assuming the total fixed costs are $320,004.
(b)   Prove the correctness of your answer.

_____

_____

_____

_____

_____

_____

_____

_____

_____

_____

_____

The
Navigator

SOLUTIONS TO REVIEW QUESTIONS AND EXERCISES

TRUE-FALSE

1. (F) The approaches only differ concerning fixed manufacturing overhead costs which are treated as a product cost under absorption costing and treated as a period cost under variable costing.
2. (T)
3. (F) In this circumstance, income is higher under absorption costing than under variable costing.
4. (T)
5. (T)
6. (F) One of the problems with absorption costing is that managers may have greater incentive to overproduce inventories.
7. (T)
8. (T)
9. (T)
10. (F) At any level of units sold, net income will be greater if more high contribution margin units are sold than low contribution margin units.
11. (F) The formula for computing the break-even point in dollars is fixed costs divided by the weighted-average contribution margin ratio.
12. (T)
13. (F) Cost structure refers to the relative proportion of fixed versus variable costs that a company incurs.
14. (T)
15. (F) A cost structure that relies on higher fixed costs has more risk and can be good when revenues are increasing, but can be bad when revenues are decreasing.

MULTIPLE CHOICE

1. (d) Under absorption costing all manufacturing costs are charged to, or absorbed by, the product. Therefore, fixed manufacturing overhead cost per unit of $7 ($140,000 ÷ 20,000) is added to $10 variable unit costs for a total unit cost of $17. Under variable costing, fixed manufacturing overhead is not included, but only the variable manufacturing cost per unit of $10.

2. (d) Under absorption costing all manufacturing costs are charged to the product. Therefore, fixed manufacturing overhead cost per unit of $2 ($200,000 ÷ 100,000) is added to $10 variable manufacturing unit costs for a total unit cost of $12. Under variable costing, fixed manufacturing overhead is not included, only the variable manufacturing cost per unit of $10.

3. (a) There are 10,000 units in ending inventory. Under absorption costing, unit cost is $11.20 [$8 + ($160,000 ÷ 50,000)]. Total costs are $112,000. Under variable costing, unit cost is $8 and total cost $80,000.

4. (c) When units produced are less than units sold income under absorption costing will be lower than under variable costing.

5.   (b)   When units produced and sold are the same, income under variable costing will be the same as under absorption costing.

6.   (b)   Contribution margin is sales less variable cost of goods sold and variable expenses. Thus, the amount is $800,000 - $420,000 ($600,000 X 70%) - $48,000 ($120,000 X 40%) or $332,000.

7.   (d)   Variable costing is compatible with responsibility accounting (a). However, it is not acceptable under generally accepted accounting principles (b) or for income tax purposes (c) because it understates inventory costs.

8.   (a)   One of the problems with absorption costing is that management may be tempted to increase income by overproducing.

9.   (b)   The variable costing method is not allowed under generally accepted accounting principles. All of the other answers (a, c, and d) are advantages of variable costing.

10.   (b)   Break-even sales can be computed for a mix of two or more products by determining the weighted average unit contribution margin of all the products.

11.   (c)   The total contribution margin for the sales mix of 4 chairs to 1 table is $140 [($80 x 1) + ($15 X 4)]. The weighted average unit contribution margin is $28 ($140/5). The computation of break-even sales in units assuming $210,000 of fixed costs is 7,500 ($210,000/$28). Therefore, Jennifer Company must sell 1,500 tables (1/5 X 7,500) and 6,000 chairs (4/5 X 7,500).

12.   (b)   The total contribution margin for the sales mix of 4 chairs to 1 table is $140 [($80 X 1) + ($15 X 4)]. The weighted average unit contribution margin is $28 ($140/5). The computation of break-even sales in units assuming $118,580 of fixed costs is 4,235 ($118,580/$28). The break-even point per the mixed units are 847 tables (1/5 X 4,235) and 3,388 chairs (4/5 X 4,235). Therefore, Jennifer Company must have $169,400 revenues in chairs (3,388 X $50).

13.   (b)   The total contribution margin for the sales mix of 3 lamps to 1 clock is $96 [($27 x 3) + ($15 X 1)]. The weighted average unit contribution margin is $24 ($96/4). The computation of break-even sales in units assuming $312,000 of fixed costs is 13,000 ($312,000/$24). Therefore, Sheltie Company must sell 9,750 lamps (3/4 X 13,000) and 3,250 clocks (1/4 X 13,000).

14.   (c)   The total contribution margin for the sales mix of 3 lamps to 1 clock is $96 [($27 X 3) + ($15 X 1)]. The weighted average unit contribution margin is $24 ($96/4). The computation of break-even sales in units assuming $149,952 of fixed costs is 6,248 ($149,952/$24). The break-even point per the mixed units are 1,562 clocks (1/4 X 6,248) and 4,686 lamps (3/4 X 6,248). Therefore, Sheltie Company must have $351,450 revenues in lamps (4,686 X $75).

15. (b) At any level of units sold, net income will be greater if more high contribution margin units are sold than low contribution margin units. Answers (c) and (d) could be true but also false depending on the circumstances.

16. (d) Operating leverage refers to the change that a company experiences in net income when there is a change in its sales revenue.

17. (a) Because of operating leverage, the more a company relies on fixed costs, the greater a company's risk.

MATCHING

1.	b		4.	f
2.	d		5.	e
3.	c		6.	a

EXERCISES

EX. 7-1

(a)

Manufacturing Costs	Absorption Costing	Variable Costing
Variable	$2,000	$2,000
Fixed ($1,800,000 ÷ 3,000)	600	
	$2,600	$2,000

(b)

FENDI COMPANY
Income Statement
For the Month Ended March 31, 2006
(Variable Costing)

Sales (2,500 X $4,000)		$10,000,000
Variable expenses		
Variable cost of goods sold		
Inventory, Mach 1	$ -0-	
Variable manufacturing costs		
(3,000 X $2,000)	6,000,000	
Cost of goods available for sale	6,000,000	
Inventory, March 31, (500 x $2,000)	1,000,000	
Variable cost of goods sold	5,000,000	
Variable selling and administrative expenses		
(2,500 X $80)	200,000	
Total variable expenses		5,200,000
Contribution margin		4,800,000
Fixed expenses		
Manufacturing overhead	1,800,000	
Selling and administrative expenses	300,000	
Total fixed expenses		2,100,000
Income from operations		$ 2,700,000

EX. 7-2

(a)   The total contribution margin for the sales mix is:

$$[(\$10 \times 1) + (\$10 \times 2) + (\$8 \times 3)] = \$54$$

The weighted average unit contribution margin is:

$$\$54/6 \text{ units} = \$9.00$$

The computation of break-even sales in units assuming $320,004 of fixed costs is as follows:

$$\$320,004 \div \$9.00 = 35,556 \text{ units}$$

In order to break even with a sales mix of 1:2:3, Smuthers must sell 5,926 yellow units (1/6 X 35,556), 11,852 blue units (2/6 X 35,556), and 17,778 red units (3/6 x 35,556).

(b)   The proof for (a) is as follows:

Product	Unit Sales		Unit CM		Total CM
Yellow	5,926	X	$10.00	=	$ 59,260
Blue	11,852	X	$10.00	=	118,520
Red	17,778	X	$ 8.00	=	142,224
	35,556				$320,004

Chapter 8

The Navigator ✓
- ■ Scan Study Objectives ☐
- ■ Read Preview ☐
- ■ Read Chapter Review ☐
- ■ Work Demonstration Problem ☐
- ■ Answer True-False Statements ☐
- ■ Answer Multiple-Choice Questions ☐
- ■ Match Terms and Definitions ☐
- ■ Solve Exercises ☐

PRICING

CHAPTER STUDY OBJECTIVES

After studying this chapter, you should be able to:
1. Compute a target cost when a product price is determined by the market.
2. Compute a target selling price using cost-plus pricing.
3. Use time and material pricing to determine the cost of services provided.
4. Determine a transfer price using the negotiated, cost-based, and market-based approaches.
5. Explain the issues that arise when transferring goods between divisions located in countries with different tax rates.
*6. Determine prices using the absorption cost approach and the contribution (variable cost) approach.

*Note: All **asterisked** (*) items relate to material contained in the Appendix to the chapter.

PREVIEW OF CHAPTER 8

Few management decisions are more important than setting prices. In this chapter, two types of pricing situations are examined. The first part of the chapter addresses pricing for goods sold to external parties. The second part of the chapter addresses pricing decisions faced when goods are sold to other divisions within the same company. The content and organization of this chapter are as follows:

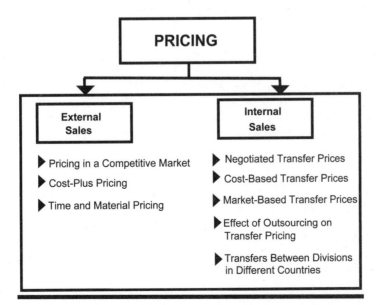

PRICING

External Sales	Internal Sales
▶ Pricing in a Competitive Market	▶ Negotiated Transfer Prices
▶ Cost-Plus Pricing	▶ Cost-Based Transfer Prices
▶ Time and Material Pricing	▶ Market-Based Transfer Prices
	▶ Effect of Outsourcing on Transfer Pricing
	▶ Transfers Between Divisions in Different Countries

CHAPTER REVIEW

External Sales

1. (S.O. 1) Some of the many factors that can affect pricing decisions include:
    a.   Pricing Objectives
         ● Gain market share
         ● Achieve a target rate of return
    b.   Environment
         ● Political reaction to prices
         ● Patent or copyright protection
    c.   Demand
         ● Price sensitivity
         ● Demographics
    d.   Cost Considerations
         ● Fixed and variable costs
         ● Short-run or long-run

2. In most cases, a company does not set prices. Instead the price is set by the competitive market (laws of supply and demand). These companies are called **price takers** and price taking often happens when the product is not easily differentiated from competing products, such as farm products (corn or wheat) or minerals (coal or sand).

3. Companies can set prices (1) where the product is specially made for a customer, (2) when there are few or no other producers capable of manufacturing a similar item, or (3) when a company can effectively differentiate its product or service from others.

Pricing in a Competitive Market

4. Once a company has identified its segment of the market, it does market research to determine the **target price**. The target price is the price that the company believes would place it in the optimal position for its target audience. Once the company has determined the target price, it can determine its target cost by setting a desired profit. The difference between the target price and the desired profit is the **target cost** of the product. The target cost includes all product and period costs necessary to make and market the product.

Cost-Plus Pricing

5. (S.O. 2) When the price is set by the company, price is commonly a function of the product or service. **Cost-plus pricing** involves establishing a cost base and adding to this cost base a **markup** to determine a **target selling price.** The size of the markup (the "plus") depends on the desired operating income return on investment (ROI) for the product line, product, or service. The cost-plus pricing formula is expressed as follows:

    Target selling price = Cost + (Markup Percentage X Cost)

6. The cost-plus approach has a major advantage: it is simple to compute. However, the cost model does not give consideration to the demand side—that is, will the customers pay the price. In addition, sales volume plays a large role in determining per unit costs. The lower the sales volume, the higher the price a company must charge to meet its desired ROI (because fixed costs are spread over fewer units and therefore the fixed costs per unit increases).

7. Instead of using both fixed and variable costs to set prices, some companies simply add a markup to their variable costs. Using variable costing as the basis avoids the problem of using poor cost information related to fixed cost per unit computations.

Time and Material Pricing

8. (S.O. 3) Under **time and material pricing,** the company sets two pricing rates—one for the labor used on a job and another for the material. The labor rate includes direct labor time and other employee costs. The material charge is based on the cost of direct parts and materials used and a **material loading charge** for related overhead costs.

9. Using time and material pricing involves three steps: (1) calculate the per-hour labor charge, (2) calculate the charge for obtaining and holding materials, and (3) calculate the charges for a particular job.

The per-hour labor charge typically includes the direct labor cost of an employee, selling, administrative, and similar overhead costs, and an allowance for a desired profit of employee time. The charge for materials typically includes the invoice price of any materials used on the job plus a material loading charge. The charges for any particular job are then a result of (1) the labor charge, (2) the direct charge for materials, and (3) the material loading charge.

10. To illustrate a time and material pricing situation, assume the following data for Rancho Park Golf Club Repair Service:

Rancho Park Golf Club Repair Service
Budgeted Costs for the Year 2006

	Time Charges	Material Charges
Repair service employee wages	$26,000	$ 5,000
Administrative assistant salary	1,950	1,000
Other overhead (supplies, depreciation, advertising, utilities)	4,940	3,000
Total budgeted costs	$32,890	$ 9,000

Step 1: During 2006 Rancho Park budgets 1,300 of hours for repair time, and it desires a profit margin of $6 per hour of labor. Computation of the hourly charges are as follows:

Per Hour	Total Cost	÷	Total Hours	=	Per Hour Charge
Hourly labor rate for repairs					
Repair service employee	$26,000	÷	1,300	=	$20.00
Overhead costs					
Administrative assistant	1,950	÷	1,300	=	1.50
Other overhead	4,940	÷	1,300	=	3.80
	$32,890	÷	1,300	=	$25.30
Profit margin					6.00
Rate charged per hour of labor					$31.30

Step 2: Rancho Park estimates that the total invoice cost of parts and materials used in 2006 will be $30,000 and it desires a 10 percent profit margin markup on the invoice cost of parts and materials. The computation of the material loading charge used by Rancho Park during 2006 is as follows:

	Material Total Cost	÷	Total Invoice Cost, Parts and Materials	=	Material Loading Charge
Overhead costs					
Parts manager salary	$5,000				
Administrative assistant	1,000				
	6,000	÷	$30,000	=	20.00%
Other overhead	3,000	÷	30,000	=	10.00%
	$9,000	÷	30,000	=	30.00%
Profit margin					10.00%
Material loading charge					40.00%

Step 3: Rancho Park prepares a price quotation to estimate the cost to fix a set of woods for a patron. Rancho Park estimates the job will require a half hour of labor and $150 in parts and materials. Rancho Park's price quotation is as follows:

Rancho Park Golf Club Repair Service
Time and Materials Price Quotation

Job: Arnold Palmer, repair of set of woods

Labor charges: half hour @ $31.30		$ 15.65
Material charges		
Cost of parts and materials	$150.00	
Material loading charge (40% X 150)	60.00	210.00
Total price of labor and materials		$225.65

Internal Sales

11. (S.O. 4) Divisions within vertically integrated companies normally transfer goods or services to other divisions within the same company, as well as to customers outside the company. When goods are transferred internally, the price used to record the transfer between the two divisions is called the **transfer price**. Three possible approaches for determining a transfer price are (1) negotiated transfer prices, (2) cost-based transfer prices, and (3) market-based transfer prices.

Negotiated Transfer Prices

12. The **negotiated transfer price** is determined through agreement of division managers. Using the negotiated transfer pricing approach, a minimum transfer price is established by the selling division, and a maximum transfer price is established by the purchasing division.

Calculating the minimum transfer price depends on whether the selling division has excess capacity or not. If the selling division has no excess capacity, then the minimum transfer price is the variable cost plus its lost contribution margin (also known as opportunity cost). If the selling division has excess capacity, then the minimum transfer price is the variable cost.

Cost-Based Transfer Prices

13.   Another method of determining transfer prices is to base the transfer price on the costs incurred by the division providing the goods. If a transfer price is used, the transfer price may be based on variable costs alone, or on variable costs plus fixed costs. A markup may be added to these cost numbers. This method, however, may lead to a loss of profitability for the company and unfair evaluations of division performance.

Market-Based Transfer Prices

14.   The market-based transfer price is based on existing market prices of competing goods or services. A market-based system is often considered the best approach because it is objective and generally provides the proper economic incentives. Unfortunately, however, there is often not a well-defined market for the good or service being transferred and thus companies resort to a cost-based system.

Transfers Between Divisions in Different Countries

15.   (S.O. 5) As more companies "globalize" their operations, an increasing number of transfers are between divisions that are located in different countries. Companies must pay income tax in the country where income is generated. In order to maximize income, and minimize income tax, many companies prefer to report more income in countries with low tax rates, and less income in countries with high tax rates. This is accomplished by adjusting the transfer prices they use on internal transfers between divisions located in different countries. The division in the low-tax-rate country is allocated more contribution margin, and the division in the high-tax-rate country is allocated less.

*Absorption Cost Approach

*16. (S.O. 6) The **absorption cost approach** is consistent with generally accepted accounting principles (GAAP) because it defines the cost base as the manufacturing cost. Both variable and fixed selling and administrative costs are excluded from this cost base. Thus, selling and administrative costs plus the target ROI must be provided through the markup.

The steps in using the absorption cost approach are as follows:
a.   Compute the unit manufacturing cost.
b.   Compute the markup percentage using the formula:

$$\frac{\text{Desired ROI per unit} + \text{Selling and Administrative Expenses Per Unit}}{} = \text{Markup Percentage} \times \text{Manufacturing Cost Per Unit}$$

c.   Set the target selling price using the formula:

$$\text{Manufacturing Cost Per Unit} + \left(\text{Markup Percentage} \times \text{Manufacturing Cost Per Unit} \right) = \text{Target Selling Price}$$

*Contribution (Variable-Cost) Approach

*17. Under the **contribution approach,** the cost base consists of all of the variable costs associated with a product, including variable selling and administrative costs. Because fixed costs are not included in the base, the markup must provide for fixed costs (manufacturing and selling and administrative) and the target ROI. The contribution approach is more useful for making short-run decisions because it displays variable cost and fixed cost behavior patterns separately.

The steps in using the contribution approach are as follows:

a.   Compute the unit variable cost.
b.   Compute the markup percentage using the formula:

$$\frac{\text{Desired ROI Per Unit} + \text{Fixed Costs Per Unit}}{\text{}} = \text{Markup Percentage} \times \text{Variable Costs Per Unit}$$

c.   Set the target selling price using the formula:

$$\text{Variable Cost Per Unit} + \left(\text{Markup Percentage} \times \text{Variable Cost Per Unit} \right) = \text{Target Selling Price}$$

The Navigator

DEMONSTRATION PROBLEM (S.O. 4)

Carter Cases is a division of Bashara Cassette Tapes, a cassette tape manufacturer. Carter produces cassette tape cases. Carter sells its products in units of 100 to Bashara Cassette Tapes, as well as to other cassette tape manufacturers. The following information is available regarding a unit of 100 of Carter's cassette cases.

Selling price of 100 cassette cases (one unit) to external customers	$22
Variable cost per 100 cassette cases (one unit)	$13
Capacity	100,000 units

Instructions
Determine whether the goods should be transferred internally or purchased externally and what the appropriate transfer price should be under each of the following independent situations.

(a) Carter Cases is operating at full capacity. There is a saving of $3 per unit for variable cost if the cassette case units are made for internal sale. Bashara Cassette Tapes can purchase a comparable unit of 100 cassette cases from an outside supplier for $18.

(b) Carter Cases has sufficient existing capacity to meet the needs of Bashara Cassette Tapes. Bashara can purchase a comparable unit of 100 cassette cases from an outside supplier for $18.

(c) Bashara Cassette Tapes wants to purchase special-order cassette cases that have a logo imprinted on the case. It needs 10,000 units. Carter has determined that the additional variable cost would be $5 per unit. Carter has no spare capacity. It will have to forgo sales of 10,000 units to external parties in order to provide this special offer.

The Navigator

SOLUTION TO DEMONSTRATION PROBLEM

(a)   Carter Cases' opportunity cost (its lost contribution margin) would be $9 ($22 - $13). Using the formula for minimum transfer price, we calculate:

$$\text{Minimum transfer price} = \text{Variable cost} + \text{Opportunity cost}$$
$$\$19 = (\$13 - \$3) + \$9$$

Since the minimum transfer price is more than the $18 it would cost if Bashara Cassette Tapes purchases from an external party, internal transfer should not take place and Bashara should purchase from the external party.

(b)   Since Carter Cases has available capacity, its opportunity cost (its lost contribution margin) would be $0. Using the formula for minimum transfer price, we determine the following:

$$\text{Minimum transfer price} = \text{Variable cost} + \text{Opportunity cost}$$
$$\$13 = (\$13) + \$0$$

Since Bashara Cassette Tapes can purchase a unit of 100 cassette cases for $18 from an external party, the most it would be willing to pay would be $18. It is in the best interest of the company as a whole, as well as the two divisions, for a transfer to take place. The two divisions must reach a negotiated transfer price between $13 and $18 that recognized the costs and benefits to each party and is acceptable to both.

(c)   Carter Cases' opportunity cost (its lost contribution margin per unit) would be $9 ($22 - $13). Its variable cost would be $18 ($13 + $5). Using the formula for minimum transfer price, we determine the following:

$$\text{Minimum transfer price} = \text{Variable cost} + \text{Opportunity cost}$$
$$\$27 = (\$18) + \$9$$

Note that in this case Carter Cases has no available capacity. Its management may decide that it does not want to provide this special order because to do so will require that it cut off the supply of the standard unit to some of its existing customers. This may anger those customers and result in the loss of customers.

REVIEW QUESTIONS AND EXERCISES

TRUE—FALSE

Indicate whether each of the following is true (T) or false (F) in the space provided.

_____ 1. (S.O. 1)   Price takers are companies that can easily set the prices on the products or services they sell.

_____ 2. (S.O. 1)   Products such as oil, gas, and corn and other products that are not easily differentiated are most often associated with companies known as price takers.

_____ 3. (S.O. 1)   The difference between the target price and the desired profit is the target cost of the product.

_____ 4. (S.O. 2)   Cost-plus pricing involves establishing a cost base and subtracting a markup to determine a target selling price.

_____ 5. (S.O. 2)   The cost-plus pricing approach has a major disadvantage: It is difficult to compute.

_____ 6. (S.O. 2)   In cost-plus pricing, if actual volume of sales is much less than budgeted volume, the company may sustain losses unless it can raise prices.

_____ 7. (S.O. 3)   Time and material pricing involves the setting of two pricing rates—one for the labor used on a job and another for the material.

_____ 8. (S.O. 3)   Time and material pricing is rarely used in service industries.

_____ 9. (S.O. 3)   The charge for labor time typically covers the costs of purchasing, receiving, handling, and storing materials.

_____ 10. (S.O. 3)   The material loading charge is expressed as a percentage of the total estimated costs of parts and materials for the year.

_____ 11. (S.O. 4)   When goods are transferred internally, the price used to record the transfer between the two divisions is the target price.

_____ 12. (S.O. 4)   Under negotiated transfer pricing, when a division has no excess capacity, the minimum transfer price should include the lost contribution margin per unit.

_____ 13. (S.O. 4)   In some instances the variable cost of units sold internally will differ from the variable cost of units sold externally.

_____ 14. (S.O. 4)   Under a cost-based approach, division performance is always evaluated fairly.

_____ 15. (S.O. 4)   A market-based system is often considered the best approach because it is objective and generally provides the proper economic incentives.

_____ 16. (S.O. 4)   Outsourcing involves contracting with an external party to provide a good or service, rather than performing the work internally.

_____ 17. (S.O. 5)   To minimize income taxes when there are transfers between divisions in different countries, the division in the high-tax-rate country is allocated more contribution margin, and the division in the low-tax-rate country is allocated less.

_____ *18. (S.O. 6)   Under the absorption cost approach, the cost base consists of all of the variable costs associated with a product, including variable selling and administrative costs.

_____ *19. (S.O. 6) Most companies that use cost-plus pricing use either absorption cost or full cost as the basis.

_____ *20. (S.O. 6)   The contribution approach is more useful for making short-run decisions because it displays variable cost and fixed cost behavior patterns separately.

The
Navigator

MULTIPLE CHOICE

Circle the letter that best answers each of the following statements.

1.   (S.O. 1) Which of the following is an **not** generally the type of product sold by a price taker?
   a.   Sand.
   b.   Corn.
   c.   A designer dress.
   d.   Coal.

2.   (S.O. 2) The cost-plus pricing formula is:
   a.   Target selling price = Cost + (Markup percentage X Cost)
   b.   Target selling price = Cost - (Markup percentage X Cost)
   c.   Target selling price = Cost + (Markup percentage ÷ Cost)
   d.   Target selling price = Cost - (Markup percentage ÷ Cost)

3.   (S.O. 2) The following information is provided for Roth Company for the new product it recently introduced:

Total unit cost	$40
Desired ROI per unit	$12
Target selling price	$52

What would be Roth Company's percentage markup on cost?
   a.   23%
   b.   30%
   c.   70%
   d.   130%

Items 4, 5, and 6 relate to the following information:

Carmalita Company is going to sell a new V1 stereo speaker system. The per unit variable cost estimates for the speaker system are as follows:

Direct materials	$45
Direct labor	25
Variable manufacturing overhead	15
Variable selling and administrative expenses	10

The fixed costs per speaker system at a budgeted sales volume of 20,000 units are as follows:

Fixed manufacturing overhead	$160,000
Fixed selling and administrative expenses	100,000

Carmalita has decided to price its new speaker system to earn a 25 percent return on its investment (ROI) of $800,000.

4. (S.O. 2) On a per unit basis, what is the desired ROI of Carmalita Company?
   a. $ 5
   b. $10
   c. $15
   d. $20

5. (S.O. 2) What is the sales price Carmalita should sell the V1 speaker system to receive the desired return on its investment?
   a. $ 95.
   b. $105.
   c. $118.
   d. $128.

6. (S.O. 2) What is the percentage markup on cost for the V1 speaker system for Carmalita?
   a.   9.26%
   b.   13.25%
   c.   14.87%
   d.   17.21%

7. (S.O. 6) Which of the following is **not** considered a limitation of cost-plus pricing?
   a.   It is difficult to compute.
   b.   The model does not give consideration to the demand side.
   c.   The model does not guarantee that customers will pay the price computed.
   d.   Sales volume plays a large role in determining per unit costs.

Items 8, 9 and 10 relate to the following information:

Juniper Computer Repairs has the following budgeted costs for the year 2006:

Juniper Computer Repairs
Budgeted Costs for the Year 2006

	Time Charges	Material Charges
Repairperson wages and benefits	$ 64,000	-
Parts manager's salary and benefits	-	$12,000
Office employee's salary and benefits	24,000	1,500
Other overhead (supplies, depreciation, property taxes, advertising, utilities)	32,000	15,000

8. (S.O. 3) If Juniper budgets 1,600 hours of repair time in 2006, and it desires a profit margin of $10 per hour of labor, what is the labor charge per hour for any particular job?
    a. $65.
    b. $75.
    c. $85.
    d. $95.

9. (S.O. 3) If Juniper estimates that the total invoice cost of parts and materials used in 2006 will be $150,000 and desires a 15 percent profit margin on the invoice cost of parts and materials, what should be the material loading charge used by Juniper in 2006?
    a.   34%
    b.   40%
    c.   44%
    d.   50%

10. (S.O. 3) Juniper estimates that a repair job for Buxter Company will require 3 hours of labor and $400 in parts and materials. Juniper's price quotation for the job should be:
    a. $487.
    b. $791.
    c. $852.
    d. $912.

11. (S.O. 4) Under negotiated transfer pricing, when the selling division has no excess capacity, how should the minimum transfer price by the selling division be calculated?
    a.   Variable cost per unit.
    b.   Variable cost per unit less its lost contribution margin per unit.
    c.   Variable cost per unit plus its lost contribution margin per unit.
    d.   Contribution margin per unit.

12. (S.O. 4) Lost contribution margin is often referred to as:
    a.   sunk cost.
    b.   contribution cost.
    c.   lost cost.
    d.   opportunity cost.

Items 13 and 14 relate to the following information:

The Howell Company primarily sells dishes, and recently purchased a cardboard box company. Howell's new cardboard box division has no excess capacity and produces and sells 40,000 boxes to outside customers. The variable cost of each box is $1.25 and usually has a contribution margin per box of $0.75. Management of Howell's dish division has decided it would like the box division to provide it with boxes.

13. (S.O. 4) What is the minimum transfer price the box division should find as acceptable?
    a. $0.50
    b. $0.75
    c. $1.25
    d. $2.00

14. (S.O. 4) Assuming that Howell's box division has excess capacity to provide all the boxes to the dish division without any loss in sales to outside customers, what is the minimum transfer price the box division should find as acceptable?
    a. $0.50
    b. $0.75
    c. $1.25
    d. $2.00

15. (S.O. 4) What transfer pricing method is known to have the disadvantage that it can lead to a loss of profitability for the company and unfair evaluations of division performance?
    a. Negotiated transfer prices.
    b. Cost-based transfer prices.
    c. Market-based transfer prices.
    d. Time and material transfer prices.

16. (S.O. 4) What transfer pricing method is often considered the best approach because it is objective and generally provides the proper economic incentives?
    a. Negotiated transfer prices.
    b. Cost-based transfer prices.
    c. Market-based transfer prices.
    d. Time and material transfer prices.

17. (S.O. 5) The Prine Company sells suit jackets and buttons. The suit jacket division is located in a country that has a tax rate of 26% and the buttons division is located in a country that has a tax rate of 32%. How should the Prine Company set transfer prices to minimize income taxes when the buttons division provides buttons to the suit jacket division?
    a. The division in the high-tax-rate country should be allocated more contribution margin.
    b. The suit jacket division should be allocated more contribution margin.
    c. The buttons division should be allocated more contribution margin.
    d. The suit jacket division should be allocated less contribution margin.

*Items 18, 19, 20 and 21 relate to the following information:

Monty Company sells a golfing aid called "The Monty Swing King" which is used to help golfers keep a steady tempo during their golf swing. Monty has the following cost information related to its production of the Swing Kings:

	Per Unit
Variable manufacturing cost	$28
Fixed manufacturing cost	$32
Variable selling and administrative expenses	$ 7
Fixed selling and administrative expenses	$12
Desired ROI per unit	$17

*18.   (S.O. 6)   What is the markup percentage assuming that Monty Company uses the absorption cost approach?
   a.   28%
   b.   36%
   c.   50%
   d.   60%

*19.   (S.O. 6) What is the target selling price assuming that Monty Company uses the absorption cost approach?
   a. $ 78
   b. $ 86
   c. $ 96
   d. $104

*20.   (S.O. 6)   What is the markup percentage assuming that Monty Company uses the contribution cost approach?
   a.   125.0%
   b.   174.3%
   c.   218.2%
   d.   229.6%

*21.   (S.O. 6)   What is the target selling price assuming that Monty Company uses the contribution cost approach?
   a. $ 78
   b. $ 86
   c. $ 96
   d. $104

The
Navigator

MATCHING

Match each term with its definition by writing the appropriate letter in the space provided.

Terms	Definitions

Terms

_____ 1. Cost-plus pricing.

_____ 2. Outsourcing.

_____ 3. Transfer price.

_____ 4. Target selling price.

_____ 5. Market-based transfer price.

_____ 6. Markup.

_____ 7. Material loading charge.

_____ 8. Cost-based transfer price.

_____ 9. Time and material pricing.

_____ 10. Target cost.

_____ 11. Negotiated transfer price.

Definitions

a. The percentage applied to a product's cost to determine the product's selling price.

b. A transfer price that is determined by the agreement of the division managers when no external market price is available.

c. A process whereby a product's selling price is determined by adding a markup to a cost base.

d. A transfer price that uses as its foundation the costs incurred by the division producing the goods.

e. The price used to record the transfer between two divisions of a company.

f. An approach to cost-plus pricing in which the company uses two pricing rates, one for the labor used on a job and another for the material.

g. The cost that will provide the desired profit on a product when the seller does not have control over the product's price.

h. A charge added to cover the cost of purchasing, receiving, handling, and storing materials, plus any desired profit margin on the materials themselves.

i. Contracting with an external party to provide a good or service, rather than performing the work internally.

j. A transfer price that is based on existing market prices of competing products.

k. The selling price that will provide the desired profit on a product when the seller has the ability to determine the product's price.

The Navigator

EXERCISES

EX. 8-1   (S.O. 2) Picture Frame, Inc. is in the process of setting a selling price on its new X1 frame. The variable cost per X1 frame is $28 and the fixed cost per X1 frame at a budgeted sales volume of 10,000 frames is $12. Picture Frame, Inc. has decided to price its new X1 frame to earn a 10% return on its investment (ROI) of $1,000,000.

Instructions
Compute the target selling price and the markup percentage that Picture Frame, Inc. should set for its X1 frame.

_____

_____

_____

_____

_____

_____

_____

_____

_____

_____

_____

EX. 8-2   (S.O. 3) Casey Tiling Company sells and installs tiles on kitchen cabinet tops. The following budgeted cost data is available:

	Time Charges	Materials Charges
Tilers' wages and benefits	$200,000	
Parts manager's salary and benefits		$45,000
Secretary's salary and benefits	24,000	5,000
Other overhead	10,000	10,000
Total budgeted costs	$234,000	$60,000

The company has budgeted for 8,000 tiler hours of time during the coming year. It desires a $26 profit margin per hour of labor and a 50% profit on parts. It estimates the total invoice cost of parts and materials in 2006 will be $500,000.

Instructions
(a) Compute the rate charged per hour of labor (round to 2 decimal places).
(b) Compute the material loading charge (round to 2 decimal places).
(c) Casey has just received a request for a bid on a new kitchen tiling job. The company estimates that it would require 8 hours of labor and $2,000 of parts. Compute the total estimated bill.

(a) _____

_____

_____

_____

_____

_____

_____

_____

_____

_____

_____

_____

_____

(b) _____

(c) _____

EX. 8-3   (S.O. 6) Williams Notebook Corporation makes the Student Spiral Notebook. The following information is available for Williams' anticipated annual volume of 10,000,000 units.

	Per Unit	Total
Direct materials	$0.10	
Direct labor	0.03	
Variable manufacturing overhead	0.02	
Fixed manufacturing overhead		$500,000
Variable selling and administrative expenses	0.04	
Fixed selling and administrative expenses		$300,000

The company has a desired ROI of 30%. It has invested assets of $2,000,000.

Instructions
(a)   Compute the total cost per unit.
(b)   Compute the desired ROI per unit.
(c)   Using the absorption cost approach, compute the markup percentage and target selling price.
(d)   Using the contribution approach, compute the markup percentage and target selling price.

(a) _____

_____

_____

_____

_____

_____

_____

_____

_____

_____

(b) _____

_____

_____

_____

_____

_____

_____

_____

_____

(c) _____

_____

_____

_____

_____

_____

_____

_____

_____

_____

_____

(d) _____

_____

_____

_____

_____

_____

_____

_____

_____

_____

_____

_____

The
Navigator

SOLUTIONS TO REVIEW QUESTIONS AND EXERCISES

TRUE-FALSE

1. (F) Price takers are companies that cannot easily set the prices on the products or services they sell. Instead, the prices are generally set by the competitive market (the laws of supply and demand).
2. (T)
3. (T)
4. (F) Cost-plus pricing involves establishing a cost base and adding a markup to determine a target selling price.
5. (F) The cost-plus pricing approach has a major advantage: It is simple to compute.
6. (T)
7. (T)
8. (F) Time and material pricing is widely used in service industries.
9. (F) The charge for labor time includes (1) the direct labor cost of the employee, including hourly rate or salary and fringe benefits; (2) selling, administrative, and similar overhead costs; and (3) an allowance for a desired profit or ROI per hour of employee time. Purchasing, receiving, handling, and storing materials are typically covered in the material loading charge.
10. (T)
11. (F) When goods are transferred internally, the price used to record the transfer between the two divisions is the transfer price.
12. (T)
13. (T)
14. (F) A cost-based approach can sometimes lead to unfair evaluations of division performance.
15. (T)
16. (T)
17. (F) To minimize income taxes when there are transfers between divisions in different countries, the division in the low-tax-rate country is allocated more contribution margin, and the division in the high-tax-rate country is allocated less.
*18. (F) Under the absorption cost approach, both variable and fixed selling administrative costs are excluded from the cost base.
*19. (T)
*20. (T)

MULTIPLE CHOICE

1. (c) Price takers generally sell a product that is not easily differentiated from competing products, such as sand, corn and coal. A designer dress is usually specially made for customer and therefore the company can more easily set the price.

2. (a) The cost-plus pricing formula is: Target selling price = Cost + (Markup percentage X Cost).

3. (b) Roth Company's percentage markup on cost is computed by dividing the desired ROI per unit by the total unit cost for 30% ($12 ÷ $40).

4.   (b)   Carmalita expects to receive income of $200,000 (25% X 800,000) on its investment. On a per unit basis, the ROI is $10 ($200,000 ÷ 20,000).

5.   (c)   The sales price of $118 is computed as follows:

Variable cost per unit	$ 95
Fixed cost per unit	13
Total cost per unit	108
Desired ROI per unit	10
Selling price	$118

6.   (a)   The percentage markup on cost for Carmalita Company is 9.26% and is computed by dividing the desired ROI per unit by the total unit cost ($10 ÷ $108).

7.   (a)   Cost-plus pricing had the advantage of being simple to compute.

8.   (c)   Computation of the hourly charges for Juniper during 2006 are shown as follows:

Per Hour	Total Cost	÷	Total Hours	=	Per Hour Charge
Hourly labor rate for repairs					
Repairpersons' wages and benefits	$ 64,000	÷	1,600	=	$40
Overhead costs					
Office employee's salary and					
benefits	24,000	÷	1,600	=	15
Other overhead	32,000	÷	1,600	=	20
Total hourly cost	$120,000		1,600	=	75
Profit margin					10
Rate charged per hour of labor					$85

9.   (a)   Computation of the material loading charge for Juniper during 2006 is shown as follows:

	Material Total Cost	÷	Total Invoice Cost, Parts and Materials	=	Material Loading Charge
Overhead costs					
Parts manager's salary and benefits	$12,000				
Office employee's salary	1,500				
	13,500	÷	$150,000	=	9%
Other overhead	15,000	÷	150,000	=	10%
	$28,500	÷	150,000	=	19%
Profit margin					15%
Material loading charge					34%

10.   (b)   The calculation of Juniper's time and material price quotation for the repair job is as follows:

Labor charges: 3 hours @ $85		$255
Material charges:		
Cost of parts and materials	$400	
Material loading charge (34% X $400)	136	536
Total price of labor and material		$791

11.   (c)   Under negotiated transfer pricing, when the selling division has no excess capacity, the minimum transfer price by the selling division should be calculated by adding the variable cost per unit to its lost contribution margin per unit. When there is excess capacity, then the selling division need only use the variable cost per unit.

12.   (d)   Lost contribution margin is often referred to as opportunity cost.

13.   (d)   Because the box division has no excess capacity, it should set a minimum transfer price equal to the variable cost per unit ($1.25) plus the contribution margin per unit ($0.75) for a total of $2.00.

14.   (c)   Because the box division has excess capacity, it should set a minimum transfer price equal to the variable cost per unit of $1.25.

15.   (b)   The cost-based transfer pricing method is known to have the disadvantage that it can lead to a loss of profitability for the company and unfair evaluations of division performance.

16.   (c)   The market-based transfer pricing method is often considered the best approach because it is objective and generally provides the proper economic incentives. Unfortunately, in many cases, there simply is not a well-defined market for the good or service being transferred and therefore cannot be used.

17.   (b)   In order to minimize income taxes, the division in the low-tax-rate country should be allocated more contribution margin and the division in the high-tax-rate country should be allocated less contribution margin. Therefore, the Prine Company should allocate more contribution margin to the suit jacket division which has a 26% tax rate and allocate less contribution margin to the buttons division which has a 32% tax rate.

*18. (d) The markup percentage is computed by solving for the following equation:

Desired ROI Per Unit	+	Selling and Administrative Expenses Per Unit	=	Markup Percentage	X	Manufacturing Cost Per Unit
$17	+	$19	=	MP	X	($28 + $32)
		$36 ÷ $60	=	MP		
		60%	=	MP		

*19. (c) The target selling price is computed by solving for the following equation:

$$\text{Manufacturing Cost Per Unit} + \left(\text{Markup Percentage} \times \text{Manufacturing Cost Per Unit} \right) = \text{Target Selling Price}$$

$$\$60 + (60\% \times \$60) = \$96$$

*20. (b) The markup percentage is computed by solving for the following equation:

Desired ROI Per Unit	+	Fixed Costs Per Unit	=	Markup Percentage	X	Variable Cost Per Unit
$17	+	($32 + $12)	=	MP	X	($28 + $7)
		$61 ÷ $35	=	MP		
		174.3%	=	MP		

*21. (c) The target selling price is computed by solving for the following equation:

$$\text{Variable Cost Per Unit} + \left(\text{Markup Percentage} \times \text{Manufacturing Cost Per Unit} \right) = \text{Target Selling Price}$$

$$\$35 + (174.3\% \times \$35) = \$96$$

MATCHING

1.	c		7.	h
2.	i		8.	d
3.	e		9.	f
4.	k		10.	g
5.	j		11.	b
6.	a			

EXERCISES

EX. 8-1

	Per Unit
Variable cost	$28
Fixed cost	12
Total	40
Desired ROI	
(10% X $1,000,000) ÷ 10,000	10
Selling price	$50
Markup percentage ($10 ÷ $40)	25%

EX. 8-2

(a)

Per Hour	Total Cost	÷	Total Hours	=	Per Hour Charge
Hourly labor rate for repairs					
Tilers' wages and benefits	$200,000	÷	8,000	=	$25.00
Overhead costs					
Secretary's salary and benefits	24,000	÷	8,000	=	3.00
Other overhead	10,000	÷	8,000	=	1.25
Total hourly cost	$234,000		8,000	=	29.25
Profit margin					26.00
Rate charged per hour of labor					$55.25

(b)

	Material Charges	÷	Total Invoice Cost, Parts and Materials	=	Material Loading Charge
Overhead costs					
Parts manager's salary and benefits	$45,000				
Secretary's salary and benefits	5,000				
	50,000	÷	$500,000	=	10%
Other overhead	10,000	÷	$500,000	=	2%
	$60,000	÷	$500,000	=	12%
Profit margin					50%
Material loading charge					62%

(c)

Casey Tiling Company
Time and Material Price Quotation

Labor charges: 8 hours @ $55.25		$ 442
Material charges		
Cost of parts and materials	$2,000	
Material loading charge (62% X $2,000)	1,240	3,240
Total price of labor and materials		$3,682

*EX. 8-3

(a)

Direct materials	$0.10
Direct labor	0.03
Variable manufacturing overhead	0.02
Fixed manufacturing overhead	
($500,000 ÷ 10,000,000)	0.05
Variable selling and administrative expenses	0.04
Fixed selling and administrative expenses	
($300,000 ÷ 10,000,000)	0.03
Total unit cost	$0.27

(b)   Desired ROI = (30% X $2,000,000) ÷ 10,000,000 = $.06

(c)   The unit manufacturing cost under the absorption cost approach is as follows:

	Per Unit
Direct materials	$0.10
Direct labor	0.03
Variable manufacturing overhead	0.02
Fixed manufacturing overhead	0.05
Total unit manufacturing cost	$0.20

The markup percentage is calculated as follows:

Desired ROI Per Unit	+	Selling and Administrative Expenses Per Unit	=	Markup Percentage	X	Manufacturing Cost Per Unit
$0.06	+	$0.07	=	MP	X	$0.20
		$0.13 ÷ $0.20	=	MP		
		65%	=	MP		

The target selling price is calculated as follow:

$$\frac{\text{Manufacturing}}{\text{Cost Per Unit}} + \left(\frac{\text{Markup}}{\text{Percentage}} \times \frac{\text{Manufacturing}}{\text{Cost Per Unit}}\right) = \frac{\text{Target}}{\text{Selling Price}}$$

$$\$0.20 \quad + \quad (65\% \quad \times \quad \$0.20) \quad = \quad \$0.33$$

(d)   The unit manufacturing cost under the contribution approach is as follows:

	Per Unit
Direct materials	$0.10
Direct labor	0.03
Variable manufacturing overhead	0.02
Variable selling and administrative expenses	0.04
Total unit manufacturing cost	$0.19

The markup percentage is calculated as follows:

$$\frac{\text{Desired}}{\text{ROI Per Unit}} + \frac{\text{Fixed Costs}}{\text{Per Unit}} = \frac{\text{Markup}}{\text{Percentage}} \times \frac{\text{Variable}}{\text{Cost Per Unit}}$$

$$\$0.06 \quad + \quad (\$0.05 + \$0.03) \quad = \quad \text{MP} \quad \times \quad \$0.19$$

$$\$0.14 \div \$0.19 \quad = \quad \text{MP}$$

$$73.684\% \quad = \quad \text{MP}$$

The target selling price is calculated as follow:

$$\frac{\text{Variable}}{\text{Cost Per Unit}} + \left(\frac{\text{Markup}}{\text{Percentage}} \times \frac{\text{Manufacturing}}{\text{Cost Per Unit}}\right) = \frac{\text{Target}}{\text{Selling Price}}$$

$$\$0.19 \quad + \quad (73.684\% \quad \times \quad \$0.19) \quad = \quad \$0.33$$

Chapter 9

*B*UDGETARY PLANNING

The Navigator	✓
■ *Scan Study Objectives*	☐
■ *Read Preview*	☐
■ *Read Chapter Review*	☐
■ *Work Demonstration Problem*	☐
■ *Answer True-False Statements*	☐
■ *Answer Multiple-Choice Questions*	☐
■ *Match Terms and Definitions*	☐
■ *Solve Exercises*	☐

CHAPTER STUDY OBJECTIVES

After studying this chapter, you should be able to:
1. Indicate the benefits of budgeting.
2. State the essentials of effective budgeting.
3. Identify the budgets that comprise the master budget.
4. Describe the sources for preparing the budgeted income statement.
5. Explain the principal sections of a cash budget.
6. Indicate the applicability of budgeting in nonmanufacturing companies.

PREVIEW OF CHAPTER 9

Our primary focus in this chapter is budgeting—specifically, how budgeting is used as a planning tool by management. Through budgeting, it should be possible for management to maintain enough cash to pay creditors, to have sufficient raw materials to meet production requirements, and to have adequate finished goods to meet expected sales. The content and organization of this chapter are as follows:

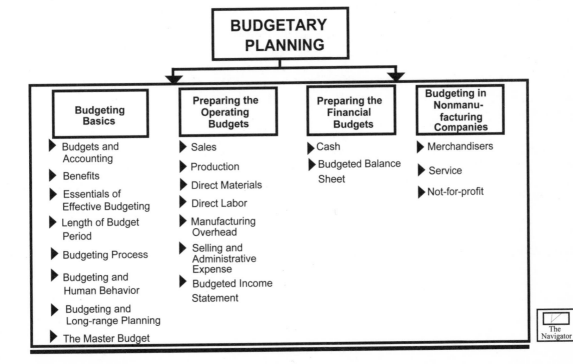

CHAPTER REVIEW

Budgeting Basics

1. (S.O. 1) A **budget** is a formal written statement of management's plans for a specified time period, expressed in financial terms.

2. The **role of accounting** during the budgeting process is to (a) provide historical data on revenues, costs, and expenses, (b) express management's plans in financial terms, and (c) prepare periodic budget reports.

Benefits of Budgeting

3. The primary benefits of budgeting are as follows:
    a.   It requires all levels of management to **plan ahead.**
    b.   It provides **definite objectives** for evaluating performance.
    c.   It creates an **early warning system** for potential problems.
    d.   It facilitates the **coordination of activities** within the business.
    e.   It results in greater **management awareness** of the entity's overall operations.
    f.   It **motivates personnel** throughout the organization.

Essentials of Effective Budgeting

4. (S.O. 2) In order to be effective management tools, budgets must be based upon
    a.   A **sound organizational structure** in which authority and responsibility are clearly defined.
    b.   **Research and analysis** to determine the feasibility of new products, services, and operating techniques.
    c.   **Management acceptance** which is enhanced when all levels of management participate in the preparation of the budget, and the budget has the support of top management.

5. The most common budget period is one year. A **continuous twelve-month budget** results from dropping the month just ended and adding a future month. The annual budget is often supplemented by monthly and quarterly budgets.

6. The responsibility for coordinating the preparation of the budget is assigned to a **budget committee.** The budget committee usually includes the president, treasurer, chief accountant (controller), and management personnel from each major area of the company.

7. A budget can have a significant impact on **human behavior.** A budget may have a strong positive influence on a manager when
    a.   Each level of management is invited and encouraged to participate in developing the budget.
    b.   Criticism of a manager's performance is tempered with advice and assistance.

8. **Long-range planning** involves the selection of strategies to achieve long-term goals and the development of policies and plans to implement the strategies. Long-range plans contain considerably less detail than budgets.

The Master Budget

9. (S.O. 3) The **master budget** is a set of interrelated budgets that constitutes a plan of action for a specified time period. It is developed within the framework of a sales forecast which shows potential sales for the industry and the company's expected share of such sales.

10. There are **two classes** of budgets in the master budget.
    a. **Operating budgets** are the individual budgets that result in the preparation of the budgeted income statement.
    b. **Financial budgets** focus primarily on the cash resources needed to fund expected operations and planned capital expenditures.

11. The **sales budget** is the first budget prepared. It is derived from the sales forecast, and it represents management's best estimate of sales revenue for the budget period. It is prepared by multiplying the expected unit sales volume for each product by its anticipated unit selling price.

12. The **production budget** shows the units that must be produced to meet anticipated sales. It is derived from the budgeted sales units plus the desired ending finished goods units less the beginning finished goods units.

13. The **direct materials budget** shows both the quantity and cost of direct materials to be purchased. It is derived from the direct materials units required for production plus the desired ending direct materials units less the beginning direct materials units.

14. The **direct labor budget** shows the quantity (hours) and cost of direct labor necessary to meet production requirements. The direct labor budget is critical in maintaining a labor force that can meet expected levels of production.

15. The **manufacturing overhead budget** shows the expected manufacturing overhead costs. The **selling and administrative expense budget** is a projection of anticipated operating expenses. Both budgets distinguish between fixed and variable costs.

Budgeted Income Statement

16. (S.O. 4) The **budgeted income statement** is the important end-product in preparing operating budgets. This budget indicates the expected profitability of operations and it provides a basis for evaluating company performance.
    a. The budget is prepared from the budgets described in review points 11-15.
    b. For example, to find cost of goods sold, it is necessary to determine the total unit cost of a finished product using the direct materials, direct labor, and manufacturing overhead budgets.

Cash Budget

17. (S.O. 5) The **cash budget** shows anticipated cash flows. It contains three sections (cash receipts, cash disbursements, and financing) and the beginning and ending cash balances. Data for preparing this budget are obtained from the other budgets.

18.   The **budgeted balance sheet** is a projection of financial position at the end of the budget period. It is developed from the budgeted balance sheet for the preceding year and the budgets for the current year.

Budgeting in Nonmanufacturing Companies

19.   (S.O. 6) The major differences in the master budget of a merchandiser and a manufacturing company are that a merchandiser (a) uses a **merchandise purchases budget** instead of a production budget and (b) does not use the manufacturing budgets (direct materials, direct labor, and manufacturing overhead).

20.   In service enterprises, the critical factor in budgeting is coordinating professional staff needs with anticipated services. Budget data for service revenue may be obtained from expected **output** or expected **input.**

21.   In the budget process for **not-for-profit organizations,** the emphasis is on cash flows rather than on a revenue and expense basis. For governmental units, the budget must be strictly followed and overspending is often illegal.

The
Navigator

DEMONSTRATION PROBLEM (S.O. 5)

The Crawford Company begins operations with a cash balance of $60,000 on January 1, 2006. Relevant quarterly budgeted data pertaining to a cash budget for the first two quarters of the year are as follows:

Sales: (1) $140,000, (2) $250,000. All sales are on account; 60% of the sales are expected to be collected in cash in the period of sale, and the balance in the following quarter.

Direct materials purchases: (1) $65,000, (2) $165,000. 40% of each purchase is paid in cash at the time of the purchase, and the balance is paid in the following quarter.

Direct labor: (1) $40,000, (2) $50,000. Wages are paid at the time they are incurred.

Manufacturing overhead: (1) $35,000, (2) $30,000. These costs include depreciation of $3,200 per quarter. All cash overhead costs are paid as incurred.

Selling and administrative expenses: (1) $18,000, (2) $19,000. These expenses include $1,000 of depreciation per quarter. All cash selling and administrative costs are paid when incurred.

The company has a line of credit at a local bank that enables it to borrow up to $30,000 per quarter. Interest on any loans and income taxes may be ignored.

The Crawford Company wants to maintain a minimum quarterly cash balance of $40,000.

Instructions
(a) Prepare schedules for (1) expected collections from customers and (2) expected payments for direct materials purchases.
(b) Prepare a cash budget by quarters for the six months ending June 30, 2006.

The
Navigator

SOLUTION TO DEMONSTRATION PROBLEM

(a) (1)   **Schedule of Expected Cash Collections from Customers**

	Quarter	
	1	**2**
First quarter sales ($140,000)	$84,000	$ 56,000
Second quarter sales ($250,000)		150,000
Total collections	$84,000	$206,000

(2)   **Schedule of Expected Payments for Direct Materials**

	Quarter	
	1	**2**
First quarter purchases ($65,000)	$26,000	$ 39,000
Second quarter purchases ($165,000)		66,000
Total payments	$26,000	$105,000

(b)

CRAWFORD COMPANY
Cash Budget
For the 6-months Ending June 30, 2006

	1	2	Total
Beginning cash balance	$60,000	$ 40,000	$ 60,000
Add: Receipts			
Collections from customers	84,000	206,000	290,000
Total available cash	144,000	246,000	350,000
Less: Disbursements			
Direct materials	26,000	105,000	131,000
Direct labor	40,000	50,000	90,000
Manufacturing overhead	31,800	26,800	58,600
Selling and administrative			
expenses	17,000	18,000	35,000
Total disbursements	114,800	199,800	314,600
Excess (deficiency) of available			
cash over disbursements	29,200	46,200	35,400
Financing			
Borrowings	10,800		10,800
Repayments	-0-	6,200	6,200
Ending cash balance	$ 40,000	$ 40,000	$ 40,000

REVIEW QUESTIONS AND EXERCISES

TRUE—FALSE

Indicate whether each of the following is true (T) or false (F) in the space provided.

_____ 1. (S.O. 1) The budget itself and the administration of the budget are entirely accounting responsibilities.

_____ 2. (S.O. 1) A primary benefit of budgeting is that it provides definite objectives for evaluating subsequent performance at each level of responsibility.

_____ 3. (S.O. 2) If a budget is effective enough, it can be a substitute for management.

_____ 4. (S.O. 2) Management acceptance of budgets occurs more frequently when the flow of input data is from the highest level of responsibility to the lowest level of responsibility.

_____ 5. (S.O. 2) Effective budgeting depends on an organizational structure in which authority and responsibility over all phases of operations are clearly defined.

_____ 6. (S.O. 2) The budget committee is usually made up of people outside the company in order to decrease bias.

_____ 7. (S.O. 2) Financial planning models and statistical and mathematical techniques may be used in forecasting sales.

_____ 8. (S.O. 3) Long-range planning usually emphasizes meeting annual profit objectives.

_____ 9. (S.O. 3) Long-range plans contain considerably less detail than short-term budgets.

_____ 10. (S.O. 3) The sales budget is derived from the production budget.

_____ 11. (S.O. 3) The production budget shows unit production data as well as cost data.

_____ 12. (S.O. 3) The direct materials budget is derived from the direct materials units required for production plus desired ending direct materials units less beginning direct materials units.

_____ 13. (S.O. 3) The direct labor budget contains only quantity data (hours) which are derived from the production budget.

_____ 14. (S.O. 3) The manufacturing overhead budget shows the expected manufacturing overhead costs.

_____ 15. (S.O. 5) The cash budget contains three sections (cash receipts, cash disbursements, and financing) and the beginning and ending cash balances.

_____ 16. (S.O. 5) In order to develop a budgeted balance sheet, the previous year's balance sheet is needed.

_____ 17. (S.O. 6) One difference between the master budget of a merchandising company and a manufacturing company is that the purchases budget is used instead of a production budget.

_____ 18. (S.O. 6) In service enterprises, the critical factor in budgeting is coordinating materials and equipment with anticipated services.

_____ 19. (S.O. 6) Not-for-profit organizations usually budget on the basis of cash flows (expenditures and receipts) rather than on a revenue and expense basis.

_____ 20. (S.O. 6) For governmental units, the budget must be strictly followed and overspending is often illegal.

The Navigator

MULTIPLE CHOICE

Circle the letter that best answers each of the following statements.

1. (S.O. 1) The responsibility for expressing management's budgeting goals in financial terms is performed by the:
   a.   accounting department.
   b.   top management.
   c.   lower level of management.
   d.   budget committee.

2. (S.O. 1) Which of the following would **not** be considered a benefit of budgeting?
   a.   Facilitates the coordination of activities.
   b.   Requires all levels of management to plan ahead.
   c.   Always motivates personnel.
   d.   Results in greater management awareness of the entity's overall operations.

3. (S.O. 2) In order for budgets to be effective there must be:
   a.   sound organizational structure.
   b.   research and analysis.
   c.   management acceptance of the budget program.
   d.   all of the above.

4. (S.O. 2) For better management acceptance, the flow of input data for budgeting should begin with the:
   a.   accounting department.
   b.   top management.
   c.   lower levels of management.
   d.   budget committee.

5. (S.O. 2) Responsibility for coordinating the preparation of the budget is assigned to the:
   a.   accounting department.
   b.   top management.
   c.   lower levels of management.
   d.   budget committee.

6. (S.O. 2) Which of the following is **not** a characteristic of long-range planning?
   a.   It encompasses a period of at least five years.
   b.   Consideration is given to the economic and political environment.
   c.   More detail is presented than in a budget.
   d.   It is used to review progress rather than as a basis for control.

7. (S.O. 3) The starting point in preparing the master budget is the:
   a.   cash budget.
   b.   budgeted income statement.
   c.   direct materials budget.
   d.   sales budget.

8. (S.O. 3) The Turlington Company has 12,000 units in beginning finished goods. If sales are expected to be 60,000 units for the year and Turlington desires ending finished goods of 15,000 units, how many units must Turlington produce?
    a.   57,000.
    b.   60,000.
    c.   63,000.
    d.   75,000.

9. (S.O. 3) The Evangelista Company has 3,000 units in beginning finished goods. The sales budget shows expected sales to be 12,000 units. If the production budget shows that 14,000 units are required for production, what was the desired ending finished goods?
    a.   1,000.
    b.   3,000.
    c.   5,000.
    d.   9,000.

10. (S.O. 3) In the Campbell Company required production for June is 44,000 units. To make one unit of finished product, three pounds of direct material Z are required. Actual beginning and desired ending inventories of direct material Z are 100,000 and 110,000 pounds, respectively. How many pounds of direct material Z must be purchased?
    a.   126,000.
    b.   132,000.
    c.   136,000.
    d.   142,000.

11. (S.O. 3) Taylor Company determines that 13,500 pounds of direct materials are needed for production in July. There are 800 pounds of direct materials on hand at July 1 and the desired ending inventory is 700 units. If the cost per unit of direct materials is $3, what is the budgeted total cost of direct materials purchases?
    a. $39,600.
    b. $40,200.
    c. $40,800.
    d. $41,400.

12. (S.O. 3) Navia Company is preparing its direct labor budget for May. Projections for the month are that 8,350 units are to be produced and that direct labor time is three hours per unit. If the labor cost per hour is $9, what is the total budgeted direct labor cost for May?
    a. $217,350.
    b. $221,400.
    c. $225,450.
    d. $243,000.

13. (S.O. 3) Porizkova Company requires that ending finished goods inventory for each month be 10% of the next month's budgeted sales. Budgeted sales in units are February 15,000, March 13,000 and April 17,000. What should be the level of production scheduled for March?
    a.   12,800.
    b.   13,000.
    c.   13,400.
    d.   14,700.

14.   (S.O. 5) On January 1, Ghauri Company has a beginning cash balance of $21,000. During the year, the company expects cash disbursements of $170,000 and cash receipts of $145,000. If Ghauri requires an ending cash balance of $20,000, the Ghauri Company must borrow:
      a. $16,000.
      b. $20,000.
      c. $24,000.
      d. $46,000.

15.   (S.O. 5) The Tennant Company has the following budgeted sales: January $40,000, February $60,000, and March $50,000. 40% of the sales are for cash and 60% are on credit. For the credit sales, 50% are collected in the month of sale, and 50% the next month. The total expected cash receipts during March are:
      a. $56,000.
      b. $53,000.
      c. $52,500.
      d. $50,000.

16.   (S.O. 5) The Auermann Company's direct materials budget shows total cost of direct materials purchases for January $125,000, February $150,000 and March $175,000. Cash payments are 60% in the month of purchase and 40% in the following month. The budgeted cash payments for March are:
      a. $165,000.
      b. $160,000.
      c. $150,000.
      d. $130,000.

17.   (S.O. 6) Which of the following statements about budgeted financial statements is **incorrect?**
      a.   The budgeted balance sheet is developed entirely from the budgets for the current year.
      b.   Once established, the budgeted income statement provides the basis for evaluating company performance.
      c.   Cost of goods sold is determined by multiplying the budgeted unit sales by the budgeted total unit production cost.
      d.   The budgeted income statement is developed from the budgets for the current year.

18.   (S.O. 6) A purchases budget is used instead of a production budget by:
      a.   merchandising companies.
      b.   service enterprises.
      c.   not-for-profit organizations.
      d.   manufacturing companies.

19.   (S.O. 6) Entities that budget on the basis of cash flows (expenditures and receipts) rather than on a revenue and expense basis are:
      a.   merchandising companies.
      b.   service enterprises.
      c.   not-for-profit organizations.
      d.   manufacturing companies.

20. (S.O. 6) Which of the following statements is **incorrect?**
a.   A continuous twelve-month budget results from dropping the month just ended and adding a future month.
b.   The production budget is derived from the direct materials and direct labor budget.
c.   The cash budget shows anticipated cash flows.
d.   In the budget process for not-for-profit organizations, the emphasis is on cash flow rather than on revenue and expenses.

MATCHING

Match each term with its definition by writing the appropriate letter in the space provided.

Terms	Definitions
_____ 1. Budget committee.	a. The projection of potential sales for the industry and the company's expected share of such sales.
_____ 2. Budget.	b. An estimate of the quantity and cost of direct materials to be purchased.
_____ 3. Cash budget.	c. The selection of strategies to achieve long-term goals and the development of policies and plans to implement the strategies.
_____ 4. Production budget.	
_____ 5. Merchandise purchases budget.	d. A formal written summary of management's plan for a specified future time period expressed in financial terms.
_____ 6. Master budget.	e. A group responsible for coordinating the preparation of the budget.
_____ 7. Manufacturing overhead budget.	f. An estimate of expected manufacturing overhead costs for the budget period.
_____ 8. Direct materials budget.	g. A projection of the units that must be produced to meet anticipated sales.
_____ 9. Sales budget.	h. A set of interrelated budgets that constitutes a plan of action for a specific time period.
_____ 10. Direct labor budget.	i. The estimated cost of goods to be purchased in a merchandising company to meet expected sales.
_____ 11. Long-range planning.	j. A projection of anticipated cash flows.
_____ 12. Sales forecast.	k. An estimate of expected sales for the budget period.
	l. A projection of the quantity and cost of direct labor to be incurred to meet production requirements.

EXERCISES

EX. 9-1   (S.O. 3) Vendela has the following sales budget for the year ending December 31, 2006:

			Quarter		
	1	**2**	**3**	**4**	**Year**
Expected unit sales	4,000	3,500	5,000	5,500	18,000

On the basis of past experiences, Vendela Company believes it can meet future sales requirements by maintaining an ending inventory equal to 10% of the next quarter's budgeted sales volume. On January 1, 2006, Vendela has beginning finished goods of 400 units. Vendela expects sales for the first quarter of 2007 to be 6,000 units.

Instructions
Prepare a production budget for Vendela Company for the year ending December 31, 2006.

VENDELA COMPANY
Production Budget
For the Year Ending December 31, 2006

EX. 9-2   (S.O. 3) Brinkley Company's production budget for 2006 by quarters is as follows: (1) 6,000, (2) 7,000, (3), 8,000, and (4) 9,000. For the first quarter of 2005, the budget is 8,000 units. The manufacture of each unit requires three pounds of direct materials and an expected cost per unit of $2. The ending inventory of direct materials is expected to be 20% of the next quarter's production needs. At December 31, 2005, Brinkley had 3,600 pounds of direct materials.

Instructions
Prepare a direct materials budget for Brinkley Company for the year ending December 31, 2006.

BRINKLEY COMPANY
Direct Materials Budget
For the Year Ending December 31, 2006

EX. 9-3   (S.O. 3 and 4) The Ireland Company has accumulated the following budget data for the year 2006.

1.   Sales 30,000 units; unit selling price $100.
2.   Cost of one unit of finished goods; direct materials $15, direct labor $30, and manufacturing overhead 60% of direct labor cost.
3.   Selling and administrative expenses: variable 5% of sales, fixed $320,000.

Instructions
Prepare a budgeted income statement for the year assuming an income tax rate of 30% on income before income taxes.

IRELAND COMPANY
Budgeted Income Statement
For the Year Ended December 31, 2006

The
Navigator

SOLUTIONS TO REVIEW QUESTIONS AND EXERCISES

TRUE-FALSE

1. (F)   The budget itself, and the administration of the budget, are entirely management responsibilities.
2. (T)
3. (F)   A budget is an aid to management; it is not a substitute for management.
4. (F)   Management acceptance of budgets occurs more frequently when the flow of input data is from the lowest level of responsibility to the highest level of responsibility.
5. (T)
6. (F)   The budget committee is usually made up of people inside the organization such as the president, treasurer, chief accountant (controller), and management personnel from each of the major areas of the company.
7. (T)
8. (F)   Budgeting is concerned with meeting annual profit objectives. Long-range planning involves the selection of strategies to achieve long-term goals and the development of policies and plans to implement the strategies.
9. (T)
10. (F)   The production budget is derived from the sales budget.
11. (F)   The production budget shows only unit production data.
12. (T)
13. (F)   The direct labor budget contains both quantity and cost data.
14. (T)
15. (T)
16. (T)
17. (T)
18. (F)   In service enterprises, the critical factor in budgeting is coordinating professional staff needs with anticipated services.
19. (T)
20. (T)

MULTIPLE CHOICE

1. (a)   The accounting department is responsible for (1) providing historical data on revenues, costs and expenses, (2) translating management's plans into financial terms, and (3) preparing periodic budget reports.

2. (c)   A budget does not always motivate personnel. If a manager views a budget as being unfair and unrealistic, he or she may become discouraged and uncommitted to the budget goals.

3. (d)   In order for budgets to be effective it is recognized that there must be (1) a sound organizational structure, (2) research and analysis, and (3) management acceptance of the budget program.

4. (c)   For management acceptance, the flow of input data for budgeting is from the lowest level of responsibility to the highest.

5. (d) The responsibility for coordinating the preparation of the budget is assigned to the budget committee.

6. (c) Long-range plans contain considerably less detail than a budget because the data are intended more for a review of progress toward long-range goals than for an evaluation of specific results to be achieved. Answers (a), (b), and (d) are correct statements.

7. (d) The sales budget is the starting point in preparing the master budget. Each of the other budgets is dependent on the sales budget.

8. (c) The production requirements are:

Expected sales	60,000
Add: Desired ending finished goods	15,000
Total required units	75,000
Less: Beginning finished goods	12,000
Units to be produced	63,000

9. (c) The desired ending finished goods is computed as follows:

Beginning finished goods	3,000
Units to be produced	14,000
Total units available	17,000
Less: Units expected to be sold	12,000
Desired ending finished goods	5,000

10. (d) The amount of direct materials to be purchased is as follows:

Units to be produced	44,000
Direct materials per unit	3
Total pounds needed for production	132,000
Add: Desired ending direct materials units	110,000
Total materials required	242,000
Less: Beginning direct materials	100,000
Direct materials purchases	142,000

11. (b) The cost of direct materials purchases is:

Total direct materials needed for production	13,500
Add: Desired ending direct materials	700
Total materials required	14,200
Less: Beginning direct materials	800
Direct materials purchases	13,400
Cost per unit	X $3
Total cost of direct materials purchases	$40,200

12. (c) The total direct labor cost is computed as follows:

Total units to be produced	8,350
Direct labor time (hours)	3
Total required direct labor hours	25,050
Direct labor cost	X $9
Total direct labor cost	$225,450

13. (c) The level of production is:

Expected units sales in March... 13,000
Add: Desired ending finished goods, March 31 (17,000
   X 10%).. 1,700
Total required units.. 14,700
Less: Beginning finished goods, March 1, (13,000 X 10%)... 1,300
Units to be produced 13,400

14. (c) The cash to be borrowed is:

Beginning cash balance .... $ 21,000
Add: Cash receipts 145,000
Total available cash.. 166,000
Less: Cash disbursements 170,000
Excess (deficiency) of available cash over disbursements .... (4,000)
Financing 24,000
Ending cash balance .... $ 20,000

15. (b) The percentage of cash collected during the month of sale is 70% [40% + (60% X 50%)]. Therefore, 30% of the February sales will be collected in March, $18,000 ($60,000 X 30%) and 70% of the March sales will be collected in March, $35,000 ($50,000 X 70%).

16. (a) In March, $60,000 will be paid on February purchases ($150,000 X 40%) and $105,000 will be paid on March purchases ($175,000 X 60%).

17. (a) The budgeted balance sheet is developed from the budgeted balance sheet from the preceding year and the budgets for the current year.

18. (a) The major differences in the master budget of a merchandising company are that (1) a purchases budget is used instead of a production budget and (2) the manufacturing budgets are not applicable.

19. (c) The budget process for not-for-profit organizations is based on cash flows (expenditures and receipts) rather than on a revenue and expense basis.

20. (b) The production budget is derived from the budgeted sales units plus the desired ending finished goods units less the beginning finished goods units.

MATCHING

1. e   7. f
2. d   8. b
3. j   9. k
4. g   10. l
5. i   11. c
6. h   12. a

EXERCISES

EX. 9-1

VENDELA COMPANY
Production Budget
For the Year Ending December 31, 2006

	Quarter				
	1	**2**	**3**	**4**	**Year**
Expected unit sales	4,000	3,500	5,000	5,500	18,000
Add: Desired ending finished goods units	350	500	550	600	600
Total required units	4,350	4,000	5,550	6,100	18,600
Less: Beginning finished goods units	400	350	500	550	400
Required production units	3,950	3,650	5,050	5,550	18,200

EX. 9-2

BRINKLEY COMPANY
Direct Materials Budget
For the Year Ending December 31, 2006

	Quarter				
	1	**2**	**3**	**4**	**Year**
Units to be produced	6,000	7,000	8,000	9,000	30,000
Direct materials per unit	X 3	X 3	X 3	X 3	X 3
Total pounds needed for production	18,000	21,000	24,000	27,000	90,000
Add: Desired ending direct materials units	4,200	4,800	5,400	4,800	4,800
Total materials required	22,200	25,800	29,400	31,800	94,800
Less: Beginning direct materials units	3,600	4,200	4,800	5,400	3,600
Direct materials purchases	18,600	21,600	24,600	26,400	91,200
Cost per pound	X $2	X $2	X $2	X $2	X $2
Total cost of direct materials purchases	$37,200	43,200	49,200	52,800	$182,400

EX. 9-3

IRELAND COMPANY
Budgeted Income Statement
For the Year Ended December 31, 2006

Sales (30,000 X $100)	$3,000,000
Cost of goods sold (30,000 X $63)	1,890,000
Gross profit	1,110,000
Selling and administrative expenses [$320,000 + ($3,000,000 X 5%)]	470,000
Income before income taxes	640,000
Income tax expense (30% X $640,000)	192,000
Net income	$ 448,000

Chapter 10

The Navigator ✓
- ■ Scan Study Objectives ☐
- ■ Read Preview ☐
- ■ Read Chapter Review ☐
- ■ Work Demonstration Problem ☐
- ■ Answer True-False Statements ☐
- ■ Answer Multiple-Choice Questions ☐
- ■ Match Terms and Definitions ☐
- ■ Solve Exercises ☐

BUDGETARY CONTROL AND RESPONSIBILITY ACCOUNTING

CHAPTER STUDY OBJECTIVES

After studying this chapter, you should be able to:
1. Describe the concept of budgetary control.
2. Evaluate the usefulness of static budget reports.
3. Explain the development of flexible budgets and the usefulness of flexible budget reports.
4. Describe the concept of responsibility accounting.
5. Indicate the features of responsibility reports for cost centers.
6. Identify the content of responsibility reports for profit centers.
7. Explain the basis and formula used in evaluating performance in investment centers.
*8. Explain the difference between ROI and residual income.

*Note: All **asterisked** (*) items relate to material contained in the Appendix to the chapter.

PREVIEW OF CHAPTER 10

In contrast to Chapter 9, we now consider how budgets are used by management to control operations. This chapter focuses on two aspects of management control: (1) budgetary control and (2) responsibility accounting. The content and organization of this chapter are as follows:

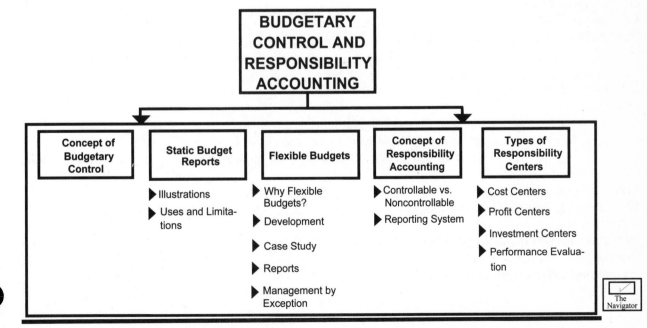

CHAPTER REVIEW

Budgetary Control

1. (S.O. 1) The use of budgets in controlling operations is known as **budgetary control.** Such control takes place by means of budget reports that compare actual results with planned objectives. The budget reports provide management with feedback on operations.

2. **Budgetary control** involves:
    a.   Developing budgets.
    b.   Analyzing the differences between actual and budgeted results.
    c.   Taking corrective action.
    d.   Modifying future plans, if necessary.

3. Budgetary control works best when a company has a formalized reporting system.   The system should
    a.   Identify the name of the budget report such as the sales budget or the manufacturing overhead budget.
    b.   State the frequency of the report such as weekly, or monthly.
    c.   Specify the purpose of the report.
    d.   Indicate the primary recipient(s) of the report.

Static Budget Reports

4. (S.O. 2) A **static budget** does not modify or adjust data regardless of changes in activity during the year. As a result, actual results are always compared with the budget data at the activity level used in developing the master budget.

5. A static budget is appropriate in evaluating a manager's effectiveness in controlling costs when (a) the actual level of activity closely approximates the master budget activity level, and/or (b) the behavior of the costs in response to changes in activity is fixed.

Flexible Budgets

6. (S.O. 3) A **flexible budget** projects budget data for various levels of activity. The flexible budget recognizes that the budgetary process is more useful if it is adaptable to changed operating conditions. This type of budget permits a comparison of actual and planned results at the level of activity actually achieved.

7. To develop the flexible budget, the following steps are taken:
    a.   Identify the activity index and the relevant range of activity.
    b.   Identify the variable costs, and determine the budgeted variable cost per unit of activity for each cost.
    c.   Identify the fixed costs, and determine the budgeted amount for each cost.
    d.   Prepare the budget for selected increments of activity within the relevant range.

8. For **manufacturing overhead costs,** the activity index is usually the same as the index used in developing the predetermined overhead rate; that is, direct labor hours or machine hours. For selling and administrative expenses, the activity index usually is sales or net sales.

9. The following **formula** may be used to determine total budgeted costs at any level of activity:

    Total budgeted costs = Fixed costs + (Total variable cost per unit X activity level)

10. Total budgeted costs at each level of activity can be shown **graphically.**
    a. In a graph, the activity index is shown on the horizontal axis and costs are shown on the vertical axis.
    b. The total budgeted costs for each level of activity are then identified from the total budgeted cost line.

11. **Flexible budget reports** are another type of internal report produced by managerial accounting. The flexible budget report consists of two sections: (a) production data such as direct labor hours and (b) cost data for variable and fixed costs. It also shows differences between budget and actual results.

12. **Management by exception** means that top management's review of a budget report is focused either entirely or primarily to differences between actual results and planned objectives. The guidelines for identifying an exception are based on materiality and controllability.

Responsibility Accounting

13. (S.O. 4) **Responsibility accounting** involves accumulating and reporting costs (and revenues, where relevant) on the basis of the manager who has the authority to make the day-to-day decisions about the items. A manager's performance is evaluated on matters directly under that manager's control.

14. Responsibility accounting can be used at every level of management in which the following **conditions** exist:
    a. Costs and revenues can be directly associated with the specific level of management responsibility.
    b. The costs and revenues are controllable at the level of responsibility with which they are associated.
    c. Budget data can be developed for evaluating the manager's effectiveness in controlling the costs and revenues.

15. Responsibility accounting is especially valuable in a decentralized company. **Decentralization** means that the control of operations is delegated to many managers throughout the organization. A **segment** is an identified area of responsibility in decentralized operations.

16. Responsibility accounting is an essential part of any effective system of budgetary control. It differs from budgeting in two respects:
    a. A distinction is made between controllable and noncontrollable items.
    b. Performance reports either emphasize or include only items controllable by the individual manager.

17. A cost is considered **controllable** at a given level of managerial responsibility if that manager has the power to incur it within a given period of time. Costs incurred indirectly and allocated to a responsibility level are considered to be **noncontrollable** at that level.

18. A **responsibility reporting system** involves the preparation of a report for each level of responsibility shown in the company's organization chart. A responsibility reporting system permits management by exception at each level of responsibility within the organization.

19. **Responsibility centers** may be classified into one of three types. A **cost center** incurs costs (and expenses) but does not directly generate revenues. A **profit center** incurs costs (and expenses) but also generates revenues. An **investment center** incurs costs (and expenses), generates revenues, and has control over investment funds available for use.

Cost Centers

20. (S.O. 5) A **responsibility report for cost centers** compares actual controllable costs with flexible budget data. Only controllable costs are included in the report, and no distinction is made between variable and fixed costs.

21. **Direct fixed costs** or **traceable costs** are costs that relate specifically to a responsibility center and are incurred for the sole benefit of the center. **Indirect fixed costs** or **common costs** pertain to a company's overall operating activities and are incurred for the benefit of more than one profit center.

Profit Centers

22. (S.O. 6) A responsibility report for a profit center shows budgeted and actual controllable revenues and costs. The report is prepared using the cost-volume-profit income statement format.

23. In the responsibility report for a profit center:
    a. Controllable fixed costs are deducted from contribution margin.
    b. The excess of contribution margin over controllable fixed costs is identified as controllable margin.
    c. Noncontrollable fixed costs are not reported.

24. Controllable margin is considered to be the best measure of the manager's performance in **controlling revenues and costs.**

Investment Centers

25. (S.O. 7) The primary basis for evaluating the performance of a manger of an investment center is **return on investment** (ROI). The **formula** for computing return on investment is: Investment Center Controllable Margin (in dollars) ÷ Average Investment Center Operating Assets = Return on Investment.
    a. **Operating assets** consist of current assets and plant assets used in operations by the center. Nonoperating assets such as idle plant assets and land held for future use are excluded.
    b. Average operating assets are usually based on the beginning and ending **cost or book values** of the assets.

26. A manager can improve ROI by (a) increasing controllable margin or (b) reducing average operating assets.

27. The return on investment approach includes **two judgmental factors:**
    a.   Valuation of operating assets—cost, book value, appraised value, or market value.
    b   Margin (income) measure—controllable margin, income from operations, or net income.

28. Performance evaluation is a management function that compares actual results with budget goals. Performance evaluation includes both **behavioral and reporting principles.**

*Residual Income

*29. (S.O. 8)   To evaluate performance using the minimum rate of return, companies use the residual income approach. **Residual income** is the income that remains after subtracting from the controllable margin the minimum rate of return on a company's average operating assets.

The residual income would be computed as follows:

Controllable Margin	$-$	Minimum Rate of Return $\times$ Average Operating Assets	$=$	Residual Income

The Navigator

DEMONSTRATION PROBLEM (S.O. 7)

Comparative data for the following investment centers of Thorson Company are shown below.

	DeKalb	Madison	Ann Arbor	Urbana
Controllable margin	$ 48,000	(b)	120,000	$100,000
Average operating assets	400,000	500,000	800,000	(d)
Return on investment	(a)	14%	(c)	12%

Instructions
Compute the missing amounts using the ROI formula.

The Navigator

SOLUTION TO DEMONSTRATION PROBLEM

(a)   12% = ($48,000 ÷ $400,000).
(b) $70,000 = (14% X $500,000).
(c)   15% = ($120,000 ÷ $800,000).
(d) $833,333 = ($100,000 ÷ 12%).

REVIEW QUESTIONS AND EXERCISES

TRUE—FALSE

Indicate whether each of the following is true (T) or false (F) in the space provided.

_____   1.   (S.O. 1)   Budget reports provide the feedback needed by management to see whether actual operations are on course.

_____   2.   (S.O. 2)   A budget prepared for a single level of activity is called a static budget.

_____   3.   (S.O. 2)   A static budget is an effective means to evaluate a manager's ability to control costs, regardless of the actual activity level.

_____   4.   (S.O. 3)   A flexible budget recognizes that the budgetary process has greater usefulness if it is adaptable to changed operating conditions.

_____   5.   (S.O. 3)   One of the steps in developing a flexible budget is the combining of variable and fixed costs into one lump-sum cost.

_____   6.   (S.O. 3)   The flexible budget report evaluates a manager's performance in two areas: (1) production and (2) costs.

_____   7.   (S.O. 3)   Management by exception means that top management will investigate every difference.

_____   8.   (S.O. 4)   Under responsibility accounting, the evaluation of a manager's performance is based on the matters directly under the manager's control.

_____   9.   (S.O. 4)   Responsibility accounting is especially valuable in a centralized company.

_____   10.   (S.O. 4)   All costs are controllable by the top management of a company.

_____   11.   (S.O. 4)   The terms controllable costs and noncontrollable costs are synonymous with variable costs and fixed costs, respectively.

_____   12.   (S.O. 4)   The responsibility reporting system begins with the lowest level of responsibility and moves upward to each higher level.

_____   13.   (S.O. 4)   A responsibility reporting system permits management by exception at each level of responsibility within the organization.

_____   14.   (S.O. 4)   A profit center incurs costs (and expenses) but also generates revenues.

_____   15.   (S.O. 5)   A responsibility report for cost centers makes a clear distinction between variable and fixed costs.

_____ 16. (S.O. 5)   Most direct fixed costs are not controllable by the profit center manager.

_____ 17. (S.O. 7)   The formula for computing return on investment in responsibility accounting is controllable margin in dollars divided by average current assets.

_____ 18. (S.O. 7)   The manager of an investment center can improve ROI by reducing average operating assets.

_____ 19. (S.O. 7)   An advantage of the return on investment ratio is that no judgmental factors are involved.

_____ 20. (S.O. 7)   Performance evaluation is a management function that compares actual results with budget goals.

The Navigator

MULTIPLE CHOICE

Circle the letter that best answers each of the following statements.

1. (S.O. 1) Which of the following would **not** be considered an aspect of budgetary control?
   a.   It assists in the determination of differences between actual and planned results.
   b.   It provides feedback value needed by management to see whether actual operations are on course.
   c.   It assists management in controlling operations.
   d.   It provides a guarantee for favorable results.

2. (S.O. 1) Budgetary control involves all but one of the following:
   a.   Modify future plans, if necessary.
   b.   Analyze differences between actual and planned results.
   c.   Take disciplinary action.
   d.   Develop the budget.

3. (S.O. 1) Which of the following is not part of a formalized reporting system?
   a.   Identify the name of the budget reports.
   b.   State the corrective action that should be taken.
   c.   Specify the purpose of the report.
   d.   Indicate the primary recipient(s) of the report.

4. (S.O. 2) In a static budget,
   a.   data are modified and adjusted according to changes in activity during the year.
   b.   the actual results are always compared with budget data at the original budgeted activity level.
   c.   it is important to select an activity index and a relevant range of activity.
   d.   only budgeted fixed costs are compared with actual fixed costs.

5. (S.O. 2) A static budget is usually appropriate in evaluating a manager's effectiveness in controlling:
   a.   fixed manufacturing costs and fixed selling and administrative expenses.
   b.   variable manufacturing costs and variable selling and administrative expenses.
   c.   fixed manufacturing costs and variable selling and administrative expenses.
   d.   variable manufacturing costs and fixed selling and administrative expenses.

6. (S.O. 3) In the Johnson Company, indirect labor is budgeted for $24,000 and factory supervision is budgeted for $8,000 at normal capacity of 80,000 direct labor hours. If 90,000 direct labor hours are worked, flexible budget total for these costs is:
   a. $32,000.
   b. $36,000.
   c. $35,000.
   d. $33,000.

7. (S.O. 3) Vidmar Company uses flexible budgets. At normal capacity of 8,000 units, budgeted manufacturing overhead is: $64,000 variable and $180,000 fixed. If Vidmar had actual overhead costs of $250,000 for 9,000 units produced, what is the difference between actual and budgeted costs?
   a. $2,000 unfavorable.
   b. $2,000 favorable.
   c. $6,000 unfavorable.
   d. $8,000 favorable.

8. (S.O. 3) A flexible budget provides a basis for evaluating a manager's performance for:

	Production Control	Cost Control
a	No	No
b.	Yes	No
c.	No	Yes
d.	Yes	Yes

9. (S.O. 3) When production levels decline within a relevant range and a flexible budget is used, what effects would be anticipated with respect to each of the following?

	Total Fixed Costs	Total Variable Costs
a.	Decrease	Decrease
b.	Decrease	No change
c.	No change	No change
d.	No change	Decrease

10. (S.O. 3) A flexible budget is appropriate for:

	Direct Labor Costs	Manufacturing Overhead Costs
a.	No	No
b.	Yes	Yes
c.	Yes	No
d.	No	Yes

11. (S.O. 3) The criteria used in identifying an exception under management by exception are:
   a. materiality and frequency.
   b. controllability and frequency.
   c. materiality and controllability.
   d. none of the above.

12.   (S.O. 4) Responsibility accounting cannot be used effectively when:
      a.   costs are allocated to the responsibility level.
      b.   budget data can be developed for evaluating the manager's effectiveness in controlling costs.
      c.   costs are controllable at the level of responsibility with which they are associated.
      d.   costs can be directly associated with the specific level of responsibility.

13.   (S.O. 4) Controllable costs for responsibility accounting purposes are those costs that are directly influenced by:
      a.   a given manager within a given period of time.
      b.   a change in activity.
      c.   production volume.
      d.   sales volume.

14.   (S.O. 4) A responsibility reporting system:
      a.   begins with the highest level of responsibility and moves downward to the lowest level.
      b.   involves the preparation of a report for each level of responsibility shown in the company's organization chart.
      c.   does not permit comparative evaluations of responsibility centers.
      d.   does not permit management by exception at each level of responsibility.

15.   (S.O. 5) Responsibility reports for cost centers will include:

	Controllable Costs	Noncontrollable Costs
a.	No	No
b.	No	Yes
c.	Yes	No
d.	Yes	Yes

16.   (S.O. 5) Which of the following is **not** a direct fixed cost of a profit center?
      a.   Timekeeping for center's employees.
      b.   Depreciation on center's equipment.
      c.   Profit center manager's salary.
      d.   General office administrative costs.

17.   (S.O. 7) In the return on investment (ROI) formula:
      a.   sales are divided by average investment center operating assets.
      b.   controllable margin is divided by sales.
      c.   controllable margin is divided by average investment center operating assets.
      d.   sales are divided by net income.

18.   (S.O. 7) Which of the following will cause an increase in ROI?
      a.   An increase in variable costs.
      b.   An increase in average operating assets.
      c.   An increase in sales.
      d.   An increase in controllable fixed costs.

19.   (S.O. 7) Which of the following is **incorrect** about average operating assets?
      a.   Both current assets and plant assets are included.
      b.   Nonoperating assets are excluded.
      c.   The assets are valued at fair market values.
      d.   The average may be based on beginning and ending recorded balances.

20. (S.O. 7) If controllable margin is $300,000 and the average investment center operating assets are $1,000,000, the return on investment is:
   a. .33%.
   b. 3.33%.
   c. 10%.
   d. 30%.

MATCHING

Match each term with its definition by writing the appropriate letter in the space provided.

Terms	Definitions
_____ 1. Budgetary control.	a. A projection of budget data for various levels of activity.
_____ 2. Flexible budget.	b. The use of budgets to control operations.
_____ 3. Static budget.	c. Costs incurred indirectly and allocated to a responsibility center that are not controllable at that level.
_____ 4. Responsibility accounting.	d. Control of operations is delegated by top management to many managers throughout the organization.
_____ 5. Noncontrollable costs.	e. Costs that a manager has the authority to incur within a given period of time.
_____ 6. Controllable costs.	f. The preparation of reports for each level of responsibility shown in the company's organization chart.
_____ 7. Responsibility reporting system.	g. A part of management accounting that involves accumulating and reporting revenues and cost on the basis of the individual manager who has the authority to make the day-to-day decisions about the items.
_____ 8. Cost center.	
_____ 9. Management by exception.	h. A responsibility center that incurs costs, generates revenues, and has control over the investment funds available for use.
_____ 10. Profit center.	
_____ 11. Investment center.	i. A projection of budget data at one level of activity.
_____ 12. Decentralization.	j. The review of budget reports by top management directed entirely or primarily to differences between actual results and planned objectives.
	k. A responsibility center that incurs costs and also generates revenues.
	l. A responsibility center that incurs costs but does not directly generate revenues.

EXERCISES

EX. 10-1   (S.O. 3)   Hartung Company is in the midst of preparing its flexible budget for manufacturing overhead. At a production level of 10,000 units, unit costs are: Indirect materials $4, Indirect labor $3, Supplies $5, Depreciation $6, and Property taxes $2. Depreciation and property taxes are fixed costs.

Instructions
Complete the following four-column flexible budget for the manufacturing costs for the Hartung Company.

HARTUNG COMPANY
Flexible Manufacturing Overhead Budget

Activity level: Units	8,000	10,000	12,000	14,000
Variable costs:				
Indirect materials				
Indirect labor				
Supplies				
Total variable				
Fixed costs:				
Depreciation				
Property taxes				
Total fixed				
Total costs				

EX. 10-2   (S.O. 3)   Gaylord Company has the following flexible budget for manufacturing overhead:

Activity level:	20,000	25,000	30,000
Direct labor hours			
Variable costs:			
Indirect materials	$10,000	$ 12,500	$ 15,000
Indirect labor	40,000	50,000	60,000
Supplies	30,000	37,500	45,000
Total	80,000	100,000	120,000
Fixed costs:			
Depreciation	30,000	30,000	30,000
Supervision	45,000	45,000	45,000
Total	75,000	75,000	75,000
Total costs	$155,000	$175,000	$195,000

In January, 22,000 direct labor hours were expected and 24,000 were worked.

Instructions
Given the following actual costs, complete the following budget report:

GAYLORD COMPANY
Manufacturing Overhead Budget Report
For the Month Ended January 31

	Budget at	Actual Costs at	Difference Favorable F Unfavorable U
Direct labor hours (DLH):			
Expected			
Actual	_____	_____	
Variable costs			
Indirect materials	$	$ 13,000	$
Indirect labor		47,500	
Supplies		35,200	
Total variable		95,700	
Fixed costs			
Depreciation		25,000	
Supervision		46,000	
Total fixed		71,000	_____
Total costs	_____	$166,700	_____

The Navigator

SOLUTIONS TO REVIEW QUESTIONS AND EXERCISES

TRUE-FALSE

1. (T)
2. (T)
3. (F) A static budget is an effective means to evaluate a manager's ability to control costs provided (1) the actual level of activity closely approximates the master budget activity level, or (2) the behavior of the costs in response to changes in activity is fixed.
4. (T)
5. (F) To develop the flexible budget, the following steps are taken:
    1. Identify the activity index and the relevant range of activity.
    2. Identify the variable costs and determine the budgeted variable cost per unit of activity for each cost.
    3. Identify the fixed costs and determine the budgeted amount for each cost.
    4. Prepare the budget for selected increments of activity within the relevant range.
6. (T)
7. (F) Management by exception does not mean that top management will investigate every difference. Exceptions are identified by materiality and controllability of the item.
8. (T)
9. (F) Responsibility accounting is especially valuable in a decentralized company.
10. (T)
11. (F) A controllable cost can be variable or fixed, and a noncontrollable cost can also be variable or fixed.
12. (T)
13. (T)
14. (T)
15. (F) There is usually no distinction between variable and fixed costs in a responsibility report for cost centers.
16. (F) Most direct fixed costs are controllable by the profit center manager.
17. (F) The basic formula for computing return on investment is controllable margin (in dollars) divided by average operating assets.
18. (T)
19. (F) A number of judgmental factors are involved such as the proper valuation of operating assets and selection of the income measure to be used.
20. (T)

MULTIPLE CHOICE

1. (d) Budgetary control assists management in controlling operations by providing feedback to see whether actual operations are on course, but budgetary control does not guarantee favorable results

2. (c) Budgetary control involves taking corrective action but not necessarily disciplinary action.

3. (b)   A formalized reporting system does not require stating the corrective action. The missing part of the reporting system is specifying the frequency of the reports.

4. (b)   In a static budget, the actual results are always compared with the budget data at the original budgeted activity level. Answers (a) and (c) are aspects of a flexible budget, and answer (d) is false because a static budget includes variable as well as fixed costs.

5. (a)   A static budget is based on one level of activity. Thus, it is not usually appropriate in evaluating a manager's performance in controlling variable costs that should change at different levels of activity.

6. (c)   Indirect labor is a variable cost that is budgeted at $.30 per direct labor hour ($24,000 ÷ 80,000). Factory supervision is a fixed cost that remains the same at each activity level. The total cost, therefore, is $35,000 [(90,000 X $.30) + $8,000].

7. (b)   The per unit variable factory overhead is $8.00 ($64,000 ÷ 8,000). Therefore, for 9,000 units produced, variable factory overhead was expected to be $72,000 ($8.00 X 9,000). The addition of $180,000 fixed factory overhead gives a total budget overhead of $252,000; thus, there is a $2,000 favorable difference ($252,000 - $250,000).

8. (d)   A flexible budget provides a basis for evaluating a manger's performance for production control and cost control.

9. (d)   As production levels decrease, total fixed costs will remain the same, and total variable costs will decrease directly and proportionately.

10. (b)   Many different types of flexible budgets may be prepared. The direct labor and manufacturing overhead budgets are usually based on hours performed.

11. (c)   The usual criteria are materiality and controllability.

12. (a)   Costs allocated to the responsibility level are considered to be noncontrollable costs which are outside the scope of responsibility accounting.

13. (a)   Controllable costs are defined as the costs a manager has the power to incur within a given period of time.

14. (b)   Choice (a) is incorrect because the reporting begins at the lowest level and moves upward to the highest level. Comparative evaluations are possible (c), and management by exception is possible (d).

15. (c)   Only controllable costs are included in the responsibility report.

16. (d)   General office administrative costs are considered common fixed costs. Answers (a), (b), and (c) are all considered direct fixed costs.

17. (c) The return on investment (ROI) formula is:

$$\frac{\text{Controllable Margin (in dollars)}}{\text{Average Operating Assets}} = \text{Return on Investment}$$

18. (c) The return on investment is equal to controllable margin divided by average operating assets; therefore, an increase in sales will increase the controllable margin which will also increase the return on investment. The other choices will cause a decrease in controllable margin or an increase in average operating assets.

19. (c) The recorded book values of these assets are used in determining average operating assets.

20. (d) The return on investment is controllable margin divided by the average investment center operating assets, 30% ($300,000 ÷ $1,000,000).

MATCHING

1.	b	5.	c	9.	j
2.	a	6.	e	10.	k
3.	i	7.	f	11.	h
4.	g	8.	l	12.	d

EXERCISES

EX. 10-1

HARTUNG COMPANY
Flexible Manufacturing Overhead Budget

Activity level: Units	8,000	10,000	12,000	14,000
Variable costs:				
Indirect materials	$ 32,000	$ 40,000	$ 48,000	$ 56,000
Indirect labor	24,000	30,000	36,000	42,000
Supplies	40,000	50,000	60,000	70,000
Total variable	96,000	120,000	144,000	168,000
Fixed costs:				
Depreciation	60,000	60,000	60,000	60,000
Property taxes	20,000	20,000	20,000	20,000
Total fixed	80,000	80,000	80,000	80,000
Total costs	$176,000	$200,000	$224,000	$248,000

EX. 10-2

GAYLORD COMPANY
Manufacturing Overhead Budget Report
For the Month Ended January 31

	Budget at 24,000 DLH	Actual Costs at 24,000 DLH	Difference Favorable F Unfavorable U
Direct labor hours (DLH):			
Expected 22,000			
Actual 24,000			
Variable costs			
Indirect materials	$ 12,000	$ 13,000	$ 1,000 U
Indirect labor	48,000	47,500	(500) F
Supplies	36,000	35,200	(800) F
Total variable	96,000	95,700	(300) F
Fixed costs			
Depreciation	30,000	25,000	(5,000) F
Supervision	45,000	46,000	1,000 U
Total fixed	75,000	71,000	(4,000) F
Total costs	$171,000	$166,700	$(4,300) F

Chapter 11

STANDARD COSTS AND BALANCED SCORECARD

The Navigator ✓
- ■ Scan Study Objectives ☐
- ■ Read Preview ☐
- ■ Read Chapter Review ☐
- ■ Work Demonstration Problem ☐
- ■ Answer True-False Statements ☐
- ■ Answer Multiple-Choice Questions ☐
- ■ Match Terms and Definitions ☐
- ■ Solve Exercises ☐

CHAPTER STUDY OBJECTIVES

After studying this chapter, you should be able to:
1. Distinguish between a standard and a budget.
2. Identify the advantages of standard costs.
3. Describe how standards are set.
4. State the formulas for determining direct materials and direct labor variances.
5. State the formulas for determining manufacturing overhead variances.
6. Discuss the reporting of variances.
7. Prepare an income statement for management under a standard costing system.
*8. Describe the balanced scorecard approach to performance evaluation.
*9. Identify the features of a standard cost accounting system.

*Note: All **asterisked** (*) items relate to material contained in the Appendix to the chapter.

PREVIEW OF CHAPTER 11

In this chapter we continue the study of controlling costs by considering additional measures that permit the evaluation of performance. The content and organization of the chapter are as follows:

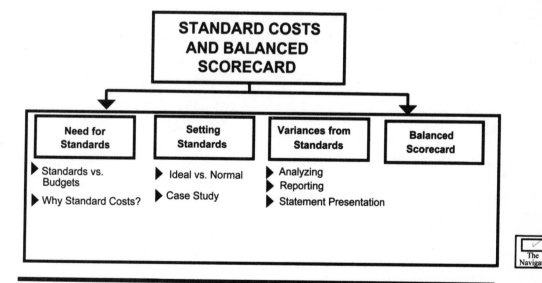

CHAPTER REVIEW

Standards and Budgets

1. (S.O. 1) In concept, **standards** and budgets are essentially the same. Both are pre-determined costs and both contribute significantly to management planning and control.
    a.   A standard is a **unit** amount, whereas a budget is a **total** amount.
    b.   Standard costs may be incorporated into a cost accounting system.

Why Standard Costs?

2. (S.O. 2) Standard costs offer the following advantages to an organization:
    a.   They facilitate **management planning.**
    b.   They promote **greater economy** by making employees more "cost conscious."
    c.   They are useful in **setting selling prices.**
    d.   They contribute to **management control** by providing a basis for the evaluation of cost control.
    e.   They are useful in highlighting variances in **management by exception.**
    f.   They **simplify the costing of inventories** and reduce clerical costs.

Setting Standard Costs

3. (S.O. 3) Setting standards requires input from all persons who have responsibility for costs and quantities. Standards may be set at one of two levels. **Ideal standards** represent optimum levels of performance under perfect operating conditions. **Normal standards** represent efficient levels of performance that are attainable under expected operating conditions.

4. To establish the standard cost of producing a product, it is necessary to establish standards for each manufacturing cost element—direct materials, direct labor, and manufacturing overhead. The standard for each element is derived from a consideration of the standard price to be paid and the standard quantity to be used.

Direct Materials

5. The **direct materials price standard** is the cost per unit of direct materials that should be incurred.
    a.   This standard is based on the purchasing department's best estimate of the cost of raw materials.
    b.   This standard should include an amount for related costs such as receiving, storing, and handling.

6. The **direct materials quantity standard** is the quantity of direct materials that should be used per unit of finished goods.
    a.   This standard is expressed as a physical measure, such as pounds, barrels, or board feet.
    b.   This standard should include allowances of unavoidable waste and normal storage.

7. The **standard direct materials cost per unit** is the standard direct materials price times the standard direct materials quantity.

Direct Labor

8. The **direct labor price standard** is the rate per hour that should be incurred for direct labor.
    a.   This standard is based on current wage rates adjusted for anticipated changes, such as cost of living adjustments included in many union contracts.
    b.   This standard generally includes employer payroll taxes and fringe benefits.

9. The **direct labor quantity standard** is the time that should be required to make one unit of the product.
    a.   This standard is especially critical in labor-intensive companies.
    b.   In setting this standard, allowances should be made for rest periods, cleanup, machine setup and machine downtime.

10. The **standard direct labor cost per unit** is the standard direct labor rate times the standard direct labor hours.

Manufacturing Overhead

11. The **manufacturing overhead standard** is based on a **standard predetermined overhead rate.**
    a.   This overhead rate is determined by dividing budgeted overhead costs by an expected standard activity index.
    b.   The **standard manufacturing overhead rate per unit** is the predetermined overhead rate times the activity index quantity standard.

Variances

12. A **variance** is the difference between total actual costs and total standard costs. An unfavorable variance suggests that too much was paid for materials, labor, and manufacturing overhead or that there were inefficiencies in using materials, labor, and manufacturing overhead. Favorable variances indicate efficiencies in incurring costs and in using materials, labor, and manufacturing overhead.

13. **Analyzing variances** begins with a determination of the cost elements that comprise the variance. For each manufacturing cost element, a total dollar variance is computed. Then this variance is analyzed into a price variance and a quantity variance.

Direct Materials Variances

14. (S.O. 4) The formulas for the direct materials variances are:

Actual Quantity X Actual Price (AQ) X (AP)	−	Standard Quantity X Standard Price (SQ) X (SP)	=	Total Materials Variance (TMV)
Actual Quantity X Actual Price (AQ) X (AP)	−	Actual Quantity X Standard Price (AQ) X (SP)	=	Materials Price Variance (MPV)
Actual Quantity X Standard Price (AQ) X (SP)	−	Standard Quantity X Standard Price (SQ) X (SP)	=	Materials Quantity Variance (MQV)

15. A **variance matrix** can be used in analyzing variances. In such cases, the formulas for each cost element are computed first and then the variances.

16. Materials price variances are usually the responsibility of the purchasing department, whereas materials quantity variances are usually attributable to the production department.

Direct Labor Variances

17. The formulas for the direct labor variances are:

Actual Hours X Actual Rate (AH) X (AR)	−	Standard Hours X Standard Rate (SH) X (SR)	=	Total Labor Variance (TLV)
Actual Hours X Actual Rate (AH) X (AR)	−	Actual Hours X Standard Rate (AH) X (SR)	=	Labor Price Variance (LPV)
Actual Hours X Standard Rate (AH) X (SR)	−	Standard Hours X Standard Rate (SH) X (SR)	=	Labor Quantity Variance (LQV)

18. Labor price variances usually result from paying workers higher wages than expected and/or misallocation of workers. Labor quantity variances relate to the efficiency of the workers and are the responsibility of the production department.

Manufacturing Overhead Variances

19. (S.O. 5) The computation of the **manufacturing overhead variances** is conceptually the same as the computation of the materials and labor variances. For manufacturing overhead, however, both variable and fixed overhead must be considered. The formulas are:

Actual Overhead	−	Overhead Applied*	=	Total Overhead Variance
Actual Overhead	−	Overhead Budgeted*	=	Overhead Controllable Variance
Fixed Overhead Rate	X (Normal Capacity Hours − Standard Hours Allowed)		=	Overhead Volume Variance

20. The overhead controllable variance shows whether overhead costs were effectively controlled.
    a. Budgeted costs are determined from the **flexible manufacturing overhead budget** for standard hours allowed.
    b. Most controllable variances are associated with **variable costs** which are controllable costs.

21. The overhead volume variance indicates whether plant facilities were efficiently used during the period.
    a. This variance relates solely to **fixed costs.**
    b. It measures the amount that fixed overhead costs are under- or overapplied.

22. In computing the overhead variances,
    a. Standard hours allowed are used in each of the variances.
    b. Budgeted costs are derived from the flexible budget.
    c. The controllable variance generally pertains to variable costs.
    d. The volume variance pertains solely to fixed costs.

23. The controllable overhead variance relates to variable manufacturing overhead and therefore is the responsibility of the production department. The overhead volume variance may be the responsibility of either the production or sales departments.

Reporting of Variances

24. (S.O. 6) All variances should be reported to appropriate levels of management as soon as possible. **Variance reports** facilitate the principle of "management by exception." Rather than analyze every variance, top management will normally look for significant variances.

Statement Presentation of Variances

25. (S.O. 7) In income statements prepared for management under a standard cost accounting system, cost of goods sold is stated at standard cost and the variances are separately disclosed. In financial statements prepared for stockholders and other external users, standard costs may be used.

Balanced Scorecard

26. (S.O. 8) Many companies use both financial and nonfinancial measures to evaluate performance. This approach is known as the **balanced scorecard.** The four most commonly employed perspectives are as follows:
    a. The **financial perspective** employs financial measures of performance.
    b. The **customer perspective** evaluates how well the company is performing from the viewpoint of those people who buy and use its product.
    c. The **internal process perspective** evaluates the internal operating processes critical to success.
    d. The **earning and growth perspective** evaluates how well the company develops and retains its employees.

The different perspectives are linked together so a company can better understand how to achieve its goals and what measures to use to evaluate performance.

Standard Cost Accounting System

*27. (S.O. 9) A **standard cost accounting system** is a double-entry system of accounting in which standard costs are used in making entries and variances are formally recognized in the accounts. A standard cost system may be used with either job order or process costing.

*28. As an example, the purchase of raw materials inventory for $5,000 when the standard cost is $6,000 would be recorded as follows:

Raw Materials Inventory..	6,000	
Materials Price Variance...		1,000
Accounts Payable..		5,000

    a.   A debit balance in a variance account indicates an unfavorable variance.
    b.   A credit balance in a variance account indicates a favorable variance.

*29. In income statements prepared for management, cost of goods sold is stated at standard cost and the variances are separately disclosed.

*30. Standard costs may be used in costing inventories in financial statements prepared for **stockholders** when there are no significant differences between actual and standard costs. However, if the difference is material, the inventories and cost of goods sold must be reported at actual costs.

DEMONSTRATION PROBLEM (S.O. 4, 5, 6, 7)

Morgan Inc. is a small company that manufactures baseball caps. For the past several years, the company has used a standard cost accounting system. Cole prepares monthly income statements for management with variances reported within the statement. In April 2006, 67,500 caps were produced. There were no finished caps on hand at either April 1 or April 30. The selling price per cap was $10.00. The following standard and actual cost data applied to the month of April when normal capacity was 14,000 direct labor hours.

Cost Element	Standard (per unit)	Actual
Direct materials	1.5 yards at $3.00 per yard	$318,600 for 108,000 yards ($2.95 yard)
Direct labor	.2 hour at $11.00 per hour	$158,760 for 14,175 hours ($11.20 per hour)
Overhead	.2 hour at $ 5.00 per hour	$49,000 fixed overhead
		$20,000 variable overhead

Overhead is applied on the basis of direct labor hours. At normal capacity, budgeted fixed overhead costs were $49,000 and budgeted variable costs were $21,000.

Instructions
(a) Compute the total, price, and quantity variances for (1) materials, (2) labor, and (3) the total, controllable, and volume variances for manufacturing overhead (assuming no beginning or ending material balances).
(b) Journalize the entries to record the variances and the completion and sale of the caps.

SOLUTION TO DEMONSTRATION PROBLEM

(a)
Direct Material Variances
Total	= $318,600 ($2.95 X 108,000)	- $303,750 (1.5 X $3.00 X 67,500)	=	$14,850 U
Price	= $318,600 ($2.95 X 108,000)	- $324,000 ($3.00 X 108,000)	=	$5,400 F
Quantity	= $324,000 ($3.00 X 108,000)	- $303,750 (1.5 X $3.00 X 67,500)	=	$20,250 U

Direct Labor Variances
Total	= $158,760 ($11.20 X 14.175)	- $148,500 (.2 X $11.00 X 67,500)	=	$10,260 U
Price	= $158,760 ($11.20 X 14,175)	- $155,925 ($11.00 X 14,175)	=	$2,835 U
Quantity	= $155,925 ($11.00 X 14,175)	- $148,500 (.2 X $11.00 X 67,500)	=	$7,425 U

Overhead Variances
Total	= $69,000	- $67,500	=	$1,500 U
	($49,000 + $20,000)	($5 X 67,500 X .2)		
Controllable	= $69,000	- $69,250	=	$250 F
		[$49,000 + ($1.50* X 67,500 X .2)]		
Volume	= $3.50 X (14,000 – 13,500)		=	$1,750 U**

*$21,000 ÷ 14,000 = $1.50
**Alternatively: $69,250 - $67,500 = $1,750 U

(b)

1. Raw Materials Inventory 324,000
       Materials Price Variance 5,400
       Accounts Payable 318,600
          (To record purchase of materials)

2. Factory Labor 155,925
    Labor Price Variance 2,835
       Wages Payable 158,760
          (To record direct labor costs)

3. Manufacturing Overhead 69,000
       Accounts Payable/Cash/Acc. Depreciation 69,000
          (To record overhead incurred)

4. Work in Process Inventory 303,750
    Materials Quantity Variance 20,250
       Raw Materials Inventory 324,000
          (To record issuance of raw materials)

5. Work in Process Inventory 148,500
    Labor Quantity Variance 7,425
       Factory Labor 155,925
          (To record ...)

6. Work in Process Inventory 67,500
       Manufacturing Overhead 67,500
          (To assign overhead to jobs)

7. Finished Goods Inventory 519,750
       Work in Process Inventory 519,750
          (To record transfer of completed work to finished goods)

8. Accounts Receivable 675,000
    Cost of Goods Sold 519,750
       Sales 675,000
       Finished Goods Inventory 519,750
          (To record sale of finished goods and the cost of
           goods sold)

9. Overhead Volume Variance 1,750
       Overhead Controllable Variance 250
       Manufacturing Overhead 1,500
          (To recognize overhead variances)

REVIEW QUESTIONS AND EXERCISES

TRUE—FALSE

Indicate whether each of the following is true (T) or false (F) in the space provided.

_____   1. (S.O. 1)   In concept, standards and budgets are essentially the same.

_____   2. (S.O. 2)   Standards may be useful in setting selling prices for finished goods.

_____   3. (S.O. 3)   Ideal standards represent an efficient level of performance under normal operating conditions.

_____   4. (S.O. 3)   The materials price standard is based on the purchasing department's best estimate of the cost of raw materials.

_____   5. (S.O. 3)   The direct labor quantity standard is based on current wage rates adjusted for anticipated changes such as cost of living adjustments included in many union contracts.

_____   6. (S.O. 3)   The standard predetermined overhead rate is based on an expected standard activity index.

_____   7. (S.O. 3)   An unfavorable variance suggests efficiencies in incurring costs and in using materials and labor.

_____   8. (S.O. 4)   The materials price variance is the difference between actual quantity of materials purchased times the standard cost and the standard quantity of materials times the standard cost.

_____   9. (S.O. 4)   The materials quantity variance is the difference between the standard cost times the actual quantity of materials used and the standard cost times the standard quantity used.

_____   10. (S.O. 4)   The materials price variance is normally caused by the production department.

_____   11. (S.O. 4)   Material quantity variances can be caused by inexperienced workers, faulty machinery, or carelessness.

_____   12. (S.O. 4)   The labor quantity variance is the difference between the actual rate times the standard hours and the standard rate times the standard hours.

_____   13. (S.O. 4)   The use of an inexperienced worker instead of an experienced employee can result in a favorable labor price variance but probably an unfavorable quantity variance.

_____   14. (S.O. 5)   The overhead controllable variance is the difference between the actual overhead costs incurred and the budgeted costs for the standard hours allowed.

_____ 15. (S.O. 5) An increase in the cost of indirect manufacturing costs such as fuel and maintenance may cause an overhead volume variance.

_____ 16. (S.O. 6) All variances should be reported to appropriate levels of management as soon as possible.

_____ 17. (S.O. 6) In using variance reports, top management normally looks carefully at every variance.

_____ *18. (S.O. 9) A standard cost system may be used with either job order or process costing.

_____ *19. (S.O. 9) Under a standard cost accounting system, a favorable labor price variance will result in a credit to Labor Price Variance.

_____ *20. (S.O. 9) The use of standard costs in inventory costing is prohibited in financial statements.

The
Navigator

MULTIPLE CHOICE

Circle the letter that best answers each of the following statements.

1. (S.O. 3) A standard that represents the optimum level of performance under perfect operating conditions is called a(n):
    a.   normal standard.
    b.   controllable standard.
    c.   ideal standard.
    d.   materials price standard.

2. (S.O. 4) The standard unit cost is used in the calculation of which of the following variances?

	Materials Price Variance	Materials Quantity Variance
a.	No	No
b.	No	Yes
c.	Yes	No
d.	Yes	Yes

3. (S.O. 4) In the Norton Company, each unit of finished goods requires one pound of direct materials at $2 per pound. In producing 50,000 units, 45,000 pounds of materials are used at $2.10 per pound. The materials price variance is:
    a. $4,500 unfavorable.
    b. $5,000 favorable.
    c. $5,000 unfavorable.
    d. $10,000 favorable.

4. (S.O. 4) Using the data in question 3 above, the materials quantity variance is:
   a. $10,500 favorable.
   b. $10,000 favorable.
   c. $10,500 unfavorable.
   d. $4,500 unfavorable.

5. (S.O. 4) In the Delaney Company, the standard material cost for the silk used in making a dress is $27.00 based on three square feet of silk at a cost of $9.00 per square foot. The production of 1,000 dresses resulted in the use of 3,400 square feet of silk at a cost of $9.20 per square foot. The materials quantity variance is:
   a. $600 unfavorable.
   b. $680 unfavorable.
   c. $3,600 unfavorable.
   d. $3,680 unfavorable.

6. (S.O. 4) The difference between the actual labor rate multiplied by the actual labor hours worked and the standard labor rate multiplied by the standard labor hours is the:
   a. total labor variance.
   b. labor price variance.
   c. labor quantity variance.
   d. labor efficiency variance.

7. (S.O. 4) The labor price variance is the difference between the:
   a. standard and actual rate multiplied by actual hours.
   b. standard and actual rate multiplied by standard hours.
   c. standard and actual hours multiplied by actual rate.
   d. standard and actual hours multiplied by the difference between standard and actual rate.

8. (S.O. 4) In the Wetzel Company 20,000 direct labor hours were worked when standard hours were 21,000 and the actual pay rate was $6.30 when the standard rate was $6.50. The labor quantity variance is:
   a. $6,300 favorable.
   b. $6,300 unfavorable.
   c. $6,500 favorable.
   d. $6,500 unfavorable.

9. (S.O. 4) Using the data in question 8, the labor price variance is:
   a. $4,000 unfavorable.
   b. $4,000 favorable.
   c. $4,200 unfavorable.
   d. $4,200 favorable.

10. (S.O. 4) An unfavorable labor quantity variance means that:
    a. the actual rate was higher than the standard rate.
    b. the total labor variance must also be unfavorable.
    c. actual hours exceeded standard hours.
    d. actual hours were less than standard hours.

11.   (S.O. 4) Information on Engstrom's direct labor costs for the month of August is as follows:

Actual rate	$7.50
Standard hours	11,000
Actual hours	10,000
Direct labor price variance—unfavorable	$5,000

What was the standard rate for August?
a. $6.95.
b. $7.00.
c. $8.00.
d. $8.05.

12.   (S.O. 4) An unfavorable material price variance generally is the responsibility of the following department:
a.   Quality control.
b.   Purchasing.
c.   Engineering.
d.   Production.

13.   (S.O. 4) Which department is usually responsible for a labor price variance attributable to misallocation of workers?
a.   Quality control.
b.   Purchasing.
c.   Engineering.
d.   Production.

14.   (S.O. 5) The total overhead variance is:
a.   the difference between actual overhead costs and overhead applied.
b.   based on actual hours worked for the units produced.
c.   the difference between overhead budgeted and overhead applied.
d.   the difference between actual overhead costs and overhead budgeted.

15.   (S.O. 5) The overhead controllable variance is the difference between the:
a.   budgeted overhead based on standard hours allowed and the overhead applied to production.
b.   budgeted overhead based on standard hours allowed and budgeted overhead based on actual hours worked.
c.   actual overhead and the overhead applied to production.
d.   actual overhead and budgeted overhead based on standard hours allowed.

16.   (S.O. 5) Budgeted overhead for the Henderson Company at normal capacity of 30,000 direct labor hours is $6 per hour variable and $4 per hour fixed. In May, $310,000 of overhead was incurred in working 31,500 hours when 32,000 standard hours were allowed. The overhead controllable variance is:
a. $5,000 favorable.
b. $2,000 favorable.
c. $10,000 favorable.
d. $10,000 unfavorable.

17. (S.O. 5) Using the data in question 16, the overhead volume variance is:
    a. $8,000 favorable.
    b. $11,000 favorable.
    c. $5,000 favorable.
    d. $10,000 favorable.

18. (S.O. 5) The overhead volume variance is the difference between the:
    a. overhead budget based on standard hours allowed and overhead budget based on actual hours worked.
    b. normal capacity hours and standard hours allowed times the fixed overhead rate.
    c. actual overhead and the overhead budget based on standard hours allowed.
    d. actual overhead and the overhead applied.

19. (S.O. 6) In reporting variances,
    a. promptness is relatively unimportant.
    b. management normally investigates all variances.
    c. the reports should facilitate management by exception.
    d. the reports are not departmentalized.

*20. (S.O. 9) A standard cost system may be used in:

	Job Order Costing	**Process Costing**
a.	No	No
b.	Yes	No
c.	No	Yes
d.	Yes	Yes

The Navigator

MATCHING

Match each term with its definition by writing the appropriate letter in the space provided.

Terms

_____   1.   Variances.

_____   2.   Materials price variance.

_____   3.   Standard hours allowed.

_____   4.   Standard cost accounting system.

_____   5.   Ideal standards.

_____   6.   Standard predetermined overhead rate.

_____   7.   Materials quantity variance.

_____   8.   Overhead controllable variance.

_____   9.   Labor price variance.

_____   10.   Normal standards.

_____   11.   Overhead volume variance.

_____   12.   Total materials variance.

_____   13.   Total overhead variance.

_____   14.   Total labor variance.

_____   15.   Labor quantity variance.

_____   16.   Standard costs.

Definitions

a.   A double entry system of accounting in which standard costs are used in making entries and variances are recognized in the accounts.

b.   Predetermined unit costs which are used as measures of performance.

c.   The difference between the actual quantity of materials times the actual price and the actual quantity times the standard price.

d.   The difference between the actual overhead incurred and overhead budgeted for the standard hours allowed.

e.   Standards based on an efficient level of performance that are attainable under expected operating conditions.

f.   The difference between actual hours times the standard rate and standard hours times the standard rate.

g.   The difference between actual hours times the actual rate and standard hours times the standard rate for labor.

h.   The difference between the actual quantity of materials times the standard price and the standard quantity times the standard price.

i.   The difference between normal capacity hours and standard hours allowed times the fixed overhead rate.

j.   Standards based on the optimum level of performance under perfect operating conditions.

k.   The difference between actual overhead incurred and overhead costs applied to work done.

l.   The differences between total actual costs and total standard costs.

m.   The difference between the actual hours times the actual wage rate and the actual hours times the standard rate.

n.   The hours that should have been worked for the units produced.

o.   The difference between the actual quantity times the actual price and the standard quantity times the standard price of materials.

p.   An overhead rate determined by dividing budgeted overhead costs by an expected standard activity index.

The Navigator

EXERCISES

EX. 11-1 (S.O. 4, 5) Barbara Company manufactures coats with fur-lined hoods. The following information pertains to the standard costs of manufacturing the hood of one coat:

Direct Material	1 yard at $30 per yard
Direct Labor	2 hours at $10 per hour
Variable Overhead	1/2 hour at $2 per hour
Fixed Overhead	1/2 hour at $3 per hour

Other data:

1. Coats produced during June—10,000.
2. 11,000 yards were purchased and used at $29 per yard.
3. Actual direct labor costs were $209,000 for 19,000 hours worked.
4. Normal capacity was 5,500 direct labor hours.
5. Actual variable overhead costs were $9,500.
6. Actual fixed overhead costs were $16,100.

Instructions
Compute the following variances for Barbara Company:

		Computation	**Amount**
a.	Total Materials		
b.	Materials Price		
c.	Materials Quantity		
d.	Total Labor		
e.	Labor Price		
f.	Labor Quantity		
g.	Total Overhead		
h.	Overhead Controllable		
i.	Overhead Volume		

*EX. 11-2   (S.O. 8) D. Brent uses a standard cost accounting system. The following transactions occurred during the year:

Feb.   20   Purchased raw materials on account, $8,800 when the standard cost was $9,300.

Mar.   5   Incurred direct labor costs, $15,200 when the standard labor cost was $14,900.

May   10   Incurred manufacturing overhead costs, $11,000 (credit Accounts Payable).

June   18   Issued raw materials for production, $8,200 when the standard cost was $9,000.

Aug.   3   Assigned factory labor to production, $14,900 when the standard cost was $14,500.

Sept.   10   Applied manufacturing overhead to production, $10,150.

Oct.   2   Transferred completed work to finished goods, $29,700.

Nov.   22   Sold the finished goods for $42,000.

Dec.   31   Recognized unfavorable overhead variances: controllable $550 and volume $300.

Instructions
Prepare the entries for D. Brent in the following general journal.

General Journal			J1
Date	Account Title	Debit	Credit

Date	Account Title	Debit	Credit
	General Journal		J

The Navigator

SOLUTIONS TO REVIEW QUESTIONS AND EXERCISES

TRUE-FALSE

1. (T)
2. (T)
3. (F) Ideal standards represent the optimum level of performance under perfect operating conditions. Normal standards represent an efficient level of performance under normal operating conditions.
4. (T)
5. (F) It is the direct labor price standard that is based on current wage rates adjusted for anticipated changes such as cost of living adjustments.
6. (T)
7. (F) An unfavorable variance has a negative connotation. It suggests that too much was paid for materials and labor or that there were inefficiencies in using materials and labor.
8. (F) The materials price variance is the difference between the actual quantity of materials purchased times the actual cost and the actual quantity times the standard cost.
9. (T)
10. (F) The materials price variance is normally the responsibility of the purchasing department.
11. (T)
12. (F) The labor quantity variance is the difference between the actual hours times the standard rate and the standard hours times the standard rate.
13. (T)
14. (T)
15. (F) An increase in the cost of indirect manufacturing costs such as fuel and maintenance may cause an overhead controllable variance.
16. (T)
17. (F) In using variance reports, top management normally looks for significant variances. The variance reports facilitate the principle of "management by exception."
18. (T)
19. (T)
20. (F) The use of standard costs in inventory costing is in accordance with generally accepted accounting principles when there are no significant differences between actual and standard costs.

MULTIPLE CHOICE

1. (c) A standard that represents the optimum level of performance under perfect operating conditions is the ideal standard. A normal standard (a) represents an efficient level of performance under normal operating conditions.

2. (d) The materials price variance is equal to the difference between the actual quantity times the actual unit cost and the actual quantity times the standard unit cost. The materials quantity variance is equal to the difference between the actual quantity times the standard unit cost and the standard quantity times the standard unit cost.

3. (a) The materials price variance is: (45,000 X $2.10) - (45,000 X $2.00) = $4,500 U.

4. (b) The materials quantity variance is: (45,000 X $2.00) - (50,000 X $2.00) = $10,000 F.

5. (c) The materials quantity variance is: (3,400 X $9.00) - (3,000 X $9.00) = $3,600 U.

6. (a) The total labor variance is equal to the difference between the actual labor rate multiplied by the actual labor hours worked and the standard labor rate multiplied by the standard labor hours.

7. (a) The labor price variance is equal to the difference between the actual hours times the actual rate and actual hours times the standard rate.

8. (c) The labor quantity variance is: (20,000 X $6.50) - (21,000 X $6.50) = $6,500 F.

9. (b) The labor price variance is: (20,000 X $6.30) - (20,000 X $6.50) = $4,000 F.

10. (c) The labor quantity variance is equal to the difference between the actual hours times the standard rate and the standard hours times the standard rate. Therefore, an unfavorable variance results when actual hours exceeds standard hours.

11. (b) The labor price variance is: (10,000 X $7.50) - ($10,000 X $X) = $5,000 U.

12. (b) Generally, the purchasing department is responsible for an unfavorable materials price variance. In some cases however, inflation may be the cause, and the production department may be responsible if a rush order caused the higher price.

13. (d) Misallocation of workers occurs when an inexperienced worker is used instead of an experienced worker and vice versa. The production department is generally responsible for a labor price variance attributable to this cause.

14. (a) The total overhead variance is the difference between actual overhead incurred and overhead applied.

15. (d) The overhead controllable variance is the difference between the actual overhead costs incurred and the budgeted costs for the standard hours allowed.

16. (b) The overhead controllable variance is: $310,000 - [(32,000 X $6.00) + (30,000 X $4.00] = $2,000 F.

17. (a) The overhead volume variance is: $4.00 X (30,000 – 32,000) = $8,000 F.

18. (b) The overhead volume variance is the difference between the overhead budgeted based on standard hours allowed and the overhead applied.

19. (c) Variances should be reported as soon as possible (a). Management normally investigates significant variances (b). The reports are usually departmentalized (d).

20. (d) A standard cost accounting system may be used in either a job order or process costing system.

MATCHING

1.	l	5.	j	9.	m	13.	k
2.	c	6.	p	10.	e	14.	g
3.	n	7.	h	11.	i	15.	f
4.	a	8.	d	12.	o	16.	b

EXERCISES

EX. 11-1

	Variances	Computations
a.	Total materials	(11,000 X $29) - (10,000 X $30) = $19,000 U
b.	Materials price	(11,000 X $29) - (11,000 X $30) = $11,000 F
c.	Materials quantity	(11,000 X $30) - (10,000 X $30) = $30,000 U
d.	Total labor	(19,000 X $11) - (20,000 X $10) = $ 9,000 U
e.	Labor price	(19,000 X $11) - (19,000 X $10) = $19,000 U
f.	Labor quantity	(19,000 X $10) - (20,000 X $10) = $10,000 F
g.	Total overhead	($9,500 + $16,100) - [5,000 X ($2 + $3)] = $600 U
h.	Overhead controllable	($9,500 + $16,100) - [(5,000 X $2) + $16,500] = $ 900 F
i.	Overhead volume	$3 X (5,500 − 5,000) = $1,500 U

EX. 11-2

General Journal

J1

Date	Account Title	Debit	Credit
Feb. 20	Raw Materials Inventory	9,300	
	Materials Price Variance		500
	Accounts Payable		8,800
Mar. 5	Factory Labor	14,900	
	Labor Price Variance	300	
	Wages Payable		15,200
May 10	Manufacturing Overhead	11,000	
	Accounts Payable		11,000

	General Journal		J2
Date	Account Title	Debit	Credit
June 18	Work in Process Inventory	9,000	
	Materials Quantity Variance		800
	Raw Materials Inventory		8,200
Aug. 3	Work in Process Inventory	14,500	
	Labor Quantity Variance	400	
	Factory Labor		14,900
Sept. 10	Work in Process Inventory	10,150	
	Manufacturing Overhead		10,150
Oct. 2	Finished Goods Inventory	29,700	
	Work in Process Inventory		29,700
Nov. 22	Accounts Receivable	42,000	
	Cost of Goods Sold	29,700	
	Sales		42,000
	Finished Goods Inventory		29,700
Dec. 31	Overhead Controllable Variance	550	
	Overhead Volume Variance	300	
	Manufacturing Overhead		850

Chapter 12

The Navigator	✓
■ *Scan Study Objectives*	☐
■ *Read Preview*	☐
■ *Read Chapter Review*	☐
■ *Work Demonstration Problem*	☐
■ *Answer True-False Statements*	☐
■ *Answer Multiple-Choice Questions*	☐
■ *Match Terms and Definitions*	☐
■ *Solve Exercises*	☐

PLANNING FOR CAPITAL INVESTMENTS

CHAPTER STUDY OBJECTIVES

After studying this chapter, you should be able to:
1. Discuss the capital budgeting evaluation process and explain what inputs are used in capital budgeting.
2. Describe the cash payback technique.
3. Explain the net present value method.
4. Identify the challenges presented by intangible benefits in capital budgeting.
5. Describe the profitability index.
6. Indicate the benefits of performing a post-audit.
7. Explain the internal rate of return method.
8. Describe the annual rate of return method.

The Navigator

PREVIEW OF CHAPTER 12

The process of making capital expenditure decisions is referred to as **capital budgeting.** Capital budgeting involves choosing among various capital projects to find the one(s) that will maximize a company's return on its financial investment. The purpose of this chapter is to discuss the various techniques used to make effective capital budgeting decisions. The content and organization of the chapter are as follows:

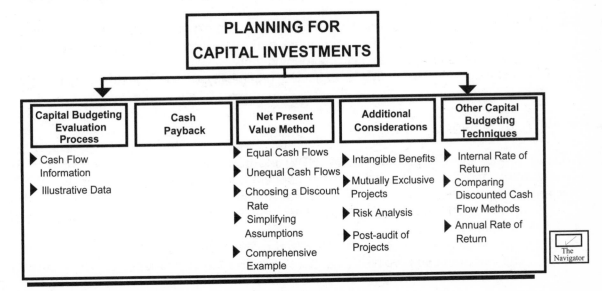

CHAPTER REVIEW

The Capital Budgeting Evaluation Process

1. (S.O. 1) The capital budgeting evaluation process generally has the following steps:
    a. Project proposals are requested from departments, plants, and authorized personnel.
    b. Proposals are screened by a capital budget committee.
    c. Officers determine which projects are worthy of funding; and
    d. Board of directors approves capital budget.

Cash Flow Information

2. While accrual accounting has advantages over cash accounting in many contexts, for purposes of capital budgeting, estimated cash inflows and outflows are preferred for inputs into the capital budgeting decision tools.

3. Sometimes cash flow information is not available, in which case adjustments can be made to accrual accounting numbers to estimate cash flows.

4. The capital budgeting decision, under any technique, depends in part on a variety of considerations:
    a. The availability of funds;
    b. Relationships among proposed projects;
    c. The company's basic decision-making approach; and
    d. The risk associated with a particular project.

Cash Payback

5. (S.O. 2) The **cash payback technique** identifies the time period required to recover the cost of the capital investment from the net annual cash inflow produced by the investment. The formula for computing the cash payback period is:

    Cost of Capital Investment ÷ Net Annual Cash Flow = Cash Payback Period

    Net annual cash flow can be approximated by adding depreciation expense to net income.

6. The evaluation of the payback period is often related to the expected useful life of the asset.
    a. With this technique, the shorter the payback period, the more attractive the investment.
    b. This technique is useful as an initial screening tool.
    c. This technique ignores both the expected profitability of the investment and the time value of money.

Net Present Value Method

7. (S.O. 3) Under the **net present value (NPV) method,** cash flows are discounted to their present value and then compared with the capital outlay required by the investment. The difference between these two amounts is the **net present value (NPV).**
    a. The interest rate used in discounting the future net cash flows is the required minimum rate of return.
    b. A proposal is acceptable when NPV is zero or positive.
    c. The higher the positive NPV, the more attractive the investment.

8. When there are **equal annual cash inflows,** the table showing the present value of an annuity of 1 can be used in determining present value. When there are **unequal annual cash inflows,** the table showing the present value of a single future amount must be used in determining present value.

9. The **discount rate** used by most companies is its **cost of capital**—that is, the rate that the company must pay to obtain funds from creditors and stockholders.

10. The net present value method demonstrated in the text requires the following assumptions:
    a. All cash flows come at the end of each year;
    b. All cash flows are immediately reinvested in another project that has a similar return; and
    c. All cash flows can be predicted with certainty.

Intangible Benefits

11. (S.O. 4) By ignoring **intangible benefits,** such as increased quality or improved safety, capital budgeting techniques might incorrectly eliminate projects that could be financially beneficial to the company. To avoid rejecting projects that actually should be accepted, two possible approaches are suggested;
    a. Calculate net present value ignoring intangible benefits, and then, if the NPV is negative, ask whether the intangible benefits are worth at least the amount of the negative NPV.
    b. Project rough, conservative estimates of the value of the intangible benefits, and incorporate these values into the NPV calculation.

Mutually Exclusive Projects

12. (S.O. 5) In theory, all projects with positive NPVs should be accepted. However, companies rarely are able to adopt all positive-NPV proposals because (1) the proposals are **mutually exclusive** (if the company adopts one proposal, it would be impossible to also adopt the other proposal), and (2) companies have limited resources.

13. In choosing between two projects, one method that takes into account both the size of the original investment and the discounted cash flows is the **profitability index.** The profitability index formula is as follows:

$$\frac{\text{Present Value of}}{\text{Future Cash Flows}} \div \frac{\text{Initial}}{\text{Investment}} = \frac{\text{Profitability}}{\text{Index}}$$

The project with the greater profitability index should be the one chosen.

14. Another consideration made by financial analysts is **uncertainty** or **risk.** One approach for dealing with uncertainty is **sensitivity analysis.** Sensitivity analysis uses a number of outcome estimates to get a sense of the variability among potential returns. In general, a higher risk project should be evaluated using a higher discount rate.

Post-Audit of Investment Projects

15. (S.O. 6) A **post-audit** is a thorough evaluation of how well a project's actual performance matches the projections made when the project was proposed. Performing a post-audit is beneficial for the following reasons:
   a. Management will be encouraged to submit reasonable and accurate data when they make investment proposals;
   b. A formal mechanism is used for determining whether existing projects should be supported or terminated;
   c. Management improves their estimation techniques by evaluating their past successes and failures.

16. A post-audit involves the same evaluation techniques that were used in making the original capital budgeting decision—for example, use of the net present value method. The difference is that, in the post-audit, actual figures are inserted where known, and estimation of future amounts is revised based on new information.

Internal Rate of Return Method

17. (S.O. 7) The **internal rate of return method** results in finding the **interest yield** of the potential investment. This is the interest rate that will cause the present value of the proposed capital expenditure to equal the present value of the expected annual cash inflows. Determining the internal rate of return can be done with a financial (business) calculator, computerized spreadsheet, or by employing a trial-and-error procedure.

18. The **decision rule** is: Accept the project when the internal rate of return is equal to or greater than the required rate of return, and reject the project when the internal rate of return is less than the required rate.

Annual Rate of Return Method

19. (S.O. 8) The **annual rate of return method** indicates the profitability of a capital expenditure and its formula is:

Expected Annual Net Income ÷ Average Investment = Annual Rate of Return

Average investment is based on the following:

$$\frac{\text{Original investment} + \text{Value at end of useful life}}{2} = \text{Average Investment}$$

20. The annual rate of return is compared with management's required minimum rate of return for investments of similar risk. The minimum rate of return (the hurdle rate or cutoff rate) is generally based on the company's cost of capital. The decision rule is: A project is acceptable if its rate of return is greater than management's minimum rate of return; it is unacceptable when the reverse is true.

21. When the rate of return technique is used in deciding among several acceptable projects, the higher the rate of return for a given risk, the more attractive the investment.

DEMONSTRATION PROBLEM (S.O. 3, 5, and 7)

Mar Vista Molding Company is considering investing in new thermokillian equipment. It has two options: Option A would have an initial lower cost but would require a significant expenditure for rebuilding after 3 years. Option B would require no rebuilding expenditure, but its maintenance costs would be higher. Since the Option B machine is of initial higher quality, it is expected to have a salvage value at the end of its useful life. The following estimates were made of the cash flows:

	Option A	Option B
Initial cost	$53,000	$58,000
Annual cash inflows	$30,000	$30,000
Annual cash outflows	$15,000	$18,000
Cost to rebuild (end of year 3)	$12,000	$ -0-
Salvage value	$ -0-	$10,000
Estimated useful life	6 years	6 years

The company's cost of capital is 8%.

Instructions
(a) Compute the (1) net present value, (2) profitability index, and (3) internal rate of return for each option.
(b) Which option should be accepted?

SOLUTION TO DEMONSTRATION PROBLEM

(a)
Net Present Value of Option A

Event	Time Period	Cash Flow	8% Discount Factor	Present Value
Equipment purchase	0	($53,000)	1.00000	$(53,000)
Equipment overhaul	3	($12,000)	.79383	(9,526)
Net annual cash inflows	1-6	$15,000	4.62288	69,343
Net present value				$ 6,817

Net Present Value of Option B

Event	Time Period	Cash Flow	8% Discount Factor	Present Value
Equipment purchase	0	($58,000)	1.00000	$(58,000)
Net annual cash inflows	1-6	$12,000	4.62288	55,475
Salvage value	6	$10,000	.63017	6,302
Net present value				$ 3,777

Profitability Index
Option A: 59,817 ÷ 53,000 = 1.13
Option B: 61,777 ÷ 58,000 = 1.07

Internal Rate of Return: The internal rate of return can be approximated by experimenting with different discount rates to see which one comes the closest to resulting in a net present value of zero. Doing this, we find that Option A has an internal rate of return of approximately 12%, while the internal rate of return for Option B is approximately 10% as shown below.

Option A

Cash Flows	X	12% Discount Factor	=	Present Value
$53,000		1.0000		$(53,000)
$12,000		.71178		(8,541)
$15,000		4.11141		61,671
Net Present Value				$ 130

Option B

Cash Flows	X	10% Discount Factor	=	Present Value
$58,000		1.00000		$(58,000)
$12,000		4.35526		52,263
$10,000		.56447		5,645
Net Present Value				$ (92)

(b)   Option A should be chosen because it has a higher net present value, a greater profitability index, and a higher internal rate of return.

REVIEW QUESTIONS AND EXERCISES

TRUE—FALSE

Indicate whether each of the following is true (T) or false (F) in the space provided.

_____   1. (S.O. 1)   The process of making capital expenditure decisions in business is known as capital budgeting.

_____   2. (S.O. 1)   While cash accounting has advantages over accrual accounting in many contexts, for purposes of capital budgeting, accrual accounting is preferred.

_____   3. (S.O. 2)   The cash payback technique identifies the time period required to recover the cost of the capital investment from the net annual cash flow produced by the investment.

_____   4. (S.O. 2)   When the payback technique is used to decide among acceptable alternative projects, the longer the payback period, the more attractive the investment.

_____   5. (S.O. 2)   The cash payback technique may be useful as an initial screening tool.

_____   6. (S.O. 3)   It is useful to recognize the timing of cash flows when evaluating projects.

_____   7. (S.O. 3)   The net present value method considers estimated total cash flows from the investment but not the time value of money.

_____   8. (S.O. 3)   Under the net present value method, a proposal is acceptable when there is a positive or zero net present value.

_____   9. (S.O. 3)   The lower the positive net present value, the more attractive the investment.

_____   10. (S.O. 3)   In most cases, a company uses a discount rate equal to its cost of capital—that is, the rate that it must pay to obtain funds from creditors and stockholders.

_____   11. (S.O. 4)   When making capital budgeting decisions, management should ignore intangible benefits.

_____   12. (S.O. 5)   "Mutually exclusive" means that if a company adopts one proposal, it is still possible to adopt the other proposal.

_____   13. (S.O. 5)   A simple method of comparing alternative projects that takes into account both the size of the original investment and the discounted cash flows is the profitability index.

_____   14. (S.O. 6)   A post-audit is a thorough evaluation of how well a project's actual performance matches the projections made when the project was proposed.

_____ 15. (S.O. 7)   The internal rate of return is the rate that will cause the present value of the proposed capital expenditure to equal the present value of the expected annual cash flows.

_____ 16. (S.O. 7)   Under the internal rate of return method, the project is rejected when the internal rate of return is less than the required rate.

_____ 17. (S.O. 7)   The internal rate of return is very rarely used in practice because most managers find the internal rate of return difficult to interpret.

_____ 18. (S.O. 8)   The annual rate of return is computed by dividing expected annual net income by average investment.

_____ 19. (S.O. 8)   Under the annual rate of return method, a project is acceptable if its rate of return is less than management's minimum rate of return.

_____ 20. (S.O. 8)   One of the principal advantages of the annual rate of return method is the simplicity of its calculation.

The
Navigator

MULTIPLE CHOICE

Circle the letter that best answers each of the following statements.

1.   (S.O. 1) Which of the following is **incorrect?**
   a.   Capital budgeting is the process of making capital expenditure decisions.
   b.   Capital budgeting decisions are the opposite of incremental analysis.
   c.   Accounting data are indispensable in capital budgeting decisions.
   d.   Capital budgeting involves the allocation of limited resources.

2.   (S.O. 1 Which of the following is typically considered a cash inflow?
   a.   Repairs and maintenance.
   b.   Increased operating costs.
   c.   Sale of old equipment.
   d.   Overhaul of equipment.

3.   (S.O. 2) The cash payback formula is:
   a.   Cost of Capital Investment ÷ Net Income.
   b.   Cost of Capital Investment ÷ Net Annual Cash Flow.
   c.   Average Investment ÷ Net Income.
   d.   Average Investment ÷ Net Annual Cash Flow.

4. (S.O. 2) Sue Bonno Company has identified that the cost of a new computer will be $40,000, but with the use of the new computer, net income will increase by $5,000 a year. If depreciation expense is $3,000 a year, the cash payback period is:
    a. 20 years.
    b. 10 years.
    c. 8 years.
    d. 5 years.

5. (S.O. 3) Melvin's annual cash inflows are expected to be $32,000 for the next 8 years. Assuming a discount rate of 10%, the present value of cash flows for Melvin is:
    a. $14,928.
    b. $16,421.
    c. $170,718.
    d. $214,723.

6. (S.O. 3) Which of the following is **not** part of the discounted cash flow techniques?
    a. Annual rate of return.
    b. Net present value method.
    c. Internal rate of return method.
    d. All of the above are part of the discounted cash flow technique.

7. (S.O. 3) Which of the following is **not** considered in the net present value method?
    a. Present value of net annual cash flows.
    b. Present value of depreciation expense.
    c. Present value of liquidation proceeds.
    d. Capital investment.

8. (S.O. 3) To approximate net annual cash flow, depreciation is:
    a. subtracted from net income because it is an expense.
    b. subtracted from net income because it is an outflow of cash.
    c. added back to net income because it is an inflow of cash.
    d. added back to net income because it is not an outflow of cash.

9. (S.O. 3) A **negative** net present value means that the:
    a. project's rate of return exceeds the required rate of return.
    b. project's rate of return is less than the required rate of return.
    c. project's rate of return equals the required rate of return.
    d. project is acceptable.

10. (S.O. 3) The salvage value on a piece of equipment is expected to be $10,000 in 12 years. If the discount rate is 8%, what is the present value of the equipment's salvage value?
    a. $3,168.
    b. $3,220.
    c. $3,971.
    d. $4,039.

11.   (S.O. 3) Mobley Corporation estimates that it will have the following future cash inflows over the next three years: 2006—$18,000; 2007—$19,000; and 2008—$20,000. If the discount rate is 6%, what is the present value of the future cash inflows?
    a. $50,683.
    b. $51,342.
    c. $53,561.
    d. $57,331.

12.   (S.O. 5) The profitability index is calculated by:
    a.   dividing the initial investment by the present value of future cash flows.
    b.   dividing the present value of cash flows by the initial investment.
    c.   multiplying the initial investment by the present value of cash flows.
    d.   multiplying the discount rate by the initial investment.

13.   (S.O. 5) Francisco Trujillo is contemplating a project with an initial investment of $50,000. Francisco also has a discount rate of 8%. If the project has estimated net annual cash flows of $12,000 for the next six years, what is the profitability index for the project?
    a.   1.03.
    b.   1.07.
    c.   1.11.
    d.   1.27.

14.   (S.O. 7) Which of the following statements about the internal rate of return method is **false?**
    a.   It is widely used in practice.
    b.   It results in finding the interest yield of the potential investment.
    c.   It does not recognize the time value of money.
    d.   The internal rate of return factor can be computed with a computerized spreadsheet.

15.   (S.O. 7)   Jesilow Company is contemplating purchasing equipment for $60,000 with expected future annual cash inflows of $18,100 for the next 4 years. What is the estimated internal rate of return?
    a.   5%.
    b.   6%.
    c.   8%.
    d.   10%.

16.   (S.O. 7) Richman Company is contemplating a project with an initial capital investment of $40,000. The expected future annual cash inflows from the project are estimated to be $7,500 for the next 8 years. What is the estimated internal rate of return for the project?
    a.   4%.
    b.   6%.
    c.   8%.
    d.   10%.

17. (S.O. 8) The formula for the annual rate of return method is:
a. Annual Cash Flow ÷ Cost of Capital Investment.
b. Annual Cash Flow ÷ Average Investment.
c. Expected Annual Net Income ÷ Cost of Capital Investment.
d. Expected Annual Net Income ÷ Average Investment.

18. (S.O. 8) In the annual rate of return method, the minimum rate of return is **not:**
a. based on the cost of capital.
b. also called the annual rate of return.
c. also called the hurdle rate.
d. also called cutoff rate.

19. (S.O. 8) Ehrlich Company had an investment which cost $260,000 and had a salvage value at the end of its useful life of zero. If Ehrlich's expected annual net income is $20,000, the annual rate of return is:
a. 7.7%.
b. 13%.
c. 15.4%.
d. 20%.

20. (S.O. 8) Which of the following is **not** correct about the annual rate of return method?
a. The calculation is simple.
b. The accounting terms used are familiar to management.
c. The time value of money is considered.
d. The timing of the cash inflows is not considered.

The
Navigator

MATCHING

Match each term with its definition by writing the appropriate letter in the space provided.

<table>
<tr><td colspan="2" align="center">**Terms**</td><td colspan="2" align="center">**Definitions**</td></tr>
<tr><td>_____</td><td>1. Postaudit.</td><td>a.</td><td>A method of determining the profitability of a capital expenditure by dividing expected annual net income by the average invest-ment.</td></tr>
<tr><td>_____</td><td>2. Discounted cash flow techniques.</td><td>b.</td><td>A method used in capital budgeting in which cash inflows are discounted to their present value and then compared to the capital outlay required by the investment.</td></tr>
<tr><td>_____</td><td>3. Profitability index.</td><td></td><td></td></tr>
<tr><td>_____</td><td>4. Capital budgeting.</td><td>c.</td><td>A thorough evaluation of how well a project's actual performance matches the projections made when the project was proposed.</td></tr>
<tr><td>_____</td><td>5. Annual rate of return method.</td><td>d.</td><td>The process of making capital expenditure decisions in business.</td></tr>
<tr><td>_____</td><td>6. Cost of capital.</td><td>e.</td><td>The average rate of return that management expects to pay on all borrowed and equity funds.</td></tr>
<tr><td>_____</td><td>7. Cash payback technique.</td><td>f.</td><td>A method used in capital budgeting that results in finding the interest yield of the potential investment.</td></tr>
<tr><td>_____</td><td>8. Net present value method.</td><td>g.</td><td>A method of comparing alternative projects that is computed by dividing the present value of cash flows by the initial investment.</td></tr>
<tr><td>_____</td><td>9. Internal rate of return method.</td><td>h.</td><td>A capital budgeting technique which identifies the time period required to recover the cost of the capital investment from the annual cash inflows produced by the investment.</td></tr>
<tr><td></td><td></td><td>i.</td><td>Capital budgeting techniques that consider both the estimated total cash inflows from the investment and the time value of money.</td></tr>
</table>

The Navigator

EXERCISES

EX. 12-1   (S.O. 2, 3, and 8) Bianca Company is considering a long-term investment project. The project will require an investment of $450,000, and it will have a useful life of 6 years. Annual net income is expected to be: Year 1, $25,000; Year 2, $27,000; Year 3, $30,000; Year 4, $32,000; Year 5, $36,000; and Year 6, $39,000. Depreciation is computed by the straight-line method with no salvage value. The company's cost of capital is 8%. (Hint: Assume cash flows can be computed by adding back depreciation expense to net income.)

Instructions
(a) Compute the cash payback period for the project.
(b) Compute the net present value for the project.
(c) Compute the annual rate of return for the project.

EX. 12-2 (S.O. 2, 3, 7 and 8) Jenny Durdil Company is considering an investment of $200,000 in new equipment which will be depreciated on a straight-line basis (8-year life, no salvage value). The expected annual revenues and costs of the new product that will be produced from the equipment are:

Sales		$292,000
Less costs and expenses:		
Manufacturing costs	$200,000	
Equipment depreciation	25,000	
Selling and administrative	43,900	268,900
Income before income taxes		23,100
Income tax expense (30%)		6,930
Net income		$ 16,170

Instructions
(Hint: Assume cash flows can be computed by adding back depreciation expense to net income.)
(a) Compute the cash payback period.
(b) Compute the net present value assuming a 12% required rate of return.
(c) Determine the internal rate of return.
(d) Compute the annual rate of return.

(a)

(b)

(c)

(d)

SOLUTIONS TO REVIEW QUESTIONS AND EXERCISES

TRUE-FALSE

1. (T)
2. (F)   While accrual accounting has advantages over cash accounting in many contexts, for purposes of capital budgeting, estimated cash inflows and outflows are preferred for inputs in the capital budgeting decision tools.
3. (T)
4. (F)   When the payback technique is used to decide among acceptable alternative projects, the shorter the payback period, the more attractive the investment.
5. (T)
6. (T)
7. (F)   The net present value method considers both estimated total cash flows and the time value of money.
8. (T)
9. (F)   The higher the positive net present value, the more attractive the investment.
10. (T)
11. (F)   When making capital budgeting decisions, management should identify intangible benefits such as increased quality or safety or employee loyalty.
12. (F)   "Mutually exclusive" means that if a company adopts one proposal, it would be impossible also to adopt the other proposal.
13. (T)
14. (T)
15. (T)
16. (T)
17. (F)   The internal rate of return is widely used in practice and most managers find it easy to interpret.
18. (T)
19. (F)   Under the annual rate of return method, a project is acceptable if its rate of return is greater than management's minimum rate of return.
20. (T)

MULTIPLE CHOICE

1.   (b)   Incremental analysis involves decision making for alternative courses of action. Capital budgeting is similar in that it involves choosing among various capital projects.

2.   (c)   The sale of old equipment is typically considered a cash inflow. Repairs and maintenance, increased operating costs and overhaul of equipment are typically considered cash outflows.

3.   (b)   The formula for computing cash payback is cost of capital investment divided by net annual cash flow.

4.   (d)   The cash payback period is calculated by dividing the cost of the capital investment by the net annual cash flow (net income + depreciation expense), [$40,000 ÷ ($5,000 + $3,000)].

5.   (c)   Using the Present Value of an Annuity Table, $32,000 at a discount rate of 10% for the next 8 years is equal to $170,718 ($32,000 X 5.33493).

6.   (a)   The discounted cash flow techniques include the net present value method and the internal rate of return method. The annual rate of return does not consider the time value of money and therefore is not part of the discounted cash flow technique.

7.   (b)   Net present value is computed as the present value of future cash flows (annual cash flows and liquidation proceeds) less the capital investment. Depreciation expense is not considered because it is not a cash flow.

8.   (d)   To approximate annual cash inflow, depreciation expense is added back to net income because it is an expense which is not an outflow of cash.

9.   (b)   A negative net present value means the project's rate of return is less than the required rate of return and is therefore unacceptable.

10.   (c)   Using the Present Value Table, $10,000 at a discount rate of 8% for 12 years is equal to $3,971 ($10,000 X .39711).

11.   (a)   The present value of the cash flows is calculated as follows:

Year	Assumed Annual Cash Flows (1)	Discount Factor 6% (2)	Present Value 6% (1) X (2)
2006	$18,000	.94340	$16,981
2007	$19,000	.89000	$16,910
2008	$20,000	.83962	$16,792
Total			$50,683

12.   (b)   The profitability index is calculated by dividing the present value of future cash flows by the initial investment.

13.   (c)   The profitability index is 1.11 [($12,000 X 4.62288) ÷ $50,000].

14. (c) The internal rate of return method recognizes the time value of money. The other answer choices are correct.

15. (c) Manipulating the present value of an Annuity equation, the internal rate of return is calculated by dividing the capital investment by the annual cash inflows to obtain 3.3149 ($60,000 ÷ $18,100). By observing the Present Value of an Annuity Table and row for four years, the closest interest rate column is the 8% column which has a factor of 3.31213.

16. (d) Manipulating the Present Value of an Annuity equation, the internal rate of return is calculated by dividing the capital investment by the annual cash inflows to obtain 5.3333 ($40,000 ÷ $7,500). By observing the Present Value of an Annuity Table and row for 8 years, the closest interest rate column is the 10% column which has a factor of 5.33493.

17. (d) The formula for the annual rate of return is expected annual net income divided by average investment.

18. (b) The minimum rate of return, also called the hurdle rate (c) or cutoff rate (d), is based on the cost of capital (a). It is not the same as the annual rate of return.

19. (c) The annual rate of return is expected annual net income, $20,000, divided by average investment of $130,000 [($260,000 + 0)/2].

20. (c) A major limitation is that this method does not consider the time value of money. The other statements are correct.

MATCHING

1. c
2. i
3. g
4. d
5. a
6. e
7. h
8. b
9. f

EXERCISES

EX. 12-1

(a) Average annual net income: ($25,000 + $27,000 + $30,000 + $32,000 + $36,000 + $39,000) ÷ 6 = $31,500

Depreciation expense: $450,000 ÷ 6 = $75,000

Cash payback period: $450,000 ÷ ($31,500 + $75,000) = 4.23

(b)

Year	Discount Factor	Cash Inflow	Present Value
1	.92593	$100,000	$ 92,593
2	.85734	$102,000	$ 87,449
3	.79383	$105,000	$ 83,352
4	.73503	$107,000	$ 78,648
5	.68058	$111,000	$ 75,544
6	.63017	$114,000	$ 71,839
			$489,425
			$450,000
			$ 39,425

(c) $31,500 ÷ ($450,000 ÷ 2) = 14%

EX. 12-2

(a) $200,000 ÷ ($16,170 + $25,000) = 4.86 years.

(b) Present value of annual cash inflows ($41,170 X 4.96764)............................ $204,518
Capital investment .... (200,000)
Positive net present value.. $ 4,518

(c) $200,000 ÷ $41,170 = 4.8579 internal rate of return factor. The approximate internal rate of return is slightly greater than 12%.

(d) $16,170 ÷ [($200,000 + $0)/2] = 16.17%.

Chapter 13

The Navigator ✓
- ■ Scan Study Objectives ☐
- ■ Read Preview ☐
- ■ Read Chapter Review ☐
- ■ Work Demonstration Problem ☐
- ■ Answer True-False Statements ☐
- ■ Answer Multiple-Choice Questions ☐
- ■ Match Terms and Definitions ☐
- ■ Solve Exercises ☐

STATEMENT OF CASH FLOWS

CHAPTER STUDY OBJECTIVES

After studying this chapter, you should be able to:
1. Indicate the usefulness of the statement of cash flows.
2. Distinguish among operating, investing, and financing activities.
3. Explain the impact of the product life cycle on a company's cash flows.
4. Prepare a statement of cash flows using one of two approaches: (a) the indirect method or (b) the direct method.
5. Use the statement of cash flows to evaluate a company.

The Navigator

PREVIEW OF CHAPTER 13

The balance sheet, income statement, and retained earnings statement do not always show the whole picture of the financial condition of a company or institution. For example, how did Eastman Kodak finance cash dividends of $649 million in a year in which it earned only $17 million? The answer to this and similar questions can be found in this chapter, which presents the **statement of cash flows.** The content and organization of this chapter are as follows:

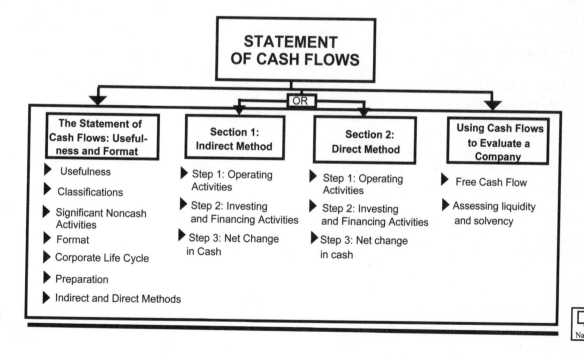

STATEMENT OF CASH FLOWS

OR

The Statement of Cash Flows: Usefulness and Format
- ▶ Usefulness
- ▶ Classifications
- ▶ Significant Noncash Activities
- ▶ Format
- ▶ Corporate Life Cycle
- ▶ Preparation
- ▶ Indirect and Direct Methods

Section 1: Indirect Method
- ▶ Step 1: Operating Activities
- ▶ Step 2: Investing and Financing Activities
- ▶ Step 3: Net Change in Cash

Section 2: Direct Method
- ▶ Step 1: Operating Activities
- ▶ Step 2: Investing and Financing Activities
- ▶ Step 3: Net change in cash

Using Cash Flows to Evaluate a Company
- ▶ Free Cash Flow
- ▶ Assessing liquidity and solvency

The Navigator

CHAPTER REVIEW

Usefulness of the Statement of Cash Flows

1. (S.O. 1) The information in the statement of cash flows should help investors to assess the
    a. entity's ability to generate future cash flows.
    b. entity's ability to pay dividends and meet obligations.
    c. reasons for the difference between net income and net cash flow provided (used) by operating activities.
    d. cash investing and financing transactions during the period.

Classification of Cash Flows

2. (S.O. 2) The statement of cash flows classifies cash receipts and cash payments by:
    a. **Operating activities** which include cash effects of transactions that create revenues and expenses and thus enter into the determination of net income.
    b. **Investing activities** which include (1) acquiring and disposing of investments and property, plant, and equipment and (2) lending money and collecting the loans.
    c. **Financing activities** include (1) obtaining cash from issuing debt and repaying the amounts borrowed and (2) obtaining cash from stockholders and providing them with a return on their investments.

3. **Significant noncash transactions** will include the conversion of bonds into common stock and the acquisition of assets through the issuance of bonds or capital stock. These transactions are individually reported at the bottom of the statement of cash flows or they may appear in a separate note or Supplementary Schedule to the financial statements.

General Format

4. The three classes of activities constitute the general **format** of the statement with the operating activities section appearing first, followed by the investing activities and financing activities sections.
    a. The **net cash** provided or used by each activity is totaled to show the **net increase (decrease) in cash** for the period.
    b. The net change in cash for the period is then added to or subtracted from the beginning-of-the-period cash balance.
    c. Finally, any significant noncash investing and financing activities are reported in a **separate schedule** usually at the bottom of the statement.

5. (S.O. 3) All products go through a series of phases called the **product life cycle.** The phases (in order of their occurrence) are often referred to as the **introductory phase, growth phase, maturity phase** and **decline phase.**

6. The statement of cash flows is not prepared from the adjusted trial balance. The information to prepare this statement usually comes from three sources: (a) a comparative balance sheet, (b) the current income statement, and (c) additional information.

The Indirect Method

7.   (S.O. 4a) The following points 9 through 14 explain and illustrate the indirect method.

The First Step--Indirect

8.   The first step is to determine **net cash provided/used** by operating activities.
   a.   Under **generally accepted accounting principles** the accrual basis of accounting is used which results in recognizing revenues when earned and expenses when incurred.
   b.   In order to determine cash provided from operations it is necessary to report revenues and expenses on a **cash basis.** This is determined by adjusting net income for items that did not affect cash.

9.   The operating section of the statement of cash flows should (a) begin with net income, (b) add (or deduct) items not affecting cash, and (c) show net cash provided by operating activities.

10.   In determining net cash provided by operating activities,
   a.   expenses for depreciation, amortization, and depletion and a loss on a sale of equipment are added back to net income, and a gain on a sale of equipment is deducted from net income.
   b.   increases in specific current assets other than cash are deducted from net income, and decreases are added to net income.
   c.   increases in specific current liabilities are added to net income, and decreases are deducted from net income.

The Second Step--Indirect

11.   The second step, **net cash provided/used by investing and financing activities** is generally determined from changes in noncurrent accounts reported in the comparative balance sheet and selected additional data.
   a.   If the account, Land, increases $50,000 and the transaction data indicates that land was purchased for cash, a cash outflow from an investment activity has occurred.
   b.   If the account, Common Stock, increases $100,000 and the transaction data indicates that additional capital stock was issued for cash, a cash inflow from a financing activity has resulted.

12.   The redemption of debt and the retirement or reacquisition of capital stock is a cash outflow from a financing activity.

The Third Step--Indirect

13.   To prepare a statement of cash flows, the third step is determining the net increase or decrease in cash. This is simply the difference between cash at the beginning of the year and cash at the end of the year.

The Direct Method

14.   (S.O. 4b) The following points 16 through 22 explain and illustrate the direct method.

The First Step--Direct

15. The first step is to determine net cash provided/used by operating activities by adjusting each item in the income statement from the accrual basis to the cash basis.
    a. If the income statement shows revenue of $120,000 and accounts receivable (net) increased $20,000 during the year, cash revenue is $100,000 ($120,000 - $20,000).
    b. If the income statement reports operating expenses of $60,000 but accounts payable have increased $12,000 during the year, cash operating expenses are $48,000 ($60,000 - $12,000).

16. In the operating activities section, only **major classes** of cash receipts and cash payments are reported as follows:
    a. **Cash receipts** from (1) sales of goods and services to customers and (2) interest and dividends on loans and investments.
    b. **Cash payments** (1) to suppliers, (2) to employees, (3) for operating expenses, (4) for interest, and (5) for taxes.

17. The formula for computing **cash receipts from customers** is:

$$\text{Revenue from sales} \begin{bmatrix} + & \text{Decrease in accounts receivable} \\ & \text{or} \\ - & \text{Increase in accounts receivable} \end{bmatrix}$$

18. The formula for computing **cash payments to suppliers** is:

$$\text{Cost of goods sold} \begin{bmatrix} + & \text{Increase in inventory} \\ & \text{or} \\ - & \text{Decrease in inventory} \end{bmatrix} \text{and} \begin{bmatrix} + & \text{Decrease in accounts payable} \\ & \text{or} \\ - & \text{Increase in accounts payable} \end{bmatrix}$$

19. The formula for computing **cash payments for operating expenses** is:

$$\text{Operating expenses (exclusive of depreciation expense)} \begin{bmatrix} + & \text{Increase in prepaid expenses} \\ & \text{or} \\ - & \text{Decrease in prepaid expenses} \end{bmatrix} \text{and} \begin{bmatrix} + & \text{Decrease in accrued expenses payable} \\ & \text{or} \\ - & \text{Increase in accued expenses payable} \end{bmatrix}$$

20. The formula for computing **cash payments for income taxes** is:

$$\text{Income tax expense} \begin{bmatrix} + & \text{Decrease in income taxes payable} \\ & \text{or} \\ - & \text{Increase in income taxes payable} \end{bmatrix}$$

The Second Step--Direct

21. The second step, **net cash provided/used by investing and financing activities** is generally determined from changes in noncurrent accounts reported in the comparative balance sheet and selected additional data.

The Third Step--Direct

22. The first step is to determine the net increase or decrease in cash by determining the difference between cash at the beginning of the year and cash at the end of the year.

Using Cash Flows to Evaluate a Company

23. (S.O. 5) The following sections demonstrates some cash-based ratios that are gaining increased acceptance among analysts.

Free Cash Flow

24. Analysts have noted that cash provided by operating activities fails to take into account that a company must invest in new fixed assets just to maintain its current level of operations, and it must at least maintain dividends at current levels to satisfy investors. **Free cash flow** is the term used to describe the cash remaining from operations after adjustment for capital expenditures and dividends. The formula for free cash flow is:

$$\text{Cash Provided by Operations} - \text{Capital Expenditures} - \text{Cash Dividends} = \text{Free Cash Flow}$$

Current Cash Debt Coverage Ratio

25. Another indicator of a company's ability to generate sufficient cash to meet its immediate obligations is:

$$\text{Current Cash Debt Coverage Ratio} = \frac{\text{Cash Provided by Operations}}{\text{Average Current Liabilities}}$$

The Navigator

DEMONSTRATION PROBLEM (S.O. 4)

Presented below is the comparative balance sheet for Kinports Company as of December 31, 2007 and 2006, and the income statement for 2007:

KINPORTS COMPANY
Comparative Balance Sheet
December 31

Assets	2007	2006
Cash	$ 52,000	$ 63,000
Accounts receivable (net)	64,000	75,000
Inventory	193,000	179,000
Prepaid expenses	21,000	27,000
Land	95,000	120,000
Equipment	277,000	221,000
Accumulated depreciation—equipment	(51,000)	(42,000)
Building	300,000	300,000
Accumulated depreciation—building	(100,000)	(75,000)
	$851,000	$868,000

Liabilities and Stockholders' Equity	2007	2006
Accounts payable	$ 34,000	$ 77,000
Bonds payable	245,000	290,000
Common stock, $1 par	275,000	230,000
Retained earnings	297,000	271,000
	$851,000	$868,000

KINPORTS COMPANY
Income Statement
For the Year Ended December 31, 2007

Sales		$600,000
Less:		
Cost of goods sold	$380,000	
Operating expenses	90,000	
Loss on sale of equipment	2,000	
Income tax expense	27,000	499,000
Net income		$101,000

Additional information:
1. Operating expenses include depreciation expense of $54,000.
2. Land was sold at book value.
3. Cash dividends of $75,000 were declared and paid.
4. Equipment was purchased for $82,000. In addition, equipment costing $26,000 with a book value of $6,000 was sold for $4,000.
5. Bonds with a face value of $45,000 were converted into 45,000 shares of $1 par value common stock.
6. Accounts payable pertain to merchandise suppliers.

Instructions
(a) Prepare a statement of cash flows for the year ended December 31, 2007 using the indirect method.
(b) Prepare a statement of cash flows for the year ended December 31, 2007 using the direct method.

The Navigator

SOLUTION TO DEMONSTRATION PROBLEM

(a)

KINPORTS COMPANY
Statement of Cash Flows
For the Year Ended December 31, 2007

Cash flows from operating activities		
Net income		$101,000
Adjustments to reconcile net income to net cash provided by operating activities		
Depreciation expense	$ 54,000	
Loss on sale of equipment	2,000	
Decrease in accounts receivable	11,000	
Increase in inventory	(14,000)	
Decrease in prepaid expenses	6,000	
Decrease in accounts payable	(43,000)	16,000
Net cash provided by operating activities		117,000
Cash flows from investing activities		
Sale of equipment	4,000	
Sale of land	25,000	
Purchase of equipment	(82,000)	
Net cash used by investing activities		(53,000)
Cash flows from financing activities		
Cash dividend to stockholders		(75,000)
Net decrease in cash		(11,000)
Cash at beginning of period		63,000
Cash at end of period		$ 52,000
Noncash investing and financing activities		
Conversion of bonds into common stock		$ 45,000

(b)

KINPORTS COMPANY
Statement of Cash Flows
For the Year Ended December 31, 2007

Cash flows from operating activities
    Cash receipts from customers (1) $611,000
    Cash payments
        To suppliers (2)... $437,000
        For operating expenses (3).................................   30,000
        For income taxes   27,000   494,000
        Net cash provided by operating activities   117,000
Cash flows from investing activities
    Sale of equipment...   4,000
    Sale of land..   25,000
    Purchase of equipment...   (82,000)
        Net cash used by investing activities ....   (53,000)
Cash flows from financing activities
    Cash dividend to stockholders...   (75,000)
Net decrease in cash ....   (11,000)
Cash at beginning of period   63,000
Cash at end of period.. $ 52,000
Noncash investing and financing activities
    Conversion of bonds into common stock................................. $ 45,000

(1)   Cash receipts from customers:
        Sales per income statement $600,000
        Add: Decrease in accounts receivable   11,000
        Cash receipts from customers $611,000

(2)   Cash payments to suppliers:
        Cost of goods sold per income statement $380,000
        Add: Increase in inventory   14,000
        Purchases   394,000
        Add: Decrease in accounts payable   43,000
        Cash payments to suppliers $437,000

(3)   Cash payments for operating expenses:
        Operating expenses per income statement $90,000
        Deduct: Depreciation expense $54,000
                Decrease in prepaid expenses   6,000   60,000
        Cash payments for operating expenses $30,000

REVIEW QUESTIONS AND EXERCISES

TRUE—FALSE

Indicate whether each of the following is true (T) or false (F) in the space provided.

_____ 1. (S.O. 1) The statement of cash flows is an optional financial statement.

_____ 2. (S.O. 1) The statement of cash flows helps investors assess the company's ability to pay cash dividends.

_____ 3. (S.O. 2) The statement of cash flows classifies cash receipts and cash payments into two categories: operating activities and nonoperating activities.

_____ 4. (S.O. 2) Investing activities pertain only to cash flows from acquiring and disposing of investments and property, plant, and equipment.

_____ 5. (S.O. 2) Financing activities include the obtaining of cash from issuing debt and repaying the amounts borrowed.

_____ 6. (S.O. 2) A cash inflow from the sale of equity securities of another entity is an investing activity.

_____ 7. (S.O. 2) Cash outflows to pay employees for services rendered are an operating activity.

_____ 8. (S.O. 2) A significant noncash transaction occurs when plant assets are acquired by issuing bonds.

_____ 9. (S.O. 2) Significant noncash transactions are reported in the body of the cash flow statement.

_____ 10. (S.O. 2) In the statement of cash flows, the operating activities section is usually presented last.

_____ 11. (S.O. 3) The phases of a product life cycle are usually in the following order: introductory phase, growth phase, maturity phase, and decline phase.

_____ 12. (S.O. 3) The adjusted trial balance is the only item needed to prepare the Statement of Cash Flows.

_____ 13. (S.O. 3) The indirect method is used more often in practice than the direct method.

_____ 14. (S.O. 3) In determining net cash provided by operating activities, accrual basis net income is converted to cash basis net income.

_____ 15. (S.O. 4a) Under the indirect method, retained earnings is adjusted for items that affected reported net income but did not affect cash.

_____ 16. (S.O. 4a) Under the indirect method, noncash charges in the income statement are added back to net income.

_____ 17. (S.O. 4a) Under the indirect method, in determining net cash provided by operating activities, an increase in accounts receivable and an increase in accounts payable are added to net income.

_____ 18. (S.O. 4b) Under the direct method of determining net cash provided by operating activities, cash revenues and cash expenses are computed.

_____ 19. (S.O. 4b) Under the direct method, the formula for computing cash collections from customers is sales revenues plus the increase in accounts receivable or minus the decrease in accounts receivable.

_____ 20. (S.O. 4b) Under the direct method, cash payments for operating expenses is computed by adding increases in prepaid expenses and decreases in accrued expenses payable to operating expenses.

The
Navigator

MULTIPLE CHOICE

Circle the letter that best answers each of the following statements.

1. (S.O. 1) The information in a statement of cash flows will **not** help investors to assess the entity's ability to:
   a. generate future cash flows.
   b. obtain favorable borrowing terms at a bank.
   c. pay dividends.
   d. pay its obligations when they become due.

2. (S.O. 2) Financing activities involve:
   a. lending money to other entities and collecting on those loans.
   b. cash receipts from sales of goods and services.
   c. acquiring and disposing of productive long-lived assets.
   d. long-term liability and owners' equity items.

3. (S.O. 2) Investing activities include all of the following **except** cash:
   a. inflows from the sale of debt securities of other entities.
   b. outflows to redeem the entity's long-term debt.
   c. outflows to purchase property, plant, and equipment.
   d. outflows to make loans to other entities.

4. (S.O. 2) Which of the following statements about significant noncash transactions is **incorrect?**
   a. The reporting of these transactions in the financial statements or notes is optional.
   b. The conversion of bonds into common stock is an example of a significant noncash transaction.
   c. These transactions can be individually reported in a separate note.
   d. These transactions can be reported in a separate section at the bottom of the statement of cash flows.

5. (S.O. 2) The statement of cash flows is generally prepared from all of the following **except:**
   a. the adjusted trial balance.
   b. comparative balance sheets.
   c. selected transaction data.
   d. current income statement.

6. (S.O. 2) Which of the following steps is **not** required in preparing the statement of cash flows?
   a. Determine the change in cash.
   b. Determine net cash provided by operating activities.
   c. Determine cash from investing and financing activities.
   d. Determine the change in current assets.

7. (S.O. 2) In determining net cash provided by operating activities it is **incorrect** to:
   a. eliminate noncash revenues from net income.
   b. eliminate noncash expenses from net income.
   c. include the issuance of the company's bonds for cash.
   d. convert accrual based net income to a cash basis.

8. (S.O. 4a) In the Ulen Company, net income is $65,000. If accounts receivable increased $35,000 and accounts payable decreased $10,000, net cash provided by operating activities using the indirect method is:
   a. $20,000.
   b. $40,000.
   c. $90,000.
   d. $110,000.

9. (S.O. 4a) Under the indirect method, when accounts receivable decrease during the period,
   a. to convert net income to net cash provided by operating activities, the decrease in accounts receivable must be added to net income.
   b. revenues on a cash basis are less than revenues on an accrual basis.
   c. to convert net income to net cash provided by operating activities, the decrease in accounts receivable must be subtracted from net income.
   d. revenues on an accrual basis are greater than revenues on a cash basis.

10. (S.O. 4a) Which of the following is the correct treatment for changes in current liabilities in the cash flow statement using the indirect method?

	Add to Net Income	Deduct from Net Income
a.	Decreases	Increases
b.	Decreases	Decreases
c.	Increases	Decreases
d.	Increases	Increases

11. (S.O. 4a) In the Freyfogle Company, land decreased $75,000 because of a cash sale for $75,000, the equipment account increased $30,000 as a result of a cash purchase, and Bonds Payable increased $100,000 from an issuance for cash at face value. The net cash provided by investing activities is:
a. $75,000.
b. $145,000.
c. $45,000.
d. $70,000.

12. (S.O. 4a) In the Tabb Company, Treasury Stock increased $15,000 from a cash purchase, and Retained Earnings increased $40,000 as a result of net income of $62,000 and cash dividends paid of $22,000. Net cash used by financing activities is:
a. $15,000.
b. $22,000.
c. $55,000.
d. $37,000.

13. (S.O. 4a) In converting net income to net cash provided by operating activities, under the indirect method:
a.   decreases in accounts receivable and increases in prepaid expenses are added.
b.   decreases in inventory and increases in accrued liabilities are added.
c.   decreases in accounts payable and decreases in inventory are deducted.
d.   increases in accounts receivable and increases in accrued liabilities are deducted.

14. (S.O. 4a) In the Hayes Company, there was an increase in the land account during the year of $24,000. Analysis reveals that the change resulted from a cash sale of land at cost $55,000, and a cash purchase of land for $79,000. In the statement of cash flows, the change in the land account should be reported in the investment section:
a.   as a net purchase of land, $24,000.
b.   only as a purchase of land $79,000.
c.   as a purchase of land $79,000 and a sale of land $55,000.
d.   only as a sale of land $55,000.

15. (S.O. 4a) In the Merrit Company, machinery with a book value of $8,000 is sold for $5,000 cash. In the statement of cash flows, the cash proceeds are reported in the:
a.   investing section and the loss is added to net income in the operating section.
b.   financing section and the loss is added to net income in the operating section.
c.   investing section and no adjustment is made to net income.
d.   financing section and no adjustment is made to net income.

16. (S.O. 4b) In the Phander Corporation, cash receipts from customers were $92,000, cash payments for operating expenses were $68,000, and one-third of the company's $4,200 of income taxes were paid during the year. Net cash provided by operating activities is:
a. $24,000.
b. $19,800.
c. $22,600.
d. $21,200.

17. (S.O. 4b) The Rotunda Company uses the direct method in determining net cash provided by operating activities. If reported cost of goods sold is $140,000, inventory increased $20,000, and accounts payable increased $15,000, cash payments to suppliers are:
    a. $135,000.
    b. $145,000.
    c. $175,000.
    d. $105,000.

18. (S.O. 4b) The Cribbets Company uses the direct method in determining net cash provided by operating activities. During the year operating expenses were $260,000, prepaid expenses increased $20,000, and accrued expenses payable increased $30,000. Cash payments for operating expenses were:
    a. $210,000.
    b. $310,000.
    c. $270,000.
    d. $250,000.

19. (S.O. 4b) The Bainbridge Company uses the direct method in determining net cash provided by operating activities. The income statement shows income tax expense $70,000. Income taxes payable were $25,000 at the beginning of the year and $18,000 at the end of the year. Cash payments for income taxes are:
    a. $63,000.
    b. $70,000.
    c. $77,000.
    d. none of the above.

20. (S.O. 5) For the year ended December 31, 2005, Geis Company had Cash Provided by Operations of $60,000, Capital Expenditures of $35,000, Cash Dividends of $10,000 and average current liabilities of $5,000. What is the Geis Company's Free Cash Flow at year end?
    a. $0.
    b. $10,000.
    c. $15,000.
    d. $25,000.

MATCHING

The Ross Company had the following transactions. In the space provided, classify each transaction by using the following code letters: (A) operating activity (indirect method), (B) investing activity, (C) financing activity, and (D) significant noncash investing and financing activity. (Note: a transaction may be reported in more than one section.)

_____ 1. Payment of cash dividends to stockholders.

_____ 2. Sale of land for cash at cost.

_____ 3. Purchase of treasury stock for cash.

_____ 4. Issuance of long-term bonds for cash.

_____ 5. Exchange of equipment for a patent.

_____ 6. Payment of cash to lenders for interest.

_____ 7. Loan of money to a supplier.

_____ 8. Purchase of equity securities of another entity for cash.

_____ 9. Cash payments to the IRS for income taxes.

_____ 10. Redemption of bonds at book value.

_____ 11. Receipt of cash dividends from another entity.

_____ 12. Sale of treasury stock for cash at a gain.

_____ 13. Sale of equity securities of another entity at book value for cash.

_____ 14. Collection of loan made to a supplier.

_____ 15. Collection from customers for sales of goods.

_____ 16. Conversion of bonds into common stock.

_____ 17. Cash payments to employees for services.

_____ 18. Purchase of land for cash.

_____ 19. Cash payments to suppliers for inventory.

_____ 20. Receipt of interest on loans to another entity.

The Navigator

EXERCISES

EX. 13-1 (S.O. 4) Lafave Inc., a service company, has the following selected information at December 31, 2006.

Balance Sheets	2006	2005
Cash	$ 83,000	$ 61,000
Accounts receivable	78,000	86,000
Prepaid expenses	12,000	6,000
Accounts payable	92,000	87,000
Income taxes payable	17,000	13,000

Income statement for 2006	
Sales revenues	$173,000
Operating expenses	160,000
Income before income taxes	13,000
Income tax expense	6,000
Net income	$ 7,000

Operating expenses include $4,000 of depreciation expense.

Instructions
(a) Using the direct method, prepare the operating activities section of the statement of cash flows for 2006.
(b) Using the indirect method, prepare the operating activities section of the statement of cash flows for 2006.

(a)   Cash flows from operating activities using the direct method.

(b)   Cash flows from operating activities using the indirect method.

EX. 13-2   (S.O. 4)   Illini Law Company reports the following condensed balance sheets at December 31:

Assets	2006	2005
Cash	$ 53,000	$ 38,000
Accounts receivable	72,000	76,000
Inventory	65,000	58,000
Property, plant and equipment (net)	196,000	172,000
Total	$386,000	$344,000

Liabilities and Stockholders' Equity		
Accounts payable	$ 48,000	$ 52,000
Notes payable, long-term	83,000	71,000
Common stock	212,000	180,000
Retained earnings	43,000	41,000
Total	$386,000	$344,000

Other information:
1. Net income was $10,000 in 2006 and $25,000 in 2005.
2. Depreciation expense was $8,000 in 2006 and $10,000 in 2005.
3. Machinery costing $62,000 was purchased for cash in 2006.
4. Dividends of $8,000 were paid during 2006.
5. Equipment was sold for cash during 2006 at $2,000 below its book value of $30,000.
6. A $12,000, long-term note payable was issued for cash in 2006.
7. Common stock of $32,000 was issued for cash in 2006.
8. Sales revenue per the income statement was $150,000 in 2006.
9. Cost of goods sold per the 2006 income statement was $110,000.
10. Operating expenses (all paid in cash) per the 2006 income statement were $20,000, excluding depreciation expense.
11. Accounts payable pertain to suppliers.

Instructions
(a) Prepare a statement of cash flows for 2006 using the indirect method.
(b) Prepare a statement of cash flows for 2006 using the direct method.

(a)

ILLINI LAW COMPANY
Statement of Cash Flows
For the Year Ended December 31, 2006

(b)

ILLINI LAW COMPANY
Statement of Cash Flows
For the Year Ended December 31, 2006

SOLUTIONS TO REVIEW QUESTIONS AND EXERCISES

TRUE-FALSE

1. (F) The statement of cash flows is the fourth basic financial statement that companies are required to prepare.
2. (T)
3. (F) The statement classifies cash receipts and cash payments into three categories of activity: investing, financing, and operating.
4. (F) Investing activities also include lending money and collecting on these loans.
5. (T)
6. (T)
7. (T)
8. (T)
9. (F) Significant noncash transactions are reported in either a separate schedule at the bottom of the statement or in a separate note or supplementary schedule.
10. (F) The operating section is always listed first.
11. (T)
12. (F) The statement of cash flows requires detailed information concerning the changes in account balances.
13. (T)
14. (T)
15. (F) It is net income and not retained earnings that is adjusted under the indirect method.
16. (T)
17. (F) An increase in accounts receivable is deducted from net income.
18. (T)
19. (F) Increases in accounts receivable are deducted and decreases in accounts receivable are added.
20. (T)

MULTIPLE CHOICE

1. (b) Information in the statement does not permit an assessment of an entity's credit rating or the borrowing terms at a bank.

2. (d) Financing activities involve long-term liability and owners' equity items and include (1) obtaining cash from issuing debt and repaying the amounts borrowed, and (2) obtaining cash from stockholders and providing them with a return on their investment. Answers (a) and (c) are investing activities and answer (b) is an operating activity.

3. (b) Cash outflows to redeem the entity's long-term debt are a financing activity.

4. (a) The reporting of significant noncash transactions in the financial statements or notes is required because they represent significant financing and investing activities that merit disclosure.

5. (a) The statement is not prepared from an adjusted trial balance.

6. (d) It is not necessary to determine the change in current assets because the statement pertains to cash flows.

7. (c) The issuance of a company's bonds is a financing transaction that is not included in determining cash provided by operations.

8. (a) The computation is:

Net income		$65,000
Deduct: Increase in accounts receivable	$35,000	
Decrease in accounts payable	10,000	45,000
Net cash provided by operations		$20,000

9. (a) To convert net income to net cash provided by operating activities, a decrease in accounts receivable must be added to net income. Also, a decrease in accounts receivable results in revenues on a cash basis being higher than revenues on an accrual basis.

10. (c) In determining net cash from operating activities under the indirect method, when there is an increase in current liabilities the amount is added to net income; and when there is a decrease, the amount is subtracted from net income.

11. (c) The issuance of bonds is a financing activity. The sale of land and the purchase of equipment are investing activities. Therefore, net cash provided by investing activities is $45,000 ($75,000 - $30,000).

12. (d) Net income is an operating activity. The other transactions are financing activities. Thus, net cash used by financing activities is $37,000 ($15,000 + $22,000).

13. (b) Increases in prepaid expenses are deducted (a). Decreases in inventory are added (c). Increases in accrued liabilities are added (d).

14. (c) Both the gross cash inflow, $55,000 and the gross cash outflow $79,000 should be reported.

15. (a) The sale of machinery is an investing activity and the cash proceeds of $5,000 should be reported in this section. The $3,000 loss is a noncash charge that must be added back to net income in the operating section.

16. (c) Cash receipts were $92,000 and cash payments for operating expenses and income taxes were $69,400 ($68,000 + $1,400) or a difference of $22,600.

17. (b) An increase in inventory is added and an increase in accounts payable is deducted. Thus $140,000 + $20,000 - $15,000 = $145,000.

18. (d) An increase in prepaid expenses is added and an increase in accrued expenses payable is deducted. Thus, $260,000 + $20,000 - $30,000 = $250,000.

19. (c) A decrease in income taxes payable is added to income tax expense. Thus $70,000 + $7,000 = $77,000.

20. (c) Free Cash Flow is calculated as Cash Provided by Operations less Capital Expenditures less Cash Dividends. Therefore the answer is $15,000 ($60,000 - $35,000 - $10,000).

MATCHING

1.	C	6.	A	11.	A	16.	D
2.	B	7.	B	12.	C	17.	A
3.	C	8.	B	13.	B	18.	B
4.	C	9.	A	14.	B	19.	A
5.	D	10.	C	15.	A	20.	A

EXERCISES

EX. 13-1

(a)   Cash flows from operating activities

Cash receipts from customers (1)	$181,000
Cash payments for operating expenses (2)	157,000
Income before income taxes	24,000
Cash payments for income taxes (3)	2,000
Net cash provided by operations	$ 22,000

    (1)   Computation of cash receipts from customers:

Sales revenues per income statement	$173,000
Add: Decrease in receivables (net)	8,000
Cash receipts from revenues	$181,000

    (2)   Computation of cash payments for operating expenses:

Operating expense per income statement	$160,000
Deduct: Depreciation expense	(4,000)
Deduct: Increase in accounts payable	(5,000)
Add: Increase in prepaid expenses	6,000
Cash payments for operating expenses	$157,000

    (3)   Computation of cash payments for income taxes:

Income taxes per income statement	$ 6,000
Deduct: Increase in income taxes payable	(4,000)
Cash payments for income taxes	$ 2,000

(b)   Cash flows from operating activities
      Net income .... $ 7,000
      Add (deduct) items not affecting cash
            Depreciation expense.. $ 4,000
            Decrease in accounts receivable   8,000
            Increase in prepaid expense ....   (6,000)
            Increase in accounts payable...................................   5,000
            Increase in taxes payable...   4,000   15,000
            Cash provided by operations.................................... $22,000

EX. 13-2

(a)   **ILLINI LAW COMPANY**
                              Statement of Cash Flows
                        For the Year Ended December 31, 2006

Cash flows from operating activities
      Net income $10,000
      Adjustments to reconcile net income to net cash
        provided by operating activities
            Depreciation expense .... $ 8,000
            Decrease in accounts receivable...............................   4,000
            Increase in inventory...   (7,000)
            Decrease in accounts payable...................................   (4,000)
            Loss on sale of equipment..   2,000   3,000
            Net cash provided by operating activities   13,000
Cash flows from investing activities
      Sale of equipment .... $ 28,000
      Purchase of machinery ....   (62,000)
            Cash used by investing activities..................................   (34,000)
Cash flows from financing activities
      Issuance of long-term note payable...   12,000
      Issuance of common stock...   32,000
      Payment of cash dividends ....   (8,000)
            Cash provided by financing activities.............................   36,000
Net increase in cash   15,000
Cash balance at beginning of period   38,000
Cash balance at end of period $53,000

(b)

ILLINI LAW COMPANY
Statement of Cash Flows
For the Year Ended December 31, 2006

Cash flows from operating activities			
Cash receipts from customers (1)..			$154,000
Cash payments			
To suppliers (2)...		$121,000	
For operating expenses		20,000	141,000
Net cash provided by operating activities			13,000
Cash flows from investing activities			
Sale of equipment..		$ 28,000	
Purchase of machinery		(62,000)	
Net cash used by investing activities...........................			(34,000)
Cash flows from financing activities			
Issuance of long-term note payable.......................................		12,000	
Issuance of common stock		32,000	
Payment of cash dividends		(8,000)	
Net cash provided by financing activities.......................			36,000
Net increase in cash			15,000
Cash balance at beginning of period			38,000
Cash balance at end of period..			$53,000

(1)   Computation of cash receipts from customers:

Sales revenue per income statement	$150,000
Add: Decrease in receivables	4,000
Cash receipts from receivables	$154,000

(2)   Computation of cash payments to suppliers:

Cost of goods sold per income statement	$110,000
Add: Increase in inventory	7,000
Add: Decrease in accounts payable	4,000
Cash payments to suppliers	$121,000

Chapter 14

FINANCIAL STATEMENT ANALYSIS: THE BIG PICTURE

The Navigator ✓

- ■ Scan Study Objectives ☐
- ■ Read Preview ☐
- ■ Read Chapter Review ☐
- ■ Work Demonstration Problem ☐
- ■ Answer True-False Statements ☐
- ■ Answer Multiple-Choice Questions ☐
- ■ Match Terms and Definitions ☐
- ■ Solve Exercises ☐

CHAPTER STUDY OBJECTIVES

After studying this chapter, you should be able to:
1. Describe and apply horizontal analysis.
2. Describe and apply vertical analysis.
3. Identify and compute ratios used in analyzing a company's liquidity, solvency and profitability.
4. Understand the concept of quality of earnings.

PREVIEW OF CHAPTER 14

Financial statement analysis, the topic of this chapter, enhances the usefulness of published financial statements in making decisions about a company. The content and organization of this chapter are shown below.

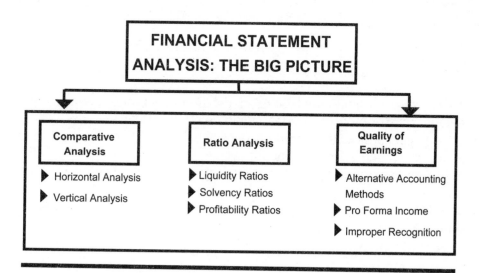

CHAPTER REVIEW

Comparative Analysis

1.   (S.O. 1) Comparative analysis may be made on a number of different bases
     a.   **Intracompany basis**—Compares an item or financial relationship within a company in the current year with the same item or relationship in one or more prior years.
     b.   **Intercompany basis**—Compares an item or financial relationship of one company with the same item or relationship in one or more competing companies.
     c.   **Industry averages**—Compares an item or financial relationship of a company with industry averages.

Tools of Financial Analysis

2.   There are three **basic tools** of analysis: (a) horizontal, (b) vertical, and (c) ratio.

Horizontal Analysis

3.   **Horizontal analysis,** also called **trend analysis,** is a technique for evaluating a series of financial statement data over a period of time to determine the increase or decrease that has taken place, expressed as either an amount or a percentage. In horizontal analysis, a base year is selected and changes are expressed as percentages of the base year amount.

Vertical Analysis

4.   (S.O. 2) **Vertical analysis,** also called **common size analysis,** expresses each item within a financial statement as a percent of a base amount. Generally, the base amount is total assets for the balance sheet, and net sales for the income statement. For example, it may be determined that current assets are 22% of total assets, and selling expenses are 15% of net sales.

Ratio Analysis

5.   (S.O. 3) A **ratio** expresses the mathematical relationship between one quantity and another as either a percentage, rate, or proportion. Ratios can be classified as:
     a.   **Liquidity ratios**—measures of the short-term ability of the enterprise to pay its maturing obligations and to meet unexpected needs for cash.
     b.   **Solvency ratios**—measures of the ability of the enterprise to survive over a long period of time.
     c.   **Profitability ratios**—measures of the income or operating success of an enterprise for a given period of time.

Liquidity Ratios

6.   The common **liquidity ratios** are: the current ratio, current cash debt coverage ratio, receivables turnover, and inventory turnover.

7.   The **current ratio** expresses the relationship of current assets to current liabilities. It is a widely used measure for evaluating a company's liquidity and short-term debt paying ability. The formula for this ratio is:

$$\text{Current ratio} = \frac{\text{Current assets}}{\text{Current liabilities}}$$

8.   The **current cash debt coverage ratio** also measures a company's liquidity but has the advantage of using the net cash provided by operating activities rather than a balance at a point in time. The formula for the ratio is:

$$\text{Current cash debt coverage ratio} = \frac{\text{Cash provided by operations}}{\text{Average current liabilities}}$$

9.   The **receivables turnover ratio** is used to assess the liquidity of the receivables. This ratio measures the number of times, on average, receivables are collected during the period. The formula for the ratio is:

$$\text{Receivables turnover} = \frac{\text{Net credit sales}}{\text{Average net receivables}}$$

Average net receivables can be computed from the beginning and ending balances of the net receivables.

10. A popular variant of the receivables turnover ratio is to convert it into an **average collection period** in terms of days. This is done by dividing the turnover ratio into 365 days.

11. The **inventory turnover ratio** measures the number of times, on average, the inventory is sold during the period. It indicates the liquidity of the inventory. The formula for the ratio is:

$$\text{Inventory turnover} = \frac{\text{Cost of goods sold}}{\text{Average inventory}}$$

Average inventory can be computed from the beginning and ending inventory balances.

12. A variant of the inventory turnover ratio is to compute the **days in inventory.** This is done by dividing the inventory turnover ratio into 365 days.

Solvency Ratios

13. Some **solvency** ratios are: debt to total assets, times interest earned, cash debt coverage ratio, and free cash flow.

14. The **debt to total assets ratio** measures the percentage of total assets provided by creditors. The formula for this ratio is:

$$\text{Debt to total assets} = \frac{\text{Total liabilities}}{\text{Total assets}}$$

The adequacy of this ratio is often judged in the light of the company's earnings. Companies with relatively stable earnings, such as public utilities, have higher debt to total assets ratios than cyclical companies with widely fluctuating earnings, such as many high-tech companies.

15. **The times interest earned ratio** measures a company's ability to meet interest payments as they become due. The formula is:

$$\text{Times interest earned} = \frac{\text{Net income} + \begin{array}{c}\text{Interest} \\ \text{Expense}\end{array} + \begin{array}{c}\text{Tax} \\ \text{Expense}\end{array}}{\text{Interest expense}}$$

16. The **cash debt coverage ratio** demonstrates a company's ability to repay its liabilities from cash generated from operating activities, without having to liquidate the assets employed in its operations.

$$\text{Cash debt coverage ratio} = \frac{\text{Cash provided by operations}}{\text{Average total liabilities}}$$

17. **Free cash flow** measures a company's ability to pay dividends or expand operations. The formula is:

$$\begin{array}{c}\text{Net Cash} \\ \text{Provided by} \\ \text{Operating Activities}\end{array} - \begin{array}{c}\text{Capital} \\ \text{Expenditures}\end{array} - \begin{array}{c}\text{Dividends} \\ \text{Paid}\end{array} = \begin{array}{c}\text{Free Cash} \\ \text{Flow}\end{array}$$

Profitability Ratios

18. Popular profitability ratios are explained as follows:

19. The **return on common stockholders' equity ratio** measures profitability from the common stockholders' viewpoint. The ratio shows the dollars of income earned for each dollar invested by the owners. The formula is:

$$\begin{array}{c}\text{Return on common} \\ \text{stockholders' equity}\end{array} = \frac{\text{Net income - Preferred stock dividends}}{\text{Average common stockholders' equity}}$$

20. The **return on assets ratio** is an overall measure of profitability. It measures the rate of return on each dollar invested in assets. The formula is:

$$\text{Return on assets} = \frac{\text{Net income}}{\text{Average assets}}$$

Leveraging or trading on the equity at a gain means that the company has borrowed money through the issuance of bonds or notes at a lower rate of interest than it is able to earn by using the borrowed money. A comparison of the rate of return on total assets with the rate of interest paid for borrowed money indicates the profitability of trading on the equity.

21. The **profit margin ratio** is a measure of the percentage of each dollar of sales that results in net income. The formula is:

$$\text{Profit margin on sales} = \frac{\text{Net income}}{\text{Net sales}}$$

22. **Asset turnover** measures how efficiently a company uses its assets to generate sales. The formula for this ratio is:

$$\text{Asset turnover} = \frac{\text{Net sales}}{\text{Average total assets}}$$

23. The **gross profit rate** indicates a company's ability to maintain an adequate selling price above its costs. The gross profit rate is:

$$\text{Gross profit rate} = \frac{\text{Gross profit}}{\text{Net sales}}$$

24. **Earnings per share** of stock measures the amount of net income earned on each share of common stock. The formula is:

$$\text{Earnings per share} = \frac{\text{Net income} - \text{Preferred stock dividends}}{\text{Average common Stockholders' equity}}$$

25. The **price-earnings ratio** measures the ratio of market price per share of common stock to earnings per share. It is an oft-quoted statistic that reflects investors' assessments of a company's future earnings. The formula for the ratio is:

$$\text{Price - earnings ratio} = \frac{\text{Stock price per share}}{\text{Earnings per share}}$$

26. The **payout ratio** measures the percentage of earnings distributed in the form of cash dividends. The formula is:

$$\text{Payout ratio} = \frac{\text{Cash dividends declared on common stock}}{\text{Net income}}$$

Companies with high growth rates generally have low payout ratios because they reinvest most of their income into the business.

Quality of Earnings

27. (S.O. 4) A company that provides full and transparent information that will not confuse or mislead users of the financial statements is said to have a high **quality of earnings.** Some factors that affect quality of earnings are (a) alternative accounting methods, (b) pro forma income, and (c) improper recognition of earnings.

The
Navigator

DEMONSTRATION PROBLEM

The condensed financial statements of Carpenter Company for the years 2007 and 2006 are presented below:

CARPENTER COMPANY
Balance Sheet
December 31

Assets

	(In thousands)	
	2007	2006
Current assets		
Cash and short-term investments	$ 276	$ 232
Accounts receivable (net)	523	379
Inventories	438	382
Prepaid expenses	97	81
Total current assets	1,334	1,074
Property, plant and equipment (net)	3,251	2,799
Intangibles and other assets	177	251
Total assets	$4,762	$4,124

Liabilities and Stockholders' Equity

	2007	2006
Current liabilities	$1,994	$1,621
Long-term liabilities	793	752
Stockholders' equity	1,975	1,751
Total liabilities and stockholders' equity	$4,762	$4,124

CARPENTER COMPANY
Income Statement
For the Year Ended December 31

	(In thousands)	
	2007	**2006**
Revenues...	$5,194	$4,873
Expenses		
Cost of goods sold...	2,596	2,364
Selling and administrative expenses	1,963	1,732
Interest expense...	52	46
Total expenses...	4,611	4,142
Income before income taxes..	583	731
Income tax expense..	175	219
Net income..	$ 408	$ 512

Instructions

Compute the following ratios for Carpenter for 2007 and 2006.

(a) Current ratio.

(b) Receivables turnover
     (Receivables 12/31/05, $373).

(c) Profit martin ratio.

(d) Rate of return on assets
     (Assets 12/31/05, $3,926).

(e) Return on common stockholders' equity
     (Equity 12/31/05, $1,492).

(f) Debt to total assets

(g) Times interest earned.

(h) Asset turnover.

The
Navigator

SOLUTION TO DEMONSTRATION PROBLEM

		2007	**2006**
(a)	Current ratio:		
	$1,334 ÷ $1,994 =	.67 : 1	
	$1,074 ÷ $1,621 =		.66 : 1
(b)	Receivables turnover:		
	$5,194 ÷ [($523 + $379) ÷ 2] =	11.52 times	
	$4,873 ÷ [($379 + $373) ÷ 2] =		12.96 times
(c)	Profit margin ratio:		
	$408 ÷ $5,194 =	7.9%	
	$512 ÷ $4,873 =		10.5%
(d)	Rate of return on assets:		
	$408 ÷ [$4,762 + $4,124) ÷ 2] =	9.2%	
	$512 ÷ [$4,124 + $3,926) ÷ 2] =		12.7%
(e)	Return on common stockholders' equity:		
	$408 ÷ [($1,975 + $1,751) ÷ 2] =	21.9%	
	$512 ÷ [($1,751 + $1,492) ÷ 2] =		31.6%
(f)	Debt to total assets:		
	$2,787 ÷ $4,762 =	58.5%	
	$2,373 ÷ $4,124 =		57.5%
(g)	Times interest earned:		
	($583 + $52) ÷ $52 =	12.21 times	
	($731 + $46) ÷ $46 =		16.89 times
(h)	Asset turnover:		
	$5,194 ÷ [($4,762 + $4,124) ÷ 2] =	1.17 times	
	$4,873 ÷ [($4,124 + $3,926) ÷ 2] =		1.21 times

REVIEW QUESTIONS AND EXERCISES

TRUE—FALSE

Indicate whether each of the following is true (T) or false (F) in the space provided.

_____   1.   (S.O. 1) Comparative analysis may be made on an intracompany basis, an intercompany basis, and on the basis of industry averages.

_____   2.   (S.O. 1) The three basic tools of analysis are horizontal analysis, vertical analysis, and ratio analysis.

_____   3.   (S.O. 1) Horizontal analysis involves determining percentage increases or decreases in financial statement data over a period of time.

_____   4.   (S.O. 1) A percentage change can be computed only if the base amount is zero or positive.

_____   5.   (S.O. 2) In vertical analysis, the base amount in an income statement is usually net sales.

_____   6.   (S.O. 3) A short-term creditor is primarily interested in the solvency of a company.

_____   7.   (S.O. 3) A long-term creditor is interested in the profitability and solvency of a company.

_____   8.   (S.O. 3) Profitability ratios measure the ability of the enterprise to survive over a long period of time.

_____   9.   (S.O. 3) Liquidity ratios include the current ratio, the acid-test ratio, receivables turnover, and inventory turnover.

_____   10. (S.O. 3) The formula for the current ratio is current liabilities divided by current assets.

_____   11. (S.O. 3) The formula for the acid-test ratio is the sum of cash, short-term investments, and net receivables divided by current liabilities.

_____   12. (S.O. 3) The receivables turnover ratio indicates how quickly receivables can be converted to cash.

_____   13. (S.O. 3) The average days to sell inventory is computed by multiplying the inventory turnover ratio by 365.

_____   14. (S.O. 3) Solvency ratios include debt to total assets, the price-earnings ratio, and times interest earned.

_____   15. (S.O. 3) The formula for the profit margin ratio is net income divided by average total assets.

_____ 16.   (S.O. 3)   The asset turnover ratio is an overall measure of profitability.

_____ 17.   (S.O. 3)   Preferred dividend requirements must be subtracted from net income when computing the rate of return on common stockholders' equity.

_____ 18.   (S.O. 3)   Trading on the equity at a gain means that the company's rate of return on total assets is less than the rate of interest paid for borrowed money.

_____ 19.   (S.O. 3)   The payout ratio measures the percentage of earnings distributed in the form of cash dividends.

_____ 20.   (S.O. 4)   A company that provides full and transparent information that will not confuse or mislead users of the financial statements is said to have a high quality of earnings.

The
Navigator

MULTIPLE CHOICE

Circle the letter that best answers each of the following statements.

1.   (S.O. 1)   Comparisons of data within a company are an example of the following comparative basis:
   a.   Industry averages.
   b.   Intercompany.
   c.   Intracompany.
   d.   None of the above.

2.   (S.O. 1)   Silva Corporation reported net sales of $200,000, $350,000, and $450,000 in the years 2005, 2006, and 2007 respectively.   If 2005 is the base year, what is the trend percentage for 2007?
   a.   129%.
   b.   135%.
   c.   164%.
   d.   225%.

3.   (S.O. 1)   Evans Enterprises reported current assets of $50,000 at December 31, 2006 and $40,000 at December 31, 2007.   If 2006 is the base year, this is a percentage increase (decrease) of:
   a.   (25%).
   b.   (20%).
   c.   25%.
   d.   80%.

4. (S.O. 2) When performing vertical analysis, the base amount for administrative expense is generally:
    a. administrative expense in a previous year.
    b. net sales.
    c. gross profit.
    d. fixed assets.

5. (S.O. 2) When performing vertical analysis, the base amount for cash is:
    a. Cash in a previous-year balance sheet.
    b. Total current assets.
    c. Total liabilities.
    d. Total assets.

6. (S.O. 2) Vertical analysis facilitates comparison of:
    a. companies of different size in the same industry.
    b. the income statement to the balance sheet.
    c. different years for the same company.
    d. more than one of the above.

7. (S.O. 3) What type of ratios best measure the short-term ability of the enterprise to pay its maturing obligations and to meet unexpected needs for cash?
    a. Leverage.
    b. Solvency.
    c. Profitability.
    d. Liquidity.

8. (S.O. 3) Which of the following is **not** a liquidity ratio?
    a. Current ratio.
    b. Inventory turnover.
    c. Payout ratio.
    d. Receivables turnover.

9. (S.O. 3) Thibodeau Co. has current assets of $80,000, long-term assets of $120,000, current liabilities of $40,000 and long-term liabilities of $90,000. What is Thibodeau's current ratio?
    a. 0.25
    b. 0.50
    c. 2.00
    d. 4.00

10. (S.O. 3) Candy Apples, Inc. has year-end cash provided by operations of $64,000 and the average current liabilities during the year was $80,000. If ending inventory was $24,000, what was Candy Apples' current cash debt coverage ratio?
    a. .20
    b. .50
    c. .80
    d. 1.25

11. (S.O. 3) Electra Company had gross sales of $120,000 during the year. In addition Electra had average net receivables of $10,000 and net credit sales of $75,000. What is Electra's receivables turnover ratio?
    a. 1.50
    b. 4.50
    c. 7.50
    d. 12.00

12. (S.O. 3) Given the same information in the previous question, what is Electra's average collection period for receivables?
    a. 25 days.
    b. 49 days.
    c. 81 days.
    d. 95 days.

13. (S.O. 3) The average net receivables for Merchant Company was $40,000, and net credit sales were $400,000. What was the average collection period?
    a. 10 days.
    b. 36.5 days.
    c. 70 days.
    d. Cannot be computed from the information given.

14. (S.O. 3) Avanti Corporation had beginning inventory $50,000, cost of goods purchased $350,000, and ending inventory $100,000. What was Avanti's inventory turnover?
    a. 3 times.
    b. 4 times.
    c. 5.33 times.
    d. 6 times.

15. (S.O. 3) The debt to total assets ratio:
    a. is a solvency ratio.
    b. is computed by dividing total assets by total debt.
    c. measures the total assets provided by stockholders.
    d. is a profitability ratio.

16. (S.O. 3) In 2006, Johnson Corporation reported net income of $225,000, interest expense $75,000, and income tax expense $120,000. Johnson's times interest earned ratio was:
    a. 1.4 times.
    b. 2.5 times.
    c. 3 times.
    d. 4 times.

17. (S.O. 3) The ratio of cash provided by operating activities to average total liabilities is called the:
    a. quick ratio.
    b. cash debt coverage ratio.
    c. times interest earned ratio.
    d. free cash flow.

18. (S.O. 3) Profitability ratios measure an enterprise's:
   a. ability to survive over a long period of time.
   b. short-term ability to meet its obligations.
   c. income or operating success for a given period of time.
   d. short-term ability to meet unexpected needs for cash.

19. (S.O. 3) Reams Corporation reported net income $36,000, net sales $300,000, and average assets $600,000 for 2006. The 2006 profit margin was:
   a. 6%.
   b. 12%.
   c. 50%.
   d. 200%.

20. (S.O. 3) Perez Company reports the following amounts for 2006:
   Net income $ 100,000
   Average stockholders' equity   1,000,000
   Preferred dividends   28,000
   Par value preferred stock   200,000

   The 2006 rate of return on common stockholders' equity is:
   a. 7.2%.
   b. 9.0%.
   c. 10.0%.
   d. 12.5%.

The
Navigator

MATCHING—TERMS

Match each term with its definition by writing the appropriate letter in the space provided.

Terms

_____ 1. Liquidity ratios.

_____ 2. Trend analysis.

_____ 3. Profitability ratios.

_____ 4. Common size analysis.

_____ 5. Solvency ratios.

_____ 6. Horizontal analysis.

_____ 7. Trading on the equity.

_____ 8. Vertical analysis.

_____ 9. Ratio.

_____ 10. Leveraging.

Definitions

a. Borrowing money at a rate of interest lower than the rate of return earned by using the borrowed money.

b. Measures of the short-term ability of the enterprise to pay its maturing obligations and to meet unexpected needs for cash.

c. An expression of the mathematical relationship between one quantity and another that may be expressed as a percentage, a rate, or a simple proportion.

d. Measures of the income or operating success of an enterprise for a given period of time.

e. A technique for evaluating financial statement data that expresses each item within a financial statement as a percent of a base amount within the statement.

f. A technique for evaluating a series of financial statement data over a period of time to determine the amount and/or percentage increase (decrease) that has taken place, expressed as either an amount or a percentage.

g. Measures of the ability of the enterprise to survive over a long period of time.

MATCHING—RATIOS

Match each ratio with its formula by writing the appropriate letter in the space provided.

Ratios		Formulas	

Ratios

_____ 1. Current ratio.

_____ 2. Inventory turnover.

_____ 3. Return on assets.

_____ 4. Price-earnings ratio.

_____ 5. Times interest earned.

_____ 6. Profit margin.

_____ 7. Return on common stock-holders' equity.

_____ 8. Payout ratio.

_____ 9. Receivables turnover.

_____ 10. Asset turnover.

_____ 11. Earnings per share.

_____ 12. Debt to total assets.

_____ 13. Cash debt coverage ratio.

_____ 14. Current cash debt coverage ratio.

_____ 15. Cash return on sales ratio.

Formulas

a. $\dfrac{\text{Cash provided by operations}}{\text{Average current liabilities}}$

b. $\dfrac{\text{Net income}}{\text{Net sales}}$

c. $\dfrac{\text{Net income} + \text{Interest Expense} + \text{Tax Expense}}{\text{Interest expense}}$

d. $\dfrac{\text{Cash provided by operations}}{\text{Average total liabilities}}$

e. $\dfrac{\text{Net sales}}{\text{Average total assets}}$

f. $\dfrac{\text{Cash dividends declared on common stock}}{\text{Net income}}$

g. $\dfrac{\text{Cash provided by operations}}{\text{Net sales}}$

h. $\dfrac{\text{Net income}}{\text{Average common stockholders' equity}}$

i. $\dfrac{\text{Stock price per share}}{\text{Earnings per share}}$

j. $\dfrac{\text{Cost of goods sold}}{\text{Average inventory}}$

k. $\dfrac{\text{Net income} - \text{Preferred stock dividends}}{\text{Average common shares outstanding}}$

l. $\dfrac{\text{Net credit sales}}{\text{Average net receivables}}$

m. $\dfrac{\text{Current assets}}{\text{Current liabilities}}$

n. $\dfrac{\text{Total debt}}{\text{Total assets}}$

o. $\dfrac{\text{Net income}}{\text{Average total assets}}$

The Navigator

EXERCISES

EX. 14-1   (S.O. 1) Using horizontal analysis, compute the percentage increase or decrease for Stevens Co. for each current asset and for current assets in total.

			Increase or (Decrease)	
Current Assets	**2007**	**2006**	**Amount**	**Percentage**
Cash	$ 50,000	$ 40,000		
Receivables (net)	54,000	72,000		
Inventories	90,000	100,000		
Prepaid expenses	42,000	35,000		
Total	$236,000	$247,000		

EX. 14-2   (S.O. 2) Using vertical analysis, prepare a common-size income statement for Larry Budd, using net sales as the base.

LARRY BUDD CORPORATION
Condensed Income Statement
For the Year Ended December 2006

	Amount	Percent
Net sales	$780,000	
Cost of goods sold	470,000	
Gross profit	310,000	
Operating expenses	140,000	
Income from operations	170,000	
Interest expense	16,000	
Income before income taxes	154,000	
Income tax expense	62,000	
Net income	$ 92,000	

EX. 14-3   (S.O. 3) Letterman Corporation decides to expand its operations by issuing $500,000 of 10% bonds. As a result of the additional financing, income from operations is expected to increase $70,000. Financial data prior to and after the expansion are as follows:

	Before Expansion	After Expansion
Total assets	$2,000,000	$2,514,000
Total liabilities	700,000	1,200,000
Total common stock equity	1,300,000	1,314,000
	$2,000,000	$2,514,000
Income from operations	$ 550,000	$ 620,000
Interest expense	50,000	100,000
Income before income taxes	500,000	520,000
Income tax expense (30%)	150,000	156,000
Net income	$ 350,000	$ 364,000

Instructions
Compute the following ratios before and after expansion. Assume year-end balance sheet amounts are representative of average balances.
1. Return on assets.
2. Return on common stockholders' equity.
3. Debt to total assets.
4. Times interest earned.

Ratio	Before Expansion	After Expansion
1. Return on assets.		
2. Return on common stockholders' equity.		
3. Debt to total assets.		
4. Times interest earned.		

The Navigator

SOLUTIONS TO REVIEW QUESTIONS AND EXERCISES

TRUE-FALSE

1. (T)
2. (T)
3. (T)
4. (F)   A percentage change can be computed only if the base year amount is positive.
5. (T)
6. (F)   A short-term creditor is primarily interested in the liquidity of a company.
7. (T)
8. (F)   Profitability ratios measure the income or operating success of the enterprise for a given period of time.
9. (T)
10. (F)   The current ratio is current assets divided by current liabilities.
11. (T)
12. (T)
13. (F)   The average days to sell inventory is computed by dividing 365 by the inventory turnover ratio.
14. (F)   The price-earnings ratio is a profitability ratio.
15. (F)   The formula for the profit margin ratio is net income ÷ net sales.
16. (F)   The asset turnover ratio measures how efficiently a company uses its assets to generate sales. It is the return on assets ratio that is an overall measure of profitability.
17. (T)
18. (F)   Trading on the equity at a gain means that the company's rate of return on total assets exceeds the rate of interest paid for borrowed money.
19. (T)
20. (T)

MULTIPLE CHOICE

1. (c)   Comparisons of data within a company are an example of the intracompany basis of comparison.

2. (d)   In trend analysis, the base year is assigned a value of 100%. The amounts for the other years are divided by the amount in the base year and expressed as a percentage. The percentage for 2007 is 225% ($450,000 ÷ $200,000).

3. (b)   Current assets decreased by $10,000 from $50,000 to $40,000. This is a percentage decrease of 20% ($10,000 ÷ $50,000).

4. (b)   When performing vertical analysis, the base amount for income statement items is that year's net sales. Answer (a), administrative expense in a previous year, would be the correct answer for horizontal analysis.

5. (d)   When performing vertical analysis, the base amount for balance sheet items is that year's total assets. Answer (a), cash in a previous-year balance sheet, would be the correct answer for horizontal analysis.

6. (a)   Vertical analysis would facilitate comparison of two companies in the same industry by making companies of different sizes comparable. Horizontal analysis would be best for comparing different years for the same company (c).

7. (d)   Solvency ratios (b) measure the ability of the enterprise to survive over a long period of time. Profitability ratios (c) measure the operating success (ability to earn income) of the enterprise for a given period of time. Leverage ratios (a) are not a type of ratio.

8. (c)   The payout ratio is a profitability ratio.

9. (c)   The current ratio is calculated by dividing current assets by current liabilities. Thus the answer is 2.0 ($80,000 ÷ $40,000).

10. (c)   The current cash debt coverage ratio is calculated by dividing cash provided by operations by average current liabilities. Thus, the answer is .80 ($64,000 ÷ $80,000).

11. (c)   The receivables turnover ratio is calculated by dividing net credit sales by average net receivables. Thus, the answer is 7.5 ($75,000 ÷ $10,000).

12. (b)   The average collection period for receivables is calculated by dividing 365 days by the receivables turnover ratio. Thus, the answer is 49 days (365 ÷ 7.5).

13. (b)   Receivables turnover is 10 times ($400,000 ÷ $40,000). The average collection period is 36.5 days (365 ÷ 10).

14. (b)   Cost of goods sold is $300,000 ($50,000 + $350,000 - $100,000). Average inventory is $75,000 [($50,000 + $100,000) ÷ 2]. Thus, the ratio is 4 times ($300,000 ÷ $75,000).

15. (a) The debt to total assets ratio is computed by dividing total debt by total assets (b). It measures the total assets provided by creditors (c), and it is not a profitability ratio (d).

16. (d) The formula for times interest earned is income before income taxes and interest expense divided by interest expense. The numerator is $300,000 ($225,000 + $75,000). Thus, the times interest earned is 4 ($300,000 ÷ $75,000).

17. (b) The ratio of cash provided by operating activities to average total liabilities is called the cash debt coverage ratio.

18. (c) Choice (a) refers to solvency ratios. Choices (b) and (d) pertain to liquidity ratios.

19. (b) The profit margin is net income ($36,000) divided by net sales ($300,000) or 12%.

20. (b) The basic computation for the rate of return on common stockholders' equity is net income divided by average common stockholders' equity. When preferred stock is present, preferred dividends must be subtracted from the numerator and the par value of preferred stock must be subtracted from the denominator.

The result is: $\dfrac{\$100,000 - \$28,000}{\$1,000,000 - \$200,000} = 9\%.$

MATCHING—TERMS

1.	b	6.	f
2.	f	7.	a
3.	d	8.	e
4.	e	9.	c
5.	g	10.	a

MATCHING—RATIOS

1.	m	9.	l
2.	j	10.	e
3.	o	11.	k
4.	i	12.	n
5.	c	13.	d
6.	b	14.	a
7.	h	15.	g
8.	f		

EXERCISES

EX. 14-1

Current Assets	2007	2006	Increase or (Decrease) Amount	Percentage
Cash	$ 50,000	$ 40,000	$ 10,000	25.0%
Receivables (net)	54,000	72,000	(18,000)	(25.0%)
Inventories	90,000	100,000	(10,000)	(10.0%)
Prepaid expenses	42,000	35,000	7,000	20.0%
Total	$236,000	$247,000	$(11,000)	(4.5%)

EX. 14-2

LARRY BUDD CORPORATION
Condensed Income Statement
For the Year Ended December 31, 2006

	Amount	Percent
Net sales...	$780,000	100.0%
Cost of goods sold	470,000	60.3%
Gross profit	310,000	39.7%
Operating expenses..	140,000	17.9%
Income from operations	170,000	21.8%
Interest expense	16,000	2.1%
Income before income taxes...	154,000	19.7%
Income tax expense..	62,000	7.9%
Net income...	$ 92,000	11.8%

EX. 14-3

	Ratio	Before Expansion	After Expansion
1.	Return on assets.	$\dfrac{\$350,000}{\$2,000,000} = 17.5\%$	$\dfrac{\$364,000}{\$2,514,000} = 14.5\%$
2.	Return on common stockholders' equity.	$\dfrac{\$350,000}{\$1,300,000} = 26.9\%$	$\dfrac{\$364,000}{\$1,314,000} = 27.7\%$
3.	Debt to total assets.	$\dfrac{\$700,000}{\$2,000,000} = 35\%$	$\dfrac{\$1,200,000}{\$2,514,000} = 47.7\%$
4.	Times interest earned.	$\dfrac{\$500,000 + \$50,000}{\$50,000} = 11 \text{ times}$	$\dfrac{\$520,000 + \$100,000}{\$100,000} = 6.2 \text{ times}$